Using Family Therapy

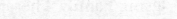

Using Family Therapy

A GUIDE FOR PRACTITIONERS
IN DIFFERENT PROFESSIONAL SETTINGS

Edited by

Andy Treacher and John Carpenter
on behalf of the
Family Therapy Cooperative

Basil Blackwell

© Basil Blackwell Publisher Limited 1984

First published 1984
Basil Blackwell Publisher Limited
108 Cowley Road, Oxford OX4 1JF, England

British Library Cataloguing in Publication Data
Using family therapy.
1. Family psychotherapy
I. Treacher, Andrew   II. Carpenter, John
616.89'156   RC488.5

ISBN 0-631-13449-2
ISBN 0-631-13456-5 Pbk

Typeset by Pioneer, East Sussex
Printed in Great Britain by Billings and Son Ltd, Worcester

Contents

vi

Contributors

Marjorie Ainley initially qualified as a nurse, and after three years as a staff nurse, transferred into further education and worked for several years as a lecturer in health education. She developed an interest in social work as a result of teaching on Home Office residential child care courses. She gained her CQSW at Bristol University, and then worked in the County of Avon for six years as a probation officer. For the past three years she has been employed in Wiltshire as a senior probation officer with special responsibility for staff development. As well as working on residential courses organized by the Probation Service Regional Staff Development Unit she is a regular visiting lecturer to the Department of Social Work at Bristol University.

John Carpenter graduated in psychology from Bristol University, and then qualified in social work. He has worked with single homeless people, young offenders, and in hospitals. From 1976 to 1982, he was employed as a social worker with the Avon Child and Family Guidance Service. During this time he took up a part-time lectureship in the Department of Social Work at Bristol University. At present he holds a joint lectureship in the Departments of Social Work and Mental Health, where he teaches medical and social work students about mental health, and social work students about family therapy. He is also convenor of the introductory course in family therapy run in conjunction with the University Department of Extra-Mural Studies. He now practises family therapy at the psychiatric day hospital in Weston-super-Mare. From 1980 to 1983 he was secretary of the National Committee of the Association for Family Therapy.

Brian Dimmock graduated in sociology and politics from Sheffield University in 1974. After three years as a community worker in

London, he joined Gloucester area social services as a social worker, and completed his CQSW at Bristol University in 1980. He has continued to work as social worker in Gloucester, but has also undertaken part-time placement in a local general practice. Since 1982 he has been teaching on the Association of Family Therapy/ Bristol University Extra-mural Department course in family therapy, and is chairman of the Gloucester branch of the Association for Family Therapy.

David Dungworth studied at Ruskin College Oxford, before moving to Sheffield University to take a degree in sociology. He then moved to Bristol University to take the Certificate of Applied Social Studies. At present he is a social worker employed by Avon County Council. He has recently completed a four-month personal social services fellowship at the Department of Social Work at Bristol University. He is chairperson of the Avon and Bristol Branch of the Association for Family Therapy.

Hugh Jenkins read French at Sussex University. He has teaching and business experience. He gained his B Phil in Social Work from Exeter University in 1975, and completed the Advanced Course in Family Therapy at the Family Institute, Cardiff in 1977. He has worked in various field social work settings and as a senior social worker at the Young People's Unit, Cardiff. He is currently team leader in the Children's Department, Maudsley Hospital. He was treasurer of the Association for Family Therapy between 1979 and 1981, and was elected chairman of the Association in 1982.

Sue Pottle graduated in German and French from Oxford University. She then worked as a research assistant at the Department of Mental Health, University of Bristol, on a project investigating deliberate self-harm. Since 1978 she has held the post of Senior Psychiatric Social Worker in the Bridgwater area of Somerset, developing a particular interest in family and network therapy.

Harry Procter graduated in psychology from Bristol University, and subsequently gained his PhD in the use of construct theory in understanding the interactional patterns of the families of schizophrenic patients. After training in clinical psychology in Nottingham he became Senior Clinical Psychologist at Southwood House, the psychiatric day hospital in Bridgwater. He specializes in family therapy and hypnotherapy.

Sigurd Reimers graduated at Cambridge in 1968 and qualified in applied social studies at University College, Cardiff in 1970. He has worked, as social worker, in an English psychiatric hospital, a Norwegian child guidance clinic, and a Welsh social services area office. He is currently employed by Somerset Social Services Department as Senior Social Work Practitioner in the field of child care and child psychiatry. He is a member of the British Association of Social Workers and NALGO, and is South West regional chairman of the Association for Family Therapy.

Trish Stephens completed her degree in sociology at the University of Bath, where she also gained her CQSW qualification. She worked in the York Probation Service before moving to work first for Bridgwater Social Services, and then at Southwood House.

Eddy Street graduated in psychology at the University of Swansea and then obtained his BPS Diploma in psychology working as a clinical psychologist in Wales. He currently works as a Clinical Psychologist within the children's section of the Department of Clinical Psychology, South Glamorgan Health Authority. He is based at Preswylfa Child and Family Centre, Cardiff, and is studying for a PhD. This will explore the ways in which training methods can influence the development of family therapy skills.

Andy Treacher graduated in psychology from Bristol University. He completed his PhD in physiological psychology at Leicester University, before moving first to Exeter and then to Bristol where he was appointed to his present job of Lecturer in Mental Health. In 1976—78 he re-trained as a clinical psychologist, spending a six-month placement with Brian Cade at the Family Institute, Cardiff. Since 1979 he has been a national committee member of the Association for Family Therapy. His main interest is in the training of family therapists, and since 1981 he has been convenor of the Training Sub-Committee of the Association for Family Therapy.

Acknowledgements

To other members of the Family Therapy Co-operative:

Susan O'Connor, Senior Registrar in Psychiatry, Barrow Hospital, Bristol;
Paul O'Reilly, Principal Clinical Psychologist, Dryden Clinic, Exeter;
Donna Smith, Social Work Team Leader, Western Wiltshire Child and Family Guidance Clinics;
Amy Urry, Family Therapist, Family Therapy Centre, Exeter;

who, in addition to their general support and encouragement, provided valuable comments and advice on many of the chapters.

To Judith Carpenter and Karen Treacher for their consistent support throughout the preparation and editing of this book.

The authors of the individual chapters would like to express their thanks to the following:

Chapter 2: Professor Phyllida Parsloe, Renee Daines and Donna Smith for their comments on the first draft. *John Carpenter*

Chapter 4: The workers on the Nansen project, Margaret Bailey, Keith Biggs, Tony Burke, George Jensen, Campbell Shaw, Hople Thane, Claire Waters and Steve Williams for their help and support. Special thanks are also owed to Sue Reardon for her patience and care in typing the many drafts of the manuscript. *Eddy Street*

Chapter 6: The Avon Probation Service for help received during the early stages of my career as a Family Therapist, Probation Officer colleagues in Swindon for their willingness to share work and learning experiences, and Philip Kingston for his constant encouragement over many years. *Marjorie Ainley*

Chapter 7: Drs Brian Cookson, William Goss and Andrew Samuel-Gibbon, and Rowena Hall, Anthea Lawrence, Kate Spreadbury and Robin Wheeler. *Brian Dimmock*

Chapter 9: Jackie Rossiter, Sarah Corrigan and Tim Forsey, fellow members of the psychogeriatric team; Dr Peter Hunt, Consultant Psychiatrist, for support and encouragement; Tony May, Area Officer, for freedom to develop new ways of working; Rosemary Collis, for advice on the initial drafts, and Natalie Hazeldine for her secretarial expertise. *Sue Pottle*

Chapter 10: Naomi Roberts, Sue O'Connor, Donna Smith and Paul O'Reilly for help in preparing his chapter. *Andy Treacher*

Chapter 11: Philip Kingston, Donna Smith and Allan Brown for allowing me to see and use material prior to publication; and Sue Jackson who worked with me for many years. *John Carpenter*

Reader's Guide

This book has been designed to be read chapter by chapter, but many readers may wish to start reading the chapter that is most relevant to the setting in which they work. However, since similar issues are explored from differing angles in some of the other chapters, readers will probably benefit from reading these overlapping chapters before considering chapters which deal with settings that are apparently less relevant to their own settings. In fact we have discovered that the chapters do overlap in all sorts of unexpected ways, but it is nevertheless clear that they can be divided into two or three groups. The three chapters dealing with Social Services settings, Residential Homes for Children and Probation are linked, while the five chapters dealing with medical settings (General Practice, Psychogeriatric Services, Day Hospitals, Mental Hospitals and Adolescent Psychiatric Units) either complement each other or share common themes. The chapter on Child Guidance Clinics perhaps overlaps least with other chapters in terms of specific content, although it explores some general theoretical issues which are of importance to all the other settings.

It is also important to stress that some of the chapters can be productively read in pairs as the following examples demonstrate. The chapter on day hospitals is logically paired with the one on psychogeriatric services, since the latter is in many ways a community-based version of the family therapy clinic system described in the Day Hospital chapter. The chapter on Residential Homes for Children is closely paired with the chapter on Social Services Departments, since many social services workers necessarily have to work closely with residential workers. The chapter on mental hospitals is closely linked with the chapter on adolescent units as both have to explore issues concerned with staff relationships in comparable institutional settings.

The reader will find that the final two chapters of the book are not concerned with specific settings — instead they seek to explore issues which are common to all settings. Chapter 11 explores the obvious fact that family therapists, irrespective of the nature of the setting in which they work, need adequate support and supervision if they are to succeed in developing their work. Chapter 12 completes the book by exploring some of the general themes that have emerged from the previous chapters. In particular it summarizes important general principles that any therapist needs to bear in mind as she attempts to develop family therapy in the setting in which she works.

Finally we should add that all the case histories referred to in the book use fictitious names in order to respect the confidentiality of the material contained in them.

1

Introduction: Using Family Therapy

JOHN CARPENTER AND ANDY TREACHER

During the last few years there has been an enormous growth in the number of publications on family therapy; perhaps another requires some justification. Family therapy texts are written almost without exception by authors who work in prestigious clinical settings, whether in the United States, Great Britain or Europe. Each reflects the author's concern with theory and, with a few exceptions, descriptions of practice focus on the techniques of therapy specifically developed to deal with the needs of families who are commonly encountered within the author's setting.

Social workers, psychiatrists, psychologists and other workers in this country have been greatly attracted to family therapy as a new and exciting approach which offers an armoury of powerful skills and the promise of effective intervention in a wide range of problems. This new generation of family therapists has been obliged, however, to rely on a mainly American literature and, whilst the theoretical and technical innovations made by the American schools have been of crucial importance in inspiring the development of family therapy in Great Britain, very real difficulties have emerged. British therapists have frequently experienced problems in putting these ideas into practice because the handbooks do not, indeed cannot, take into account either the many different settings in which they work or the variety of roles which are an integral part of their everyday work within their employing agencies.

In particular, few British family therapists are able to work within a straightforward therapist—client relationship. Indeed, it is misleading to describe British workers as 'family therapists' in the first place. If we ignore the tiny proportion who work in private practice, then the number of people employed in Great Britain with the job title of 'family therapist' can probably be counted on the fingers of two hands. This is hardly surprising, since the vast majority of health and social service workers in this country are employed by the state. They are required to fulfil a number of roles which depend on their profession and the agency for which they work. The tasks they undertake can range from committing people to mental hospitals to providing aids for disabled people; from investigating and supervising families in which child abuse is suspected to furnishing reports to the courts on the circumstances of offenders. They are probation officers, social workers, nurses, doctors, educational or clinical psychologists first, and family therapists second.

During the last ten years or so, workers from many agencies have found that a perspective informed by the theoretical contributions of family therapists, and interventions derived from a knowledge of their technical skills, have been enormously useful — whether or not they have been engaged in the accepted forms of family therapy which are described in the major textbooks. However, little has been written which acknowledges the roles and responsibilities of the average worker who seeks to make use of this perspective in settings that are not similar to the clinical settings in which family therapy has been developed. This book has therefore been specifically designed to fill this important gap.

THE FAMILY THERAPY COOPERATIVE

The origins of this book lie in the Family Therapy Cooperative, a support group established in 1979. We began as a number of individual practitioners, drawn from a variety of professional backgrounds, who worked in a diversity of settings in South West England and South Wales. We shared a desire to develop our understanding and skills in family therapy and to establish it as a primary method of working in our agencies. Since that time we have met for a day every two or three months in order to share ideas and problems, to review video-tape recordings of our work, and occasionally to invite a presentation from someone working else-where.

In many respects the strength of the Cooperative has been the diversity of its members. Thus, whilst we have often found ourselves struggling with similar problems, the different perspectives afforded by our employment in different agencies have contributed immensely to the search for new solutions. This has been particularly so when we have discussed the question of how to develop the use of family therapy in our day-to-day work. We soon discovered that it was not so much the technicalities of therapy with which we were all preoccupied, but rather with the problems of developing family therapy in the settings in which we worked. We were faced with the problem of how to introduce family therapy into our agencies in such a way that it became more than just an esoteric activity practised with a small group of 'suitable' and willing clients. In other words, if family therapy was to achieve its potential we had to establish it as a valid approach to the problems of the whole range of clients encountered by workers in the health and social services.

In this book the Cooperative has set out to describe how the theories and techniques of family therapy can be put into practice. As editors, we asked the contributors to discuss how to introduce family therapy into the settings in which they are employed, and to outline how they use the approach in their day-to-day work. It will be apparent that our colleagues have decided to emphasize different aspects of this task. Some are virtually autonomous practitioners who can choose which approach they will adopt to their clients' problems. Others are more tightly bound by the statutory and other functions of their agencies, or by the prevailing theoretical orientation of, and methods of working in, tightly structured and hierarchical staff groups. For some the central issue is one of roles — how to combine therapeutic interventions with statutory roles; for others it is one of staking the claim of family therapy to be a valid and useful approach to treatment.

FAMILY THERAPY AS AN APPROACH TO CLIENTS' PROBLEMS

We should stress at the outset that we intend to use the term 'family therapy' in the broader sense of a 'systems approach'. As one of us (J.C.) argues in chapter 2 it is an unfortunate fact that a narrow and restricted use of the term has led to an over-emphasis on conjoint family therapy (that is, of seeing all of the family members together) as an exclusive method of therapeutic intervention.

Indeed, we would agree with those who have criticized family therapy for its failure to consider the importance of wider social systems (Kingston 1979; Jordan 1981). By its concentration on therapy involving nuclear families within clinic settings, the vision of family therapy has become myopic. The family has replaced the individual as the locus of pathology. Its social context has been ignored and it has been assumed that all its problems can be easily revealed to the gaze of a group of therapists who cluster behind a one-way screen. As we have pointed out before (Treacher and Carpenter 1982), such a narrow approach to understanding change within a family system cannot be defended at a theoretical level — change is often best effected by an intervention at another system level. For example, a worker who is attempting to produce change in a family which is experiencing many problems may be better advised to assist in the formation of a housing action group, designed to influence the housing department, than to concentrate on a more limited goal of defining boundaries between the members of a family who are crowded into a small, damp and decaying flat at the top of a tower block with no working lifts.

Similarly, some family therapists, in their efforts to 'sell' the new product, have implied that all other theories and methods of intervention are misguided or useless. For example, family therapy and individual counselling and psychotherapy have been inappropriately and unhelpfully polarized. We believe that the skills of working individually with members of a family are often indispensible to a systems approach — especially when the therapeutic task is to help an individual detach himself from the family system.

A systems approach places the emphasis on the individual as a member of various social systems of which the most important is often, but not always, the family. Likewise, the family as a system should always be considered in terms of its interaction with other systems such as the neighbourhood, schools, and health and social service agencies. The usefulness of this model is, first, that it does not assume that the family is 'the problem', and second, that it illustrates the many possible targets for a worker's intervention. The contributors to this book describe a variety of interventions, both within the family system and at the 'interfaces' between the family and other systems. In many cases it is the interface with agency systems that proves to be of crucial importance — a discovery that leads to the implication that unless we are prepared to move beyond the family system, *family* therapy alone will prove to be useless.

FAMILY THERAPY AND AGENCY FUNCTION

We have already noted that few of us are employed as family therapists. This is scarcely surprising since our agencies have to perform a variety of functions. These functions are most obvious in the case of social services and probation departments, but they also exist in other settings — child guidance clinics have to make 'assessments' for special education; residential homes have to deter children from running away; psychogeriatric clinics have to decide whether old people should be admitted to hospital. These functions are not necessarily 'therapeutic'. Indeed, agencies may develop procedures whose function is to safeguard the interests or good name of the agency — the efforts that have gone into devising schemes for *monitoring* child abuse, as opposed to *treating* it, are a case in point.

In some agencies, some people come directly to ask for help with a problem. Of course when this happens (for instance in child guidance clinics, or in social service departments) the kind of help they envisage may be rather different from that which they are offered (Mayer and Timms 1970; Lerner 1972; Rees 1979; Merrington and Corden 1981). However, if the worker is careful to establish the clients' 'positions' on the nature of the problems and on an acceptable approach to them, contract-making is relatively straightforward, as Lorion (1978) has shown.

Other people are referred by health and social service agencies and also by friends, neighbours, priests, the police, and so on. Most of our contributors consider how referrals are made, and how the family and important members of their social network can be 'engaged' in the effort to create change. The process is often not as simple as it might first appear. Particularly difficult are those instances where a referral of an individual or family has been made without their consent. Thus an Education Department may refer a family because one of the children is not attending school. From the family's point of view this may not be a problem, except that it provokes the unwelcome attentions of the Education Department. In this case it is the latter which should more accurately be considered as the 'client'. The family which the department has identified can be considered only as *potential clients* unless and until some sort of agreement is reached so that the family can sanction the worker's involvement in their lives.

This issue of client 'consent' is not, however, restricted to the statutory agencies. In fact it is usually families whose attitude to change is ambivalent which present would-be therapists with the trickiest problems. They may well have consented to being referred by other professionals but this does not mean that they are ready to change. It is not surprising that this topic recurs throughout the book.

Finally, it should also be acknowledged that workers in this country frequently wield considerable power because of their relationship to the state and the mechanisms through which important administrative decisions are executed. They may therefore have the power to take a member of a family to court, to remove a child from home, or to prescribe compulsory medication. They may have the power of controlling access to resources: special education, a bed in an old people's home, an Intermediate Treatment adventure camp or a relatives' support group. They may also have the ability to influence other agencies such as schools, charitable trusts, police and the Courts, or the Housing Department. It is important that such power and authority should not be ignored if we are to help the families we see. Clearly these important aspects of our role can and must be utilized on their behalf in effecting change both within the family and in relation to the social systems with which they interact.

INTRODUCING FAMILY THERAPY INTO AGENCIES

It should already be apparent that we consider the introduction of family therapy into new settings to be no easy task. In the first place it requires considerable thought about the question of how to integrate a therapeutic role with the other roles that the worker may be required to undertake. Second, it demands flexible and creative answers to the questions of where to intervene, and third, it requires sensitivity to the structure and ethos of the agency itself. In particular, evangelical fervour is no substitute for respect and consideration when seeking to persuade our professional colleagues of the usefulness of family therapy. We believe that family therapy has a great deal to offer. In this book we explore its use in nine of the most important settings in the health and social services in Britain. We hope to demonstrate that it is a practical and workable approach.

2

Child Guidance and Family Therapy

JOHN CARPENTER

A cursory examination of Child Guidance Clinics might indicate that they were designed for the practice of family therapy. Child Guidance Clinics were, after all, established to help troubled children, and children are, by definition, members of families. However, although family therapy has gained some acceptance as a new therapeutic method, its overall impact has been rather disappointing. I will suggest in this chapter that 'family therapy' has been too narrowly defined and, as such, it has been seen by some as posing a threat to the Child Guidance Service. If, on the other hand, it is used in the broader sense of a 'systems approach', family therapy has much to contribute.

THE DEVELOPMENT OF FAMILY THERAPY IN CHILD GUIDANCE

The history of family therapy in Great Britain has yet to be written, but when it is, I have no doubt that some of the pioneering workers in Child Guidance Clinics will be given a prominent place. Indeed as early as 1949, Bowlby, who was then working in the Children's Department at the Tavistock Clinic, described an 'experimental' technique which involved the therapists holding one or two joint interviews with both the child, and her parents. These interviews were part of a systematic attempt to contact the father before commencing individual treatment of the child and to enlist his cooperation. It also gave an opportunity for the workers to convey their opinion of the problem to parents and children together, stressing that no one was to blame (Bowlby 1949).

In Britain there was little published until the late 1960s, but as

Walrond-Skinner (1981) remarks, there was much quiet experimentation taking place within workers' own practices. Martin and Knight (1962) described the assessment of family dynamics as part of the intake procedure at the Tavistock Clinic, and Robinson (1968) lists conjoint family therapy as being one of the possible outcomes of this approach. Elsewhere in London, Woodberry Down Child Guidance Unit had also instituted the co-therapy of some families by psychiatrists and psychiatric social workers (Roberts 1968).

The impression one gains from reading this early work is of family interviewing as a useful adjunct to the psychotherapy of the child. On the other hand, it was also being advanced as a promising method for working-class families who would not comply with the regime of weekly visits to the clinic for 'intensive' work. They might nevertheless be helped by family meetings at home (Parsloe 1967), or by a single, dramatic session at the clinic (Roberts 1968). In other words, family therapy was not yet established as a main method of treatment in child guidance clinics.

It is difficult to ascertain how family therapy came to be accepted as a worthwhile approach, but it seems clear that Skynner's (1969; 1976) major theoretical contributions were very influential, since they created a niche for family therapy within the established tradition of group analysis. He pioneered early training courses under the highly respected umbrella of the Institute of Group Analysis and in collaboration with other psychiatric colleagues who had trained in psychoanalytic psychotherapy. Later, Byng-Hall (1973), Bentovim (1979), and Dare (1981), demonstrated that family therapy was compatible in many respects with developments in psychoanalysis, particularly of the object-relations school. (See Dare 1981 for further discussion of this point.) These writers all worked in prestigious child guidance or child psychiatric units in London. Their work, and that of their colleagues, during the 1970s played an important role in establishing family therapy as an approach which had its own validity.

The Family Institute in Cardiff, founded in 1970, introduced many to family therapy through study-days and training courses. Many social work students who trained there later found jobs in child guidance clinics. Sue Walrond-Skinner's book (1976) provided a clearly written practical guide to therapy.

A series of annual conferences was organized by the Tavistock Clinic in conjunction with the Ackerman Clinic of New York during the mid 1970s. They were attended by many child guidance workers eager to develop theoretical and practical skills. Harry Aponte, then Director of the Philadelphia Child Guidance Clinic was the major speaker at the 1977 conference, and his presentation of structural family therapy coincided with the ever increasing sales of the books by Minuchin (1974) and Haley (1976). Minuchin's structural approach rapidly became popular and influential. Originally designed for a child guidance setting, it was developed with poor families, and presented clear goals and techniques for their improvement (Minuchin et al. 1967).

Family therapy in child guidance clinics developed rapidly and spread widely during the 1970s. Nevertheless, it has not taken over; the family-systems theory has not been established as *the* theoretical model, and family therapy is probably practised rather less than it is discussed. Why has there been no family therapy-inspired revolution in child guidance? In order to try to answer this question it is necessary to consider the history and structure of the service.

THE STRUCTURE OF THE CHILD GUIDANCE SERVICE

Like so many other innovations in mental health, including family therapy, child guidance originated in the United States. The first demonstration clinics were established with a psychiatric orientation and under medical directorship. (See Gath et al. 1977; and Sampson 1980, for historical reviews.)

Community-based child guidance and hospital-based child psychiatry services developed separately and, with the establishment of the National Health Service, this split was consolidated. Child psychiatry services including in-patient units for children and adolescents were set up, and remain, under medical control (Gath et al. 1977). The situation in child guidance clinics is rather more confused. Hugh Jenkins considers adolescent in-patient units in chapter 4, so I will confine my discussion here to community-based services.

There is unfortunately no comprehensive survey of the organization and functioning of child guidance clinics. The Underwood Report (1955) gave its seal of approval to the original model which saw multi-disciplinary teams headed by a psychiatrist with overall care and responsibility, and the major diagnostic role; the psychiatrist was the person who provided the intensive treatment for disturbed children. Psychiatric social workers played an important ancillary role, obtaining background case histories from the child's parents and counselling the mother (and sometimes the father). They saw their task as helping parents to examine their feelings with respect to their child's problem, and to acquire insight into their relationship with him (British Association of Social Workers (BASW) Report 1975). The educational psychologist worked mainly with children in schools and aided the psychiatrist's diagnosis by administering psychological tests; he or she might also be responsible for the schools psychological service (Dessent 1978).

However, the available evidence, although limited, strongly suggests that by the late 1960s child guidance practice bore slight resemblance to its founders' original vision. Timms (1968) in a comparative study of six clinics found that in three of them only 6 per cent of children on average were taken on for psychiatric treatment. In the other three clinics, about 25 per cent were recommended for it, but most soon stopped attending or were discharged. Treatment tended to be very brief and provided little opportunity for intensive work, the majority of children being seen by non-psychiatrists. Furthermore, as the report from BASW noted, by the mid-1970s the behaviour and attitudes of the various disciplines no longer conformed so neatly to their original role allocations.

Family therapy was first introduced, therefore, at a time when the original model of child guidance was beginning to be questioned (Rehin 1972). For some workers it represented an exciting new approach which promised to revitalize the child guidance movement; for others it threatened an attack on the essence of their work. These fears were highlighted by Haley (1975) who, in provocative vein, insisted:

> It is a fundamental error to assume that family therapy can be added as additional treatment procedure in a mental health clinic in the same way as one can add group therapy or one of the behavioural approaches.

He cited two major problems: that differences in theories on causation and change would lead to disagreement, and that family therapy would threaten professional hierarchies. He saw a challenge both to the medical model of child guidance and to its established structure. However, I doubt that Haley intended his arguments to be accepted uncritically and I will therefore consider these two 'problems'.

CHILD *v.*|FAMILY THERAPY: DIFFERENCES IN THEORY AND METHOD

Two American child psychiatrists, McDermott and Char, set out their concerns about family therapy in 1974. They argued that the 'mythology' fostered by the family therapists was leading to the therapeutic neglect of children for both theoretical and practical reasons. In particular, they were critical of family therapists who made the assumption that children's problems were merely extensions of parental and marital difficulties as, for example, Satir (1964) seems to suggest. They pointed out:

> The child is not simply a pawn in the game-playing between adults in which ploys and counter-ploys enmesh the child as a victim in adult dominated coalitions, alliances and psychopathology. The child himself can be ingeniously active in creating and solving problems for himself and his family.

This is true, but as we have argued elsewhere (Carpenter and Treacher 1982) both positions are untenable, when one views the family as a system. Family therapy should not be reduced to marital therapy in the presence of the children. Indeed, as Haley and Montalvo (1973), have argued the child is a necessary, integral part of the problem and its resolution in child guidance settings. Thus, whilst therapy for the family might necessarily include work with the marital dyad, the therapist in a child guidance clinic should not forget that her ticket of entry is the help she presumes to offer to the child and that her initial 'leverage' comes through his problem. Her approach should respect the parents' own perception and, even if there is a buried conflict between the spouses which manifests itself in difficulties with the child, it should stay buried — at least until they acknowledge it themselves and ask for help.

McDermott and Char also concluded that many family therapists do not have skills in relating to children and simply treat them as miniature adults. This may well be true, and I would certainly agree that family therapists who work with children must develop the necessary skills to include them as active participants. This calls for a child-focused family therapy in which the therapist takes care to listen, to observe and to speak the children's language. Dare and Lindsey (1979) present a psychoanalytically inspired account which places an emphasis on understanding the *meaning* of the children's behaviour in the session and interpreting it to the parents. My preference is for a structural approach which focuses on what the children do as their contribution to sequences of verbal and non-verbal behaviour which involve other members of the family. The observation of such sequences provides the key which 'unlocks' the family structure and thus the therapist's initial task is to create the opportunity through play, drawing, or 'enactment' for those patterns to be revealed (Carpenter and Treacher 1982).

However, even if family therapists do give sufficient weight to the child's contribution to family problems and include him actively in therapy, psychoanalysts might still be concerned about his intra-psychic life. They might doubt that the changes in personality structure sought in individual psychoanalytic psychotherapy occur in family therapy. From the systems point of view, individual psychotherapy is seen as creating an artificial dichotomy between the individual and his social context. Minuchin (1974, p. 9) has therefore been careful to argue that his structural family therapy approach causes 'changes in a family structure which contribute to changes in the behaviour and the inner psychic processes of the members of that system.' That is, intrapsychic representations, though they undoubtedly exist, are maintained in a context and seem to require persistent reinforcement to maintain them. As Combrinck-Graham (1980, p. 118) observes: 'This is not a new notion, nor is it exclusive to family therapy. It has long been the basis of residential treatment; change the context, take the child away from the family, and then the pathological process within the child can change.' Family therapy simply attempts a more direct approach to alter the child's immediate context.

I would not want to argue for the superiority of family therapy over individual psychotherapy, but rather for the use of a *systems model* in understanding and treating children's problems. A systems model always considers the child as a member of a social group, usually, but not necessarily, the family. The family, in turn, is considered as a system in interaction with other systems, such as the neighbourhood, schools, work and social agencies. It follows that there are many possible 'target' systems for the worker's intervention:

the individual child; his parents; the family group; the neighbour-hood. She can also intervene at the 'interface' between two systems, for example the family and the school.

It is unfortunate that the use of the term 'family therapy' has led to an over-emphasis, by Haley amongst others, on the family as the target system. Minuchin (et al. 1978, p. 91), however, notes that family therapy can deny the individual whilst enthroning the system. He points out that even within the most enmeshed family systems, individual members have a 'margin of choice'. The goal of therapy, he declares, is to facilitate the growth of a family system which encourages its members' freedom to be themselves, whilst preserving their sense of belonging. In order to achieve this goal, a variety of therapeutic interventions may be used. As he argues:

> The jump to the systems model frees the therapist for the utilisation of every school's insights and techniques. All techniques of individual therapy are available to the therapist, for the systems model does not abandon the individual. It recognises, however, that the individual is in continuous dialogue with the external [world].

Thus, in undertaking the treatment of anorexic patients and their families, he describes taking the child into hospital, a behaviour modification programme to encourage her to eat, family 'lunch' sessions, individual therapy for the child, and marital therapy for the parents. Each of these interventions are, nevertheless, only separate steps towards achieving the goal of changing patterns of behaviour in the family system, which he sees as maintaining the symptom in the child. Families with anorexic children, he argues, are character-ized by 'enmeshment' — the absence of boundaries in the family system. All therapists' interventions are therefore designed to create boundaries, to support autonomy and to enable the system to 'grow'. (See also Rosenberg 1978; and Black 1979 on this point.)

It is a mistake, therefore, to equate a systems approach with the method of seeing all the family together and to imply that all other theories and forms of intervention are misguided and useless. It is certainly true, as Haley suggests, that differences in theories of causation and change can lead to disagreement, but I would argue that this need not necessarily be the case. The systems model (it does not really merit the term 'theory') operates at a higher level of abstraction, seeking to augment 'linear' models of causality by using a more complex interactional framework. Thus 'linear' explanations such as those offered by psychoanalysis or behaviourism are not wrong, but partial. The systems model attempts to integrate partial explanations into a more complex whole. As a corollary, it therefore assumes (according to the principle of equifinality) that there are many ways to 'skin a rabbit', or treat a child. We are not so rich in therapeutic methods that we can afford to abandon any — unless or until they are proved to be ineffective or harmful.

Similarly, the use of a systems approach requires a therapist to consider when and where to intervene in systems outside the family. Family therapists have been rightly criticized for failing to take into account the importance of wider social systems. From this standpoint, it is indefensible to restrict 'family' therapy merely to families; the assumption that the family is the locus of pathology and that its problems are created and maintained within its own boundaries, is short-sighted. If the introduction of family therapy to child guidance clinics serves only to provoke disagreement over whether the child or the family is the 'cause' of the problem, little will have been gained. On the other hand, if 'family therapy' brings with it an appreciation of the part that both individuals *and* wider systems play in the genesis and the resolution of children's problems, then much will have been achieved.

PROFESSIONAL RELATIONSHIPS AND THE INTRODUCTION OF FAMILY THERAPY

Haley's second concern was with the effect that the introduction of family therapy has on professional hierarchies within clinics. It is difficult to establish the responses of the different disciplines, but, at the risk of over-generalization, I would make the following observations.

Psychoanalysts

In spite of the efforts, cited above, of Skynner and others to shelter family therapy under the well-respected umbrella of psychoanalysis, it has not been welcomed by most analysts. On one level this has been because of the theoretical debate which I reviewed earlier, but on another, I would note that many family therapists have not been eager to acknowledge and respect the analysts' special skills in the treatment of individual children and the contribution that they can make to a systems approach (Montalvo and Haley 1973).

Psychiatrists

The majority of child psychiatrists who were not trained in London receive no formal psychoanalytic training and tend to adopt a multi-axial medical model. Such a position is described most articulately by Rutter (1975; 1982) who sees 'family therapy' as one of a range of treatment approaches, which would be indicated when the main problems lie in family interaction. This is, of course, quite consistent with a systems approach, if family therapy is used in its more limited sense of conjoint family sessions. Problems can arise, however, when there is a disagreement over how a particular case should be tackled; for example, if a family therapist assumes that it can *only* be tackled at the level of the family system. Here, a difference of opinion can overlay a more fundamental disagreement over who should be in control, especially if the 'family therapist' is a junior psychiatrist or social worker. Such disagreements are important and I will discuss them in greater detail later on.

Social workers

The 1970s saw the decline of the psychoanalytically-based casework model in social work education and the swallowing up of psychiatric social work into the new Local Authority Social Services Departments. The supposedly 'elitist' position of child guidance workers came under attack from their new colleagues who began to reflect either the generic training they had received in the universities and colleges, or their previous practice as district team social workers. Thus, whilst many psychiatric social workers were resistant to family therapy on much the same grounds as the analysts, those from a generic background have tended to be the most enthusiastic of its protagonists, for a number of reasons. There has been the opposition to psychodynamic ideas and the casework model and, under the general influence of 'anti-psychiatry', to the 'medical' model. Family therapy is more congruent with new directions in social work which stress an active approach to the client and her problems. Further, by adopting a family therapy approach social workers have gained more influence over the way the clinics are run.

Educational psychologists

Educational psychologists have reacted against the restrictive expectation that their function is one of 'assessment'. They have spent more time engaged either in the direct behavioural treatment of children, or in advisory, planning and indirect work, especially with schools (British Psychological Society 1980). Some may have little interest in family therapy unless it has implications for their activities in schools. For others, family therapy has provided yet another opportunity to work with other members of the child guidance team in a directly therapeutic role.

The introduction of family therapy in a clinic

I have already indicated that most child guidance clinics are organized hierarchically, with a consultant psychiatrist having overall 'case responsibility'. Family therapy, or indeed any other 'new' treatment approach, can undoubtedly be used to mount a challenge to professional hierarchies which are committed to an existing orientation. However, Haley's implication that this challenge is an inevitable consequence of introducing family therapy is surely incorrect. Whilst it is true that some evangelical 'family therapists' have sought to convert all and sundry, family therapy as a method of intervention stresses a rather different approach. The initial task in intervening in a family system is to join with its members, to accommodate to the family's organization and to respect its hierarchy. The method of introducing family therapy to a clinic should be essentially similar. Thus, the extent to which family therapy has failed to become established in some child guidance clinics is probably a function of the degree to which its initiators have failed to follow this path.

For example, because most junior child guidance social workers and psychiatrists have a large degree of autonomy, there may be a temptation to introduce family therapy 'on the quiet'. This is usually a mistake. The danger, of course arises when one of the cases 'goes wrong' (often one of the more difficult cases has been selected in order to prove the method). Fearing failure, the 'family therapists' redouble their efforts, thus compounding the problem, until they have to be 'rescued' by the consultant. This demonstrates both the foolhardiness of the method and the arrogance of its proponents. Alternatively, there can be a dogmatic insistence on conjoint family therapy as being the only valid form of intervention. I pointed out above that such a position does not form part of a systems approach, but it is regrettably true that some 'family therapists' have made such a claim. However, claims like this are not an inherent feature of family therapy itself — and, indeed, proponents of other approaches, notably behaviour modification, have made similar assertions. To suggest, as Haley does, that there is something peculiar about the introduction of family therapy, is unwarranted. In my experience, family therapy can be successfully established in child guidance clinics providing that dogma is avoided, hierarchy is respected, and the existing skills of other workers acknowledged.

A more effective strategy recalls the history of family therapy in child guidance. Family therapy is probably best introduced by way of family 'assessment' interviews which are designed both to enlist the cooperation of the parents and to assess which form of intervention is most appropriate. In the absence of a dogmatic insistence on conjoint family interviews as the only 'correct' therapeutic method, this approach is usually seen by the other members of the team as being of value for the majority of referrals. The assessment itself may indeed recommend conjoint family therapy, but interventions at other systems levels, for example, the medical, intrapsychic or wider systems, will also be indicated. Further, the method of treatment recommended will make use of the existing skills of the clinic staff (for example, individual psychotherapy, behaviour modification) as well as the developing skills in family therapy.

It is advisable to take on for family therapy only those cases which the workers feel reasonably confident they can handle — if they begin to feel out of their depth, they need to request the advice of senior, more experienced members of the clinic team. To assume that because someone does not practice family therapy they have nothing to offer is simply arrogant. To acknowledge that you are inexperienced with a particular type of case or, indeed, that an intervention at a different systems level may be appropriate, is an essential survival skill for the would-be family therapist.

Working together

One of the advantages of introducing a systems approach to a child guidance clinic is that it provides an opportunity for members of the various disciplines to work much more closely together. Thus, co-therapy has been readily and extensively applied as a working method in child guidance. However, effective co-therapy relationships require considerable openness and willingness to share opinions, feelings and experiences outside the therapy sessions. It is unfortunate that the structure of many child guidance clinics does not facilitate co-therapy. In particular the part-time nature of many of the staff, the frequent turnover of junior psychiatrists, and the heavy pressure of work in many clinics, limit the therapists' attempts to cultivate and sustain good co-therapy relationships. Nevertheless, these efforts are not only essential for effective practice but they can also be a most rewarding aspect of multidisciplinary work. The subject of co-working will be discussed further in chapter 11.

Will family therapy disrupt child guidance?

Black (1982, p. 493), in a somewhat uncritical reflection of Haley's position, asserted that: 'The shift in conceptual thinking brought about by a systems approach . . . has been one of the main disruptive influences on child guidance organisations.' However, I do not agree that the problem lies at a conceptual level for, as I have suggested above, a true systems approach (as opposed to a narrow focus on conjoint family therapy, assumes that effective interventions can be made at many levels. Therefore, child guidance workers are not being invited to abandon their existing skills and knowledge, which will continue to be relevant to their work. A systems approach should, rather, enable 'family therapists' to see their colleagues' contributions in a more productive light.

Similarly, I have tried to demonstrate that multi-disciplinary conflicts are not an inevitable consequence of the introduction of a systems approach. Such conflicts pre-date the advent of family therapy by some decades and, indeed, one might argue that they are inevitable since they are founded on differences of opinion about power and influence (Child Guidance Trust 1982). However, Black (1982, p. 494) is undoubtedly correct when she observes that 'unless the family of professionals in child guidance can solve their problems of rivalry, hierarchy, autonomy and leadership, they will not be able to heal the families in trouble who come to them for help.' However, to ascribe these problems to the introduction of 'family therapy' would surely be inappropriate. On the contrary, family therapy, used in the broad sense of a systems approach, can open up new and fruitful areas of co-working, not only within the clinic team itself, but also in relation to other agencies, such as schools and social service area teams. Child guidance professionals can shrug off their original restrictive role allocations to good effect, not by discarding their existing skills, but rather by learning how to integrate them with those of their colleagues in the provision of a comprehensive service to the child in his social contexts.

USING A SYSTEMS APPROACH IN A CHILD GUIDANCE CLINIC

In this section, I shall consider two topics — methods for handling referrals, and for intervening in wider systems. A genuinely systems approach invites child guidance workers to adopt a wide-angled approach which does not narrowly focus on the nuclear family.

Referrals to child guidance clinics — who is the 'customer'?

All the available epidemiological evidence suggests that child guidance clinics only treat a fraction of the potential population of maladjusted children. The Isle of Wight survey (Rutter et al. 1970), for example, estimated the prevalence of 'psychiatric disorder' amongst all ten to twelve year-olds on the island at 6.8 per cent. Only one in ten of those children was under specialist care, though one-third were thought probably, and a further one-third possibly, to require treatment. In other words, the existing services appeared to be meeting only from 15 to 30 per cent of the need.

Reviewing the evidence from several studies, Gath et al. (1977, p. 21) concluded that:

> child guidance patients *are* drawn from among the more disturbed members of the child population; that in terms of severity and duration of symptoms they are roughly comparable to a much larger group of children who are not referred, and that the most important selective factor in referral is the presence of disturbed behaviour, as distinct from neurotic symptoms.

So, why are some children referred to clinics and others not? To some extent, this depends on availability and quality of the service provided in a given area, including the number of staff, size of catchment area, proximity to other services and its standard of communication with local schools and doctors. The crucial factor, however, is the *response* to the child's behaviour and this will be governed by attitudes of parents and teachers, mediated by the attitudes of referring agents such as doctors and head teachers (Gath et al. 1968; Shepherd et al. 1971). In Gath's study, for example, it appeared that the family situation was at least as important a factor as the child's symptoms, in the doctor's decision to refer. Further, in most cases the GP regarded the child's behaviour as trivial or even normal, and had referred them simply to placate their anxious or over-protective parents.

Similarly, it is now well-established not only that the ethos of a school has a profound effect on the behaviour of its pupils and especially on delinquency (Power et al. 1967; Rutter et al. 1979), but also that different schools in similar neighbourhoods show marked differences in the rate of referral (Gath et al. 1977). What is bad behaviour in one school, deserving the cane, is ignored in a second and construed as evidence of psychiatric disorder in a third. Not surprisingly, parents and teachers often have divergent opinions on the same child for, not only may the child behave differently at home and at school but also the same behaviour may be evaluated differently. (Indeed, Rutter et al. (1970), and Shepherd, et al. (1971), found poor agreement between parents' and teachers' responses to their questionnaires.)

Given that it is the response to the child's behaviour which appears to determine referral, rather than the child's behaviour *per se*, and given too that responses may be very different, careful evaluation of a referral to a clinic is essential. It is apparent that, despite its name, the primary clients of the child guidance service are rarely children. It is more accurate to consider as clients *those who respond* to the child's behaviour. In fact, it is best to treat them only as *potential clients* since it is dangerous to assume that they will automatically accept the clinic's approach to their problem.

Receiving a referral

Most referrals to child guidance clinics are received by letter and are considered at a team meeting of a more or less formal nature. The responsibility of a systems worker is to ensure that each referral receives an adequate assessment in its family *and* its wider context: it is not simply to replace an assessment of the identified problem child with a whole-family assessment, for this could simply be to assume family rather than individual pathology. The first task therefore is to read the referral letter carefully in order to identify the client system.

Thus, if the indications are that a parent was summoned to see the referrer (for example, called in to see the head teacher to discuss her son's bad behaviour), then such a simple assumption that she is a 'client' would be unwarranted. In this case, it is possible that it is the school staff who are the potential clients rather than the family. They may be taking a necessary first step in securing the permanent removal of a troublesome child from their school. In other words, they might simply be going through the motions in order to demonstrate to the Education Department that they have 'tried everything, including child guidance, but regrettably. . . .'

Convening a family

If, on reading the letter carefully, the problem appears to be confined to the family system and if the referrer is reliable and appears simply to be acting as a go-between, then a straightforward letter, such as the following, can be sent to the parents.

> We understand from X [referrer] that you are concerned about your son/daughter and have agreed with his/her suggestion that you make contact with the Child Guidance Clinic. We would like to offer you an appointment, etc. . . . We would like to meet all the members of your family, at least on the first occasion because we find that everyone sharing their view of a problem helps all of us to understand it better. If the time or day is inconvenient, please contact the secretary Y, who will try and arrange an alternative appointment.

Such a letter stresses the parents' *agreement* to the referral and implicitly invites them to contact the clinic to point out if their agreement is lacking. However, if doubts have been indicated in the referral letter, it is better to speak to the referrer directly, asking for these doubts to be elaborated. The parents can then be contacted by telephone, or by making a home visit, in order to establish their views and to explain the clinic's policy.

A preliminary discussion with the parents is usually sufficient to ensure the attendance of both at an assessment interview. In a study by Churven (1978), 80 per cent of fathers and 96 per cent of mothers in a deprived area of East London said that they would be prepared to participate in a family assessment and their subsequent attendance confirmed their intentions. These are surprisingly high figures if one considers parents' views expressed to Burck (1978) in a small-scale study of a similar group of families. She noted that only two out of ten families agreed with the clinic's policy of seeing the whole family, and a similar impression is gained from Merrington and Corden (1981). The implication therefore is that if the purpose of a family assessment is adequately explained by the referrer or by the clinic, then most families will attend.

Thus it is usually inadvisable to invite a family for 'family therapy' because this carries the implication that they all have problems. As Merrington and Corden (1981, p. 258) have pointed out: 'the idea that problems may arise out of skewed or disturbed family interaction is not yet readily accepted by many families . . . and is probably another instance of the "clash in perspective" between worker and clients.' Indeed, many parents, most especially mothers, feel guilty and expect to be blamed for their children's problems; the more the therapist tries to re-define the problems as 'family problems', the more some parents will insist on the madness or badness of their child. Such confrontations are unhelpful at best, and at worst precipitate disengagement. If we assume that structural and behavioural change are more important than the insistence that the family share their therapist's special insight, it no longer seems quite so necessary for there to be a struggle over the definition of the problem.

Similarly, Burck's study (1978) confirms the impression that for the therapist to jump in with an immediate offer of marital therapy is a powerful disincentive for further attendance. In any case, as I argued earlier, it is not sufficient to assume that the children can be ignored in favour of an attack on the 'fundamental' marital difficulties. Nevertheless, there are occasions when a worker using a systems approach might think it appropriate to focus on the marital sub-system. In my experience, this is often a difficult area in child guidance work and I will therefore consider the issues in more detail.

Working with marriages in child guidance

I have suggested that, in the first instance, it is best to respect the parents' own perceptions and to approach them as parents rather than marital partners. However, difficulties sometimes arise because the couple are unable to function effectively as an 'executive' sub-system, for example by failing to complete the therapist's tasks. In this case an interview without the children is advisable in which the are invited to discuss the extent to which they are prepared to share the *parenting*. (This is often an essential discussion to have with parents of 'blended' families.) Even if the parents reveal that they are planning to separate, they still retain their responsibilities to their children. Haley (1980) in discussing the therapy of 'problem' adolescents, even goes so far as to suggest that the raising of marital issues early in therapy is a diversion from dealing with the problem at hand: what to do about their child's behaviour. Of course, to some extent, a therapist's position on this issue is a function of the theoretical model she adopts. Some therapists would argue that one should *only* work with the presented problem, the child's behaviour, and that the marriage is irrelevant. As Segal (1981, p. 243) points out:

> They can have a rotten marriage and you could teach them to be a little better with the kid and the marriage may still stay rotten. And if they come in saying I want to do something about my kid and they don't say anything about the marriage I think that's their business.

Others, especially Ackerman (1966), have contended that, since the marriage is the fundamental part of the family it is inevitably part of the therapy of the family. Thus a child-focused phase would be followed by a focus on the marriage. Ackerman's prescription is the one usually avowed by family therapists in child guidance, but my impression is that there is not a great deal of pure marital (as opposed to parental) therapy being undertaken in child guidance settings. We might assume, therefore, that this is largely a function of the name of the agency and of clients' expectations. In many cases it is possible to conduct indirect work on the marital relationship and thus for some clients it seems best not to be explicit but rather to remember that they 'know' better than the therapist what the implications of her intervention are for their marriage. For example, they are unlikely to be fooled by a suggestion that they should spend an evening out together 'to increase their child's sense of independence', but they may well be open to more sensitive suggestions as to how to improve their marriage, so long as these are presented in terms of what is good for their child.

As I have indicated, a focus on the marital relationship can derive from the struggle that some parents have in agreeing and implementing parental tasks assigned in the sessions. In my experience it is best to offer or agree to help the marriage, while retaining the primary goal of helping them to be better parents.

One of my cases, for example, made little progress in the early stages. The couple involved had not discussed their children's behaviour at home, although they regularly agreed to do so as part of a homework assignment. Instead of working out a joint strategy, the husband had alternately taken over sole charge or abdicated total responsibility, while his wife had become more and more helpless and depressed and complained bitterly about him. I therefore decided on an 'unbalancing' tactic and, rather than siding with the wife, I criticized her for failing to appreciate the emotional pressure he was under at work (in a cemetery); she was to listen to his problems (which, incidentally, following a family rule, he had never previously acknowledged) before he could listen to hers. There followed, in the session, a competition between the two over who had the worse problems before they were able to recognize that the most important ones were between themselves. How would they be able to make space in their lives for each other and, most urgently, *for the children?* The focus was then temporarily switched back to the children and, with these difficulties more easily resolved, it was possible to negotiate a return to problems in the marital relationships. On subsequently being questioned in the review interview about this changing focus, the couple stressed the importance of the therapist's timing — to have moved into the marital arena too quickly and without a clear rationale would have precipitated their withdrawal. They were eventually able, for the first time, to consider their marriage as a topic for discussion, because the initial interventions were limited and they could clearly see their relevance to their immediate problems with the children. Ultimately, it was because they had been successful in dealing with the children that they had sufficient confidence in the therapist to return to the sensitive area of their marriage.

INTERVENING IN WIDER SYSTEMS

In advocating the importance of understanding and, if necessary, intervening in systems beyond the family, I do not intend to suggest that child guidance workers should simply give up their caseloads in order to mount an attack on social problems in general or even those in the local neighbourhood — the task of workers in the agency is to provide direct help to individuals and families.

Brown and Levitt (1979) have argued that a therapist's concern is with 'problem systems' rather than social problems. Social problems, mass unemployment, urban decay, poverty and racism, for example, are evidenced in society in a broad sense and can only be effectively addressed through social policy measures and large-scale social programmes. Individual clients and their families are unlikely to conceive of themselves as having a 'social problem' in this sense, but they do typically experience a number of specific problems in their interaction with a limited number of other people (for example, the neighbours) and agencies and institutions (the courts, the DHSS). The family and other systems which interact to produce the problem can be termed the 'problem system' — it revolves around the client system's concern and is limited to those persons and agencies directly involved in maintaining the problem.

Thus, the essential elements of an assessment are to determine *who is involved* and *how* they are involved, to identify the participants in the problem system and to clarify how those participants interact to produce and maintain the problematic behaviour. Thus, to assess the problems of a client system requires extensive information about the system as well as a comprehensive knowledge of the multifarious systems (for example, health, education, work, neighbourhood) which might be presumed to impinge upon it. Although not all these systems are certain to play significant roles in the problems of any given client system, an assessment which overlooks relevant systems will be at best partial, and at worst irrelevant or wrong. Furthermore, interventions based on such a limited assessment are likely to be ineffective or even detrimental and, as we have discussed before

(Treacher and Carpenter 1982), may lead to the deleterious labelling of the client system as 'resistant'.

For example, an eleven year-old boy had been sent away to a residential school for maladjusted children because of his disruptive behaviour both at home and at school. After a brief honeymoon period at his new school he began to steal and to engage in destructive pranks such as breaking windows and putting dead animals in other boys' beds. He took great care not to be caught red-handed although the circumstantial evidence pointed unequivocally to him. The residential school staff worked according to a philosophy which encouraged the boys to acknowledge responsibility for their own actions and therefore spent many hours trying to persuade him to own up to his misdemeanours. The more he misbehaved and denied his actions the more time he spent with the school staff and the more his actions intensified: however, because he was never caught in the act nor admitted his culpability, he was never punished. For this reason his parents were not informed that he had done anything wrong, although they were given indications that he was having 'some difficulty in adjusting'. The school staff had also been told that his mother had been depressed when he was at home and they did not want to worry her.

Similarly, his behaviour at home at weekend visits and half-term was also getting worse, especially when he was in his mother's charge. However, she played it down when his father came home because he was on short-time working, in danger of being made redundant, and she did not want to worry him. She spent a great deal of time trying to persuade her son to behave himself, especially when her husband's mother came to visit, since past experience led her to believe that her mother-in-law would pass on any information to her husband.

Of course, the boy's father was not entirely in the dark about his son's behaviour. He had been very suspicious when he found him playing with a new watch, but reluctantly accepted the explanation that it had been 'swapped' at school. Naturally, he did not tell his wife lest she became worried and depressed, nor did he attempt to corroborate his son's explanation with the school because he suspected it was false and he feared he might be expelled if the deed was discovered. The boy had been somewhat reluctantly accepted by the school for a trial period and it appeared to the family that the next step would be Borstal.

The clinic worker, and indeed the district team social worker responsible for a Supervision Order which had been made on the boy, had both been informed by the mother of his difficult behaviour at home. Both independently interpreted this as a reaction to leaving home, punishing his mother for having sent him away. Similarly, both shared father's anxiety that the trial period might be unsuccessful and knew that he would be difficult to place elsewhere. Therefore, neither acted on the mother's information for fear of 'rocking the boat'. The whole edifice of secrecy, founded on the wish to protect others, was but a house of cards and inevitably collapsed.

It is clear in this example that many people and agencies, through their action or inaction, were directly involved in maintaining the problem. The context of the problem is not confined to home or school and a definition of the problem system must necessarily include the residential school (including sub-systems comprising headmaster, housemaster, boys), the nuclear family (including father and mother), the father's work, the paternal grandmother, the child guidance worker, and the district team social worker. Such a definition might nevertheless prove too limited as the problems and its consequences develop. So the list might have to be extended to include other members of the extended family, the clinic team, officials of the Education Department, the father's employers (if he has to take time off work) and the mother's GP (if she becomes depressed).

In the case described, it was apparent that there were a number of different targets which had to be tackled. The method of intervention was essentially the same as one would use in engaging a family, except that, in my role as the clinic worker, I had to recognize that I was already part of the problem system. In fact, this recognition only came about when I was contacted by the head of the residential school who was at his wits' end about the boy's behaviour. I confessed that his mother was also worried and explained why neither of us had informed him. He readily agreed to my suggestion that I convene a meeting of everybody involved, since it was apparent that his pupil's misdemeanours were not solely his school's fault and also that he had not been protecting the mother from anything she did not already know about. Once I had met both parents the secret was exposed and they were eager to take part in a meeting. Interestingly they decided spontaneously to see grandmother together to explain what had been happening.

At the meeting itself, which also included an official from the Education Department and the district team social worker, we quickly identified how we had all interacted in such a way as to keep the secret. Acknowledging the part we had all played ensured that the problem could then be resolved.

Intervening in schools

As I have already suggested, a discrepancy in views often exists between family and school; this may concern whether or not there is a problem to be resolved. Thus, to confine the assessment and therapy to the family system would obviously be quite inappropriate. Fortunately, child guidance usually has a degree of influence in relation to schools. It is rarely difficult therefore, to convene meetings between school staff, parents and child, in order to make an assessment of difficulties between the two, and to engage both parties in an effort to tackle a mutual problem (Skynner 1976; Aponte 1976). (See also chapter 5.)

An appreciation of the importance of schools in influencing both the behaviour of children and how that behaviour is defined, has led some child guidance workers to intervene directly with school staff. Daines (et al. 1982) has described and evaluated a project in Bristol which involves two clinic staff in meeting with the pastoral care staff of a comprehensive school in order to provide advice and support to teachers in dealing with difficult children. At this meeting children who are causing concern are discussed, and although some of them might later be referred to the clinic itself, in very many cases the problem is dealt with at school. As Daines (1982, p. 178) points out, this avoids stigmatizing the children and it can also be an effective preventive method.

> Many children at some stage in their school careers go through a period when they are emotionally disturbed. With sensitive handling this never becomes a huge problem and need never go for psychiatric referral. The better understanding and increased skills of teachers who have the opportunity for regular meetings with mental health professions can be very important in the prevention of more chronic problems in children.

Such a consultation service can lead to more effective work in the clinic with those children who are referred, because the school staff acquire a better understanding of those cases which the clinic can help and the clinic staff can gain more helpful and specific information. Further, more children can be reached more quickly, both because the meetings can encourage teachers to discuss children at an earlier stage of their difficulties and because the formalities usually involved in making a referral are unnecessary.

In their list of recommendations for improving the service, Daines (p. 177) and her colleagues go one step further in suggesting:

> A shift to include more consideration of the system of the school and the part it plays in the problems of the child. . . . We thought that the consultation could usefully address itself to problems created for the child by the institution of the school. This might involve, for example, a consideration of the particular class a child was in, a particular structure in the school, the question of tensions in staff relationships etc. and their effects on the child.

From a systems perspective this would obviously be a most appropriate, if threatening, direction in which to move: the parallel with intervening in the marital sub-system in the family is apparent since the school defines the children and not itself as the problem. Nonetheless, some educational psychologists have experimented with such an approach. Thus Burden (1978) has described a series of projects based on the School of Education at Exeter University.

In one newly-formed comprehensive school a large number of children had been referred to the Educational Psychology Service but there had been little change in the way these 'problem children' were dealt with, despite (or perhaps because of) the psychologist's expressed view that the cause of the problem did not lie within the children themselves. A team of trainees was moved in, but as Burden underlines, they did not immediately abandon individual testing of the children, but rather tried to use the results of each investigation to 'widen the teachers' appreciation of the context within which problem behaviour is occurring.' After a while, they were able to persuade a full staff meeting to discuss the underlying issues relating to the referral of 'problem children' by asking such questions as: What is the schools' attitude to problems? Is there a school ethos? What does the school think should be done about problems? What are the school's expectations of the psychologist? By asking these questions, they were able to establish that:

> the amalgamation of secondary modern school pupils into an

existing grammar school to form a comprehensive, whilst seeking covertly to maintain the ethos and much of the curriculum of the grammar school, was having a disastrous effect on the attitudes and responses to school of a significant proportion of the pupils. Moreover the lack of clearly defined rules of pastoral responsibility or structure within the school was making it impossible for even those with the children's best interests at heart to be sure of what was appropriate with regard to their level and involvement (Burden 1978, p. 119).

To a family therapist there is something reassuringly familiar about the way in which such a formulation is couched and also, I might add, the structural changes that are apparently required. It is no coincidence perhaps that Burden and his colleagues have gone on to adopt systems theory as their working model, or indeed that they have, arguably, over-focused on the school system in exactly the same way that family therapists have over-focused on the family system.

CONCLUSION

The effects of family therapy on child guidance clinics

If the one lasting effect of family therapy on child guidance clinics is that their name was changed to child *and family* guidance, or even family consultation centres, then they will have gained little and lost much. If the only change is that the family rather than the child is viewed as the problem and that conjoint family therapy becomes the only and automatic form of intervention, then the crucial insight, that an individual and his family must be understood in their context, will have been lost.

Family therapy claims to be based on an 'open' systems model, (see Skynner 1976). Nevertheless, there is a danger that some 'family therapists' will try to create a new orthodoxy, founded on a narrow definition of family therapy and regulated by a 'metaprofession'. Even if this was possible, in my opinion it would merely elevate family therapy to a restricted domain, equivalent to that occupied by child psychotherapy, where it would be practised by a well-trained few, on 'suitable' cases.

I have argued, instead, that a systems approach can transcend a dogmatic insistence on the rights and wrongs of different treatment methods. The skills of individual psychotherapy are just as relevant as those of conjoint family therapy, if we are not to make the mistake of ignoring the individual and enthroning the family system. Similarly, if we are to avoid the myopic assumption that the problem is always located in the family, we must make serious and consistent attempts to extend our analysis and intervention beyond the family system. The introduction of a systems approach to Child Guidance Clinics can help us to avoid these errors. If this is achieved family therapy will enhance child guidance rather than disrupt it.

3

Family Therapy with adolescents in in-patient psychiatric units

HUGH JENKINS

The treatment of adolescents in psychiatry falls uneasily between the well-defined areas of child guidance and adult psychiatry. This 'between age' poses organizations and practitioners with problems about treatment and management of adolescents whose behaviour appears bizarre or in some way dangerous. The dilemma is frequently whether placement should be made in a setting designed primarily for children or for adults. Psychiatric hospitals prefer not to admit people below the age of seventeen, and social service departments frequently lack a comprehensive range of resources for young people beyond the age of fifteen or sixteen. Adolescent units are one of the solutions that society provides for some youngsters who fall between the clearer categories of child and adult.

According to a recent review (ACPP 1978), there are some 45 adolescent psychiatric units in the UK which offer an in-patient service to families. Many also offer a complementary out-patient service. They are funded by regional health authorities, and overall responsibility for clinical work is taken by a consultant psychiatrist. The other professional disciplines represented in these units include nursing, social work, clinical psychology and teaching. In some instances there will be occupational therapists and art therapists as full- or part-time members.

TREATMENT ISSUES

Adolescent units aim to help adolescents and their families cope with difficulties about personal identity and maturation which often accompany the physiological and psychological changes of puberty

(Feinstein et al. 1980). They also focus on stresses associated with separation from the family, and the uncertainties both for the adolescent and the family as he becomes more involved in the adult world. Conflicts which precipitate crises at this stage generally occur in families, and it is to families that most adolescents will return on discharge. So it is usual for units to claim a 'family focus' — which many would describe as 'family therapy'.

However, Harbin (1979) points out that 'family therapy' is often used in the restricted sense of interviewing the patient's family, so that information can be gathered, and discharge planned. For example, Orvin (1974) insists that 'the keystone of the adolescent's treatment is individual psychotherapy with the resident psychiatrist assigned to him. All other treatment modalities are intimately related to the basic therapeutic foundation between resident and adolescent.' While taking account of the family, the model proposed by Orvin is essentially an individual model of psychotherapy with other approaches taking supporting roles. He would allow the adolescent to decide when he is ready for discharge. This gives little or no authority to the family who receive him back, but instead locates the power, and a strong professional alliance, with the adolescent and his psychiatric (medical) resident. Although an apparently reasonable approach, especially as it is generally agreed that one of the tasks in adolescence is for the individual to take more responsibility for his own actions, it has something of a hit or miss quality as regards the family and others who may be directly involved and responsible. It does not respect the existing hierarchy of responsibilities and decision-making in the family, and it implicitly reinforces the adolescent's central organizing position. In this chapter, I will outline a more thorough systems approach to adolescents and their families.

Creating boundaries

One aspect of this approach involves establishing a sufficient psychological distance between the family and the adolescent, so that the adolescent can re-enter the family on a different basis once the initial crisis is over. Usually, this can be achieved in direct work with the family. Sometimes, and especially in very enmeshed families (Minuchin et al. 1978), where considerable difficulties exist in the open expression and resolution of conflict, it can be faster and more effective to achieve this 'distance' by physical separation, as the following case-history illustrates.

Peter was a fourteen year-old only son of late middle-aged parents. His isolated behaviour caused his parents concern. He was not attending school and his father usually slept with him if he had night fears. Peter was particularly hostile about the referral, influenced no doubt in large part by his previous experience of going to a child guidance clinic when his father had said they were going to watch a cricket match. Comparing the visit to a psychiatrist unfavourably with the promise of cricket, he punched his 6 foot 2 inch father on the nose in the waiting room.

From the start of my involvement with Peter and his parents, I made it a condition that both should accompany him during the pre-admission visits and discuss openly the plans being made. A further condition of Peter's treatment stipulated that the parents should be jointly involved. In a relatively short time they were helped to renegotiate their routines with Peter, which also involved them changing their ways of dealing with each other. Mother now had a more active role, and father no longer telephoned Peter at the unit to make sure he had dried his hair properly after washing it. Peter was now going to a new school, which involved more travelling than before and less direct parental involvement.

If this family-system focus is not established from the outset, it is much easier for an individual's removal to an in-patient unit to confirm the family's view of him as 'the problem'. When this happens, the rest of the family merely become therapist's aides, working with the unit to 'cure' the individual. It is the work put into setting the scene that determines the way the play will be performed.

Establishing goals

Given that the primary goal at admission is the adolescent's eventual discharge, the only uncertainty concerns the length of time he will stay in the unit. The adoption of any other aim increases the likelihood that the needs of the unit, such as having a good take-up of beds, or even of demonstrating the need for a psychiatric unit, will predominate (Byng-Hall and Bruggen 1974). A second goal, of equal importance, is that the first admission should not become an apprenticeship for a long-term career of psychiatric stays, which then become incorporated into the family's pattern for dealing with its 'problem' member.

Psychiatric in-patient units tend not to heighten conflict but to damp it down. Once this has happened, and the patient is quieter, he is usually returned home. Madanes (1980) has pointed out this danger: 'After some time [the adolescent] begins to cause trouble again and, if rehospitalised, the chances are that he has begun a career as a mental patient.' When this occurs, psychiatric institutions are in effect colluding with the family system to support the status quo. They therefore become powerless to produce changes that could interrupt this sequence of events. Both are 'forced' by the adolescent to react to his unacceptable behaviour in a way which does not allow him or the family to develop more appropriate coping strategies.

One of the central issues in adolescence concerns who is to be in charge and on what terms. Families with severe difficulties during the adolescent phase behave as though the adolescent is in control, with everyone's behaviour being organized around the problems he presents. Haley argues that the central theme for the adolescent is one of failure to begin making separate arrangements for his own life. For the family, it is failure to disengage successfully from their adolescent member. He suggests that 'one way the young person can stabilise the family is to develop some incapacitating problem . . . so that he or she continues to need the parents' (Haley 1980). By the time parents ask for help, they tend to feel powerless to reverse the pattern of failing behaviour, and much traditional professional assistance encourages them in this pattern when they relinquish their son or daughter into the hands of the 'experts'. A systems-orientated therapist will not be interested in taking over parenting functions as a goal of treatment. He will aim to support families so that they assume appropriate responsibility for the behaviour of their adolescent. It is therefore crucial that the therapist does not take charge of the decision-making process regarding admission and discharge (Byng-Hall and Bruggen 1974; Bruggen and O'Brian 1982; Madanes 1980). The decision to admit the adolescent to an in-patient unit should clearly be that of the parents. Once they have taken that decision, the unit can respond by offering the family a resource which they can use in a variety of ways to develop more appropriate problem-solving (Jones 1980). Such an approach means that the unit does not supplant the executive function of the parents,

who are thus encouraged to be aware of their continuing responsibility to indicate when they are ready for discharge to take place.

ADMISSIONS: PRACTICAL CONSIDERATIONS
AND PROCEDURES

Most references to in-patient work with adolescents include aspects
of the family's involvement (Campbell 1975; Hersov and Bentovim
1976; Van de Lande 1979; Looney et al. 1980; Jones 1980; Singh
1982; Bruce 1982). Even so, little attention is paid to how the
issues of responsibility are negotiated between the time of the first
contact with the family and the time of admission to the unit.

However, the importance of the admission phase is emphasized in
excellent accounts by Bruggen et al. (1973); Byng-Hall and Bruggen
(1974); and Bruggen and O'Brian (1982). They note that if the
negotiations which surround admission are vague, and family/unit
staff responsibilities not made clear, the criteria for discharge will
also be vague. Negotiations about admission do not precede treatment
— they are part of treatment. As it becomes clear that something
different is expected of the family, so the family will begin to
organize and behave differently. Part of this process will involve
some agreement about a clear definition of desired changes. They
must be verifiable and concrete, rather than general and abstract.
Changes in attitude or motivation for behaving in a certain way are
difficult to measure unless specific different activities are identified
which provide sufficient proof that change has occurred.

REFERRALS

Referrals to in-patient units may be made directly by the family or by
a third party — another professional agency. It is extremely rare for
an adolescent to refer himself, so that it is unusual for him to be 'the
customer'. Usually someone else complains or is concerned about
him. Negotiations about possible admission should include 'the
customer' — the person who says the adolescent has a problem. This
should happen even when the referrer is acting as 'honest broker' on
behalf of the family. However neutral he feels himself to be, the
honest broker still concurs implicitly with the request for admission

by agreeing to pass it on. It should be assumed that he will have some impact on the family, especially if the unit decides that admission is not in the best interests of all concerned at that time.

A conjoint meeting involving the family and members of the unit staff should be held. It must include the person who would be the primary therapist if admission is agreed. In cases where the family has been seen in the out-patient clinic, it is preferable for their existing therapist to continue in the primary role. Where the third-party referrer comes from another agency such as a school or social services department, it is advisable to involve a suitably powerful member from that system in the negotiations (Aponte 1976).

The next stage involves a formal visit to the unit, where the adolescent spends a day joining in the usual routine. The family are also seen, both at the start of the day and again at the end. This allows time for questions to be asked and doubts aired. The family also tour the unit buildings and meet the staff informally. The second meeting at the end of the day allows them to hear how their child has fared, and what issues, if any, have arisen. If the youngster is involved in this process, it short-circuits the first opportunity for any splitting between parents and staff to occur, since he is prevented from telling horror stories of his experience without having to substantiate them! The family leaves the unit and has to decide whether it wants to go ahead with the admission. This procedure permits the whole staff team to review the visit on the following day, and to formulate an overall strategy should the family request in-patient help.

'PARENTAL' RESPONSIBILITY

Sometimes the choices offered to the family are not straightforward, as the following case history illustrates. Louis began to have considerable difficulties in attendance at the end of his first year at secondary school. The current crisis occurred around the first anniversary of Louis' father's departure from home. His mother was the primary caretaker, but this was confused by support and interference from the maternal grandmother. Both women indulged in alcohol binges, and either Louis or the grandmother's man friend would try to cope. Attempts to engage the father, who was in contact with Louis, and his separated wife, were totally unsuccessful.

At the time of referral I could have had statutory grounds to arrange for Louis and his younger sister to be placed in the care of the local authority because of concern for their general well-being. The education authorities were putting court proceedings into operation in the case of Louis. In other words, two powerful agencies could have taken over parental rights from the mother. Instead, as a result of two family sessions involving mother, grandmother, her man friend, Louis, and his sister, the *mother* was encouraged to make a choice about Louis' future. She had said that she could neither persuade Louis to go to school, nor bear to force him. She was therefore allowed to 'choose' between a care order, via the education department, or admission to the adolescent unit. The former meant a probable residential placement some 30 miles away from home, a point which I explored in some detail, while the latter required her to be committed to a much more active involvement with her son. At this, she threatened to harm herself, cried, and then said that she would have to run out of the room. I opened the door for her and she remained in her chair. She eventually agreed to go away and return a week later with a decision. I promised to ask the education department not to act during this period.

Her decision at the end of the second session signified her willingness to be dealt with as a competent adult, and not as a chronic psychiatric patient. This was the first step in a process which ended with Louis back in school and enjoying it; grandmother living back in her own flat, Louis and his sister in more regular contact with their father, and mother no longer abusing alcohol. She appeared to have a much better self-image at this stage.

It is also important to make similarly firm agreements with local authorities when they, rather than the family, have 'parental' responsibilities in relation to adolescents. The process of negotiating such an agreement is often similar to the process of negotiating with a family, as the following case demonstrates.

Diana was a fifteen year-old girl whose mother's unpredictable life-style meant that the local authority would not allow Diana to live with her. An adolescent unit was asked to take her from a children's home. After a number of weeks, it became clear that the local authority were sending Diana at weekends to children's homes where there happened to be a vacant bed. The official carers were providing no more stability than her mother. The unit only agreed to continue work with Diana on condition that she could have a permanent base in one children's home. The local authority were not allowed to hand over their 'parental' responsibility to another agency.

When admission is dealt with in a cooperative manner, without the professional team usurping the family's responsibilities, it becomes easier to maintain that focus. If hasty admissions which undermine parental authority are allowed to happen, it will be difficult to re-establish parental responsibility at a later stage. It would be better for admission not to take place in the first instance, since there are few short-term advantages which can outweigh the long-term losses.

PROBLEMS WHICH ARISE WHEN FIRST CONTACTS WITH A
FAMILY ARE MISHANDLED

The following case history indicates some of the problems which arise when initial contact with a family is mishandled, and issues concerning the nature of the hierarchy within the family are not adequately formulated. Family and staff quickly become caught up in repetitive difficulties which maintain the problems that brought the adolescent and his family for help. It underlines the importance of establishing a working hypothesis about problem-maintaining behaviour so that professional help can be orientated to interrupt that pattern from the very first contact with the family (Watzlawick et al. 1974).

Patrick was the sixteen year-old son of parents who had separated in the previous 18 months. He continued to live with his mother, and had diminishing contact with his father. He had attacked his mother a number of times. His behaviour had become unpredictable and seemingly 'psychotic'. She felt unable to cope, and had initiated the referral. At her request, he was subsequently admitted to an adolescent unit, but at that time the unit did not establish a clear agreement between her and her estranged husband concerning parental responsibilities in relation to Patrick's behaviour.

It became clear during his stay at the unit that Patrick had considerable sexual difficulties, causing the girls and female staff justifiable anxiety by his provocative behaviour. The male staff tended to become more involved with him following either his violent outbursts or sexual provocation. When staff were angry with

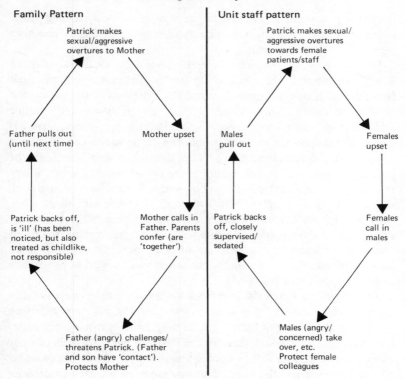

FIGURE 3.1 Patterns of interaction centred around Patrick
In both instances, although Patrick is the 'ill' person, and clearly very distressed, it is hard to ignore the 'power' which his actions have to organize other people's behaviour.

him, he usually responded with inappropriate laughter. As figure 3.1 demonstrates, it was apparent that the staff group was replicating the same patterns of interaction as occurred within Patrick's family. It was also evident that Patrick's 'psychotic' behaviour had achieved something for him and his family that nothing else had. It had brought his parents together, for they now met regularly at the unit over their shared concern for Patrick, and father was more involved when crises erupted at home during weekend leave. Patrick's behaviour also brought male and female staff together in concern and protection for each other. This had a 'healing' function for existing staff splits, but did not produce any long-term effect on the underlying dynamics. Patrick at least offered some respite from covert conflict for family, and staff, while they united to try and help him.

In Haley's terms, Patrick's behaviour served a social function of attempting to stabilize and reunite his family, and a metaphorical function of highlighting the sexual and aggressive nature of the conflictual relationships (Haley 1980). The fight between father and son was made overt and sexual. Patrick recounted how his father had threatened to 'cut my bollocks off' following one incident at home during weekend leave. This threat, around the theme of potency, is an explicit example of some of the unresolved conflicts that troubled families frequently experience. A male who is 'castrated' is unable to be a complete adult, while an anorexic girl inhibits her own normal sexual development and remains 'asexual'. These are the very real developmental costs for families which are unable to reorganize themselves in the face of the emerging needs of their adolescent members, and unable to adapt to the process of leaving and letting go (Jenkins 1981).

The effects of Patrick's behaviour on the staff team were equally complex. Ironically, the parents' view that Patrick was sick was echoed by the intrapsychic understanding of his primary therapist. He advocated individual therapy for Patrick, but also insisted that Patrick must be helped to express his anger openly to his parents. The nursing staff in the team, who had most to do with Patrick on a daily basis, focused on the distress of his home life and attempted to offer something better. At the same time they were constantly split by his behaviour in their attempts to get closer to him. Intimacy with either biological parent spelt doom for him, so it was unlikely that surrogate professional parenting would be allowed to fare any better. At another level, the nursing staff and the primary therapist began to compete over who was more competent, with the nurses protecting Patrick at times from the perceived 'potency' of the primary therapist.

In order to deal directly with the family's dilemmas, a first stage would have involved the staff agreeing on a framework for understanding the meaning of Patrick's problem in the context of his parents' relationship. Without agreement at this level, it was inevitable that similar patterns would develop within the staff group. To the extent that these particular matters were not satisfactorily resolved, it is probable that they inadvertently contributed to Patrick's eventual transfer to an adult psychiatric day hospital.

STAFF TEAMS AND THE INTRODUCTION OF FAMILY THERAPY

A staff team on an adolescent unit may number 30 or more people. The members of the team will be drawn from different professional disciplines and their status will vary. An individual wishing to develop a family therapy service, especially if not the most senior member of the team with clear executive and overall treatment responsibility, is faced with a daunting task. Anderson and Reiss (1982) identify the problems involved, and implicitly suggest a solution: 'A major reason for the failure of family therapy in an in-patient unit is the polarisation that often occurs between family and medical approaches to treatment, suggesting that one type of intervention is less important than another.'

The professional system, as shown in figure 3.2, has a web-like quality. The strength or otherwise of these links between staff will vary from unit to unit. When so many people are involved, it is important for someone with overall responsibility to be the primary therapist. The example of Patrick illustrates some of the ways in which staff can become involved in covert struggles to define how best to offer help. A family systems therapist is both at an advantage and a disadvantage when planning strategies. The advantage comes from an awareness of how systems operate, both in the here-and-now, and over time. This awareness provides a tool for working at an organizational level within the staff team. The disadvantage is that the family therapist will often want to see and work with the whole family. Others may view him as attempting to undermine their roles within the unit. There also exists the problem of proposing a new, apparently unproven treatment method which draws from many other approaches, but which does not neatly fit any existing therapeutic category.

A family systems therapist who wishes to introduce family therapy to an in-patient unit has many difficulties to overcome and pitfalls to avoid. There are the problems of complexity, of shared, and at times diffuse, responsibility, of medical versus non-medical models of treatment, and of new ideas being grafted onto established practice. He would do well, in fact, not to introduce 'family therapy' as such. To become involved in struggles about which method is best is a futile and exhausting exercise. Hurley (1982) emphasizes the

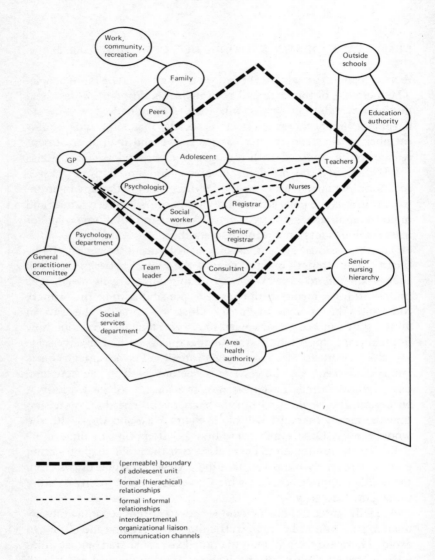

FIGURE 3.2 Unit/family systems map
In the interests of simplicity, this figure focuses on the adolescent, and not the wider family in relation to professional staff. Nor does it include other staff who might be involved on a sessional basis.

importance of not entering into battle with other agencies in out-patient treatment, and obviously it is crucial, when working in in-patient units, to avoid alienating different staff groups. It is also true that nothing is gained by setting out to prove oneself right and the rest of the staff wrong.

Time spent discussing ideas with the most powerful members of the unit hierarchy (who can both facilitate referrals and give key support to work undertaken) will pay dividends. Such discussion will establish in advance whether (and under what conditions) support will be forthcoming when difficulties arise.

Initially it is useful to avoid trying to establish an approach that is totally different, since by implication this would communicate that what others have been doing is somehow second best, or worse still, of no use at all. Instead, it is best to look for areas of common ground and practice from which to share ideas. Grandiose claims about the efficacy of family therapy should be avoided since it is not a particular therapist, but the professional system of which he is part which has the power to allow the approach to work. (See figure 3.2.)

Probably the most effective way of influencing in-patient work is to begin by establishing an *out-patient* family therapy service. This allows practice to be established in parallel, while not directly impinging on the in-patient team. It is an area where the family therapist can control involvement of other staff to a large degree, and allows him, with like-minded others, to begin to develop some expertise and professional confidence. At a later stage, the family therapist can share his experiences with students on placement from other disciplines as part of their training. This is greatly facilitated if a one-way screen, or video, is available.

Each in-patient unit will differ in the extent to which new ways of conceptualizing problems and working with them are felt to threaten the existing integrity of the team. Whether extreme or mild, there *must* be resistance to new ideas, since they involve an implied message that the old ways can be improved upon. This means that cherished beliefs may have to be modified or discarded. Just as families can respond to change during the transition phase from adolescence to adulthood by reinforcing outworn patterns of behaviour, so too professional systems may respond in the same way. A good family therapist will take time to 'join' the family and accommodate to its particular ways of dealing with its members and outsiders before shifting the focus of his behaviour towards activating change, and therefore towards some degree of crisis. Equally, an individual 'joining' a professional system must use the same respectful approach when proposing a new therapeutic framework.

CONCLUSION

I have underlined the importance of paying attention to the organizational aspects of staff teams, as well as the wider systems which impinge on the adolescent, the family, and of course, the unit itself. Inevitably, the picture is one of complexity and, when working from the inside, often seems to be one of confusion. If this is so for the staff, how much more is it likely to be so for the family who may feel powerless and divested of responsibility. For this reason, I have emphasized the importance of paying careful attention to the admission procedure which inevitably involves the contradiction of acting *in loco parentis* while at the same time emphasizing the parents' continuing responsibility for the future of their adolescent son or daughter.

The guidelines for introducing family therapy into an in-patient unit are reasonably straightforward. Initially, it is essential to avoid the error of making too many claims about the value of family therapy. It is also important not to ignore the skills of others, since their support will be crucial in the long term. Whether a systemic orientation already exists, or whether this is being introduced, it is clear that at all levels of activity the unit's organization must be considered and worked with. The pace of progress cannot be forced, but it is clear from the work of Bruggen and his colleagues that staff can and will respond positively to a family-orientated approach, particularly when it is applied to the crucial admission phase of the adolescent's stay in the unit. Staff are often sympathetic to the idea of contracts since they tend to feel manipulated both by adolescents and their families, who often triangulate them into conflicts which originate in the family. A family-orientated admission procedure can become a stepping-stone to a more consistent systems approach which is able to absorb other forms of concurrent work such as individual and group sessions.

4

Family Therapy in Residential Homes for Children

EDDY STREET

Despite their claims to be general system theorists, many family therapists tend to concentrate on the family system to the exclusion of other systems. Curiously this has even been true when families have been disrupted through a crisis which leads to the institution-alization of the person who is the 'identified patient'. For example, in their classic study *Families of the Slums*, Minuchin and his colleagues (Minuchin et al. 1967) described a research project involving boys who had been placed in a residential school. However, Minuchin made no mention of either the problems of separation experienced by the boys and their families as the boys left home to go to the school, or the organizational issues that were faced in attempting family therapy under these conditions. Strangely, there is also only passing reference to the relationship between the family, the residential staff, the child's caseworker and the therapists.

The psychological processes involved in the crisis that leads to the removal of a child into a residential establishment are undoubtedly very complex and cannot be adequately discussed here. Scott's work, concerned with a similar process in families who scapegoat and 'extrude' an adult member (Scott and Ashworth 1967), is an interesting starting point for such a discussion, but the only issue that I wish to stress here is the issue of rejection. If the family has adopted a stance of rejecting the child then it is important that the professional workers involved do not accept this position as fixed and unchanging. The case of Simon which is summarized in the chapter by Dave Dungworth and Sigurd Reimers is an excellent example of the approach that needs to be adopted. By keeping the child and the family in contact with each other, the social worker involved was able to create the grounds for a later reconciliation.

Families which reject their children are undoubtedly very difficult to work with and they often also create hostility in the professional workers who have to cope with them. The rejection of a child is seen as an immoral and largely incomprehensible act which serves to intensify the residential worker's right to take charge of the child. Given this context it is not surprising to find that residential care and family care have been seen as mutually exclusive and incompatible (Clough 1982).

Clough has noted however that there have been some isolated attempts to plan and organize residential facilities that allow for programmes involving a variety of direct work with families. He is cautious and even pessimistic about the likelihood of these schemes working because of his perception of the tensions that exist between families, the practices of residential establishments, and the context within which the establishments are expected to operate. Nevertheless, some residential workers are struggling to establish a means of involving themselves with the families of individuals within their care. Jacobs (1982), for example, has described how the staff group at a particular assessment centre for children made attempts to be involved in family sessions run by a visiting consultant psychiatrist — the outcome of this effort was not particularly encouraging because of difficulties between the staff involved.

Family therapists working with the families of children in residential care have had few guidelines; this chapter attempts to provide some. Initially, I shall focus my discussion on the systems that conflict and contend with each other when a child is separated from his or her family. I will then go on to discuss tactics for developing a family therapy programme involving a worker who is not a member of the staff of the residential institution. Finally, since residential workers are often keen to undertake family therapy themselves, I shall describe the development of a family therapy programme within a community home.

THE CONTENDING SYSTEMS WHEN A CHILD SEPARATES
FROM THE FAMILY

When a child is placed in care the authorities become responsible not only for the child but also for the relationship between the parents and the child. When separation occurs the parents tend to give up their sense of responsibility for what is happening to their child. They see the problem as no longer their concern, and hence perceive themselves as not requiring help. The authorities are now responsible for their child.

The responsibility issue is indeed a very complex one, for the child is a member of several overlapping systems. First, there is the family of which the child is a natural member. Second, there is the system of the social services department, which contains the non-residential social worker (field worker) who carries responsibility for the case. These two systems overlap to create the social worker/family system. It is this overlapping system that presents itself to the third system (the residential unit) when the child is received into care. This is a system which bears some similarity to the family since it is composed of a mixture of adults and children who collectively deal with the daily tasks of living. There is a veritable Aladdin's Cave of other professionals and their agencies whose responsibilities can and do involve the child. These include child psychiatrists from child guidance clinics, educational psychologists from schools psychological services, school counsellors and education welfare officers from schools, probation officers from the probation service and so on. Each of these systems impinge on the child, the family and each other.

The social—professional network of children in care is, therefore, an exceptionally complex one. With the multiplicity of agencies and professionals involved, it is little wonder that, on occasions, the family, and even the professionals, are confused as to where the focus of power and authority lies. However, for the sake of simplicity this analysis assumes that three systems (the family, the residential establishment and the social services department) dominate the overall network. It is between these three systems that the central issues governing the child's stay in care are contested. It is precisely these issues that have to be confronted if any therapeutic work is to be attempted. Haley (1980) has stressed that the central theme of therapy revolves around the issues of power and control between parent and child, family and therapist, and therapist and institution.

It can be argued that long-term residential care must involve the sharing of parenting responsibility between the residential unit and family in a way that safeguards the interests of the child. For the family and the child, residential care raises the question as to whether or not they belong together anymore and whether the role of natural parent confers any rights. The staff of the children's home have responsibility for the day-to-day care of the child. The professionals outside the residential unit typically have the responsibility of being involved with the major decisions central to the child's management, and not infrequently one of these carers, a social worker, bears the responsibility for the liaison and organization involved in these decisions.

With such a division of function it is commonplace to hear staff of children's homes complain that they are being requested to offer daily care and containment for a child, whilst other professionals busy themselves with the decision-making process which the unit perceives as being much more status-enhancing than their own work. Similarly, social workers complain that they are asked to remedy situations which they believe to have been created by the residential staff's management of the child; they sometimes complain too that they are not informed about important aspects of the child's behaviour. Contests of power and control can take the form of residential staff attempting to demonstrate both to the child's family and the social worker their capacity to care for the child.

Social workers also attempt to demonstrate their centrality by trying to support and care for the child. They do this by emphasizing the primary importance of activities that take place outside the residential unit, and they may spend time in forming a meaningful relationship with the child. The family, faced by all this professionally mobilized competence, may elect finally to dispense with the last remnants of their own competence by adopting a passive 'don't care' attitude. Or they may insist aggressively on their own competence, and develop a hostile, anti-authority attitude: 'He's my child. Who the hell are you to tell me what to do?' The other strategy open to the family is publicly to select one group of staff as being the most able carers, and then reinforce this group with their loyalty, while withdrawing support from the other staff groups. This latter strategy has the advantage of being highly flexible since at any moment the family can switch their preference. It is a controlling strategy since it creates confusion and competition. Such contests therefore maintain patterns of family/professional interaction in which issues of responsibility remain unresolved.

Some changes may occur in the family home, allowing for the

child to be re-accommodated within the family. The child's behaviour itself could alter in a way that would make him or her more acceptable to the family. Similarly a change could occur in the interaction between the family and the child. These changes may occur spontaneously or, on the other hand, they could be the outcome of experiences which are provided by the different professional groups. Change could result from the interview sessions between parents and field worker in the family home. Alternatively it could be through the residential experiences provided by the unit's staff. Obviously it is almost impossible to attempt to clarify the differing levels of importance that may be assigned to these processes. It is likely, however, that within this dialectical process each element is important at different times for each family.

Given that there are a variety of explanations for change when issues of power and control are being contested between systems, it is not unusual for each system to conceive of the process of change as occurring in different ways. When professional carers stress the value of the residential experience, together with the aid and assistance that is provided by a visiting social worker, then the family may perceive that it need not do any work. On the other hand, residential staff may feel that the unit should do no more than provide containment, if change is seen as occurring solely as a result of a field worker's intervention with the family. Similarly field workers can become less involved when a family and residential care staff agree that the residential experience will change the child. Often when these issues are being discussed, the different parties not only develop different ideas about the way change will occur, but also about the events that need to occur to demonstrate that change has taken place.

For example, it is a common experience that the problem behaviour, for which the child was placed in care, disappears immediately he or she enters the unit. If a non-school attender who sniffs glue is placed in a reasonably well-organized community home, with educational facilities on the premises, it is likely that these two problems will cease. For the family, and particularly for the child, the reason for being placed in care centred around these problems, but professional staff will probably perceive the problem areas differently. Their understanding will be based on notions such as attitude to authority figures, tolerance of frustration, peer relationships, chaotic family organization with vague parental boundaries, etc. If these issues between family and professional groups are never resolved, then the child simply needs to 'commit' the problem behaviour at infrequent intervals to demonstrate to himself, his family, and his carers, that he is not ready to leave and that nothing has altered. Again, because of a lack of clarity between the professional carers, the child is placed in an impossible position. Since the professionals define the situation in their own terms and not the family's, then control of the situation has passed not just to the family but directly to the child. In their work in a psychiatric hospital, Stanton and Schwartz (1954) found that agitation in particular patients was associated with conflicting attitudes and directives concerning the patients' behaviour from two staff members (authority figures) who at the same time denied their disagreeement and defined their overall position as one of benevolence. This is clearly a parallel situation to that in which children in care and their families can find themselves.

Obviously, any worker who wishes to establish family therapy as a method of working in a children's home must take these issues of power and shared responsibility into consideration when planning any work. However, since it is likely that family therapy will be initiated either by a staff member of the children's home or by a worker from another agency, it is important to discuss the different approaches that need to be taken in each case. The first approach to be discussed involves a worker from an outside agency.

FAMILY THERAPY INITIATED BY A NON-RESIDENTIAL MEMBER OF STAFF

A therapist who comes from outside the residential unit must recognize that she is intervening in the unit's system as well as the family's. Both these subsystems are, therefore, potential targets for therapeutic intervention. Whether the therapist is involved in just one case, or is in the process of establishing a regular consultant therapist role, there is a need to be aware of the processes within the staff group.

In order that the parenting function may be shared, a balance needs to be maintained between working with the family and the residential unit. At the same time, however, it is essential to maintain and reinforce the appropriate family boundary *vis-à-vis* the unit's staff. The solution to this problem is for the therapist to recruit a collaborator from the unit to assist in all sessions with the family. This enables the family to see that the residential unit itself plays an important part in the therapeutic process. Additionally, the unit's staff will feel part of the process and not become alienated from the activities which the therapy helps to organize.

The notion of collaboration, rather than co-therapy, is used here since co-therapy can imply a peer relationship in which both individuals have equal skill and equal responsibility in the decision-making process. Collaboration implies joint involvement but without equality. A collaborative relationship allows the role of the therapist to be safeguarded with respect to the responsibility for taking decisions that flow from the needs of therapy. Such a relationship stresses the primacy of the therapist and therefore permits her to deal with all issues that develop in the target system. It has to be recognized that some of these issues will involve the staff group, and that a collaborative relationship allows for some distancing between therapist and staff group members. Collaboration can be considered on a continuum from a member of the unit's staff being a silent observer at family sessions through to an active participant in the sessions. Naturally, familiarity and trust will lead to more active collaboration and involvement between a therapist and a unit, but the therapist can never fully share the responsibility of her role with unit members.

Many residential facilities do not include the notion of external work with the families in their aims, even though family therapy may have been recommended to them by a case conference. Consequently the request to involve a member of staff in family therapy could create tensions within the staff group. The therapist thus needs to be aware of the features of staff groups which may effect the process of therapy (see Street 1981).

The fundamental task of the staff group

Each staff group generates a set of ideas about its task. These conceptualizations of what the group must do in order to survive and exist within the constraints of its immediate environment are not normally negotiated, but spontaneously assumed, and hence reacted to implicitly. Within residential care the fundamental task can be perceived in a multitude of ways. It may range from merely offering physical care and refuge to children, to offering a wide variety of strategies which in their contexts would be considered as treatments. Some conceptions of these fundamental tasks may require involvement with children's families, whilst others may view communication between unit and family as only a polite information-giving exercise. In fact some staff groups may see families as 'psycho-noxious'. An important aspect of functioning for every staff group is whether or not they perceive the fundamental task as being something over which they have control, or whether they see it as being assigned to them from above. Fundamental tasks for staff groups lead to the production of rules governing behaviour; these rules in many ways resemble family rules. They have to be flexible enough so that individual members can negotiate about them. They need to be firm enough to offer members some guidelines, but not so firm as to become rigid, and not so flexible as to become chaotic. The issue of the fundamental task always raises the question of what goals are seen as being desirable for the total staff group and how these goals can be achieved. Hence the manner in which the fundamental task is conceived and maintained determines the experience of residential care that the staff provide.

Of course the relative degree of flexibility or rigidity with which the staff regard their fundamental task has important implications for the feasibility of therapeutic intervention. Flexibility of approach has to be part and parcel of therapeutic work so that it may be successful. Additionally, disagreement between unit staff can create the distinct possibility that one staff member will subtly recruit the therapist into a coalition against her colleagues in an attempt to change the conception of the fundamental task of the whole unit.

A unit unfamiliar with collaborative work with family therapists is faced with a difficulty should it be suggested that family therapy be undertaken with the family of one of their children. For it has to be appreciated that any invitation to involve a staff member in family work is in fact a covert request to have the staff group open up negotiations concerning the nature of their fundamental task. Such an invitation should therefore be treated with sensitivity and an awareness of how the staff group see their task.

Decision-making in residential homes

It is important to gain some insight into the way the staff of a residential unit arrive at decisions. Usually the staff do not make any formal decisions about their fundamental task, though much of their activity with any child is linked to decisions they have made about that child.

Staff groups differ in the extent to which members feel that they have to follow laid-down procedures, rather than exercise their professional judgement. This will determine how they will react to situations that are thrown up by a particular child and family. The therapist will therefore need to assess how the staff will deal with crises that inevitably arise during the course of therapy. For staff experienced with the problems of therapy, the therapist will be able to trust them to exercise their own judgement, whilst with a group unused to therapy, the therapist will be aiming to establish a number of procedures and rules to guide their activity.

In the early days of collaboration with a unit, the external therapist may need to outline a procedure, so that if there are difficulties, she is informed directly. Any decision that subsequently needs to be taken, will therefore involve the therapist. The nature of the calls from the unit to the therapist about these difficulties indicate a great deal about how that unit is dealing with the decisions and processes of therapy. The person who calls, the frequency of the calls, the time of day they occur, and the nature of the difficulty, will all reveal the way in which the staff group is functioning. The therapist must therefore ascertain the nature of the communication that lies behind direct requests for assistance. It may be that therapy in general, or a specific situation, is causing the staff to act in a way which contravenes some of the instructions they have received from their managers, or which flies in the face of the group's fundamental task. The staff group may be informing the therapist that they feel out of their depth with what is expected of them in family work. In effect they may be saying: 'If the therapist wants control, then she can control the whole lot.' The therapist must decide whether the request is to be dealt with over the telephone with one staff member, or at a staff meeting, or with staff and family together. It needs to be determined too whether the difficulty is simply a part of that specific situation, or whether it is symptomatic of general processes within the staff group which do not assist therapy. The manner in which these communications are dealt with by the therapist must be given just as much thought as any intervention with the family.

Of course, every problem is different and requires its own solution.

Through her attempts to solve such problems, the therapist will be attempting to build a positive relationship with the staff group, so that eventually there will be an agreement about the decisions which are the responsibility of the unit alone, and those which are the responsibility of both therapist and unit. Once again it has to be appreciated that the invitation to a unit to be involved in family therapy is an invitation to contribute to changing their custom and practice. Hence, by the introduction of new types of decisions, the staff are continually being asked to alter their ideas about the decisions that they can take, as well as their ideas about the nature of the unit's fundamental task.

Staff group hierarchies

Within residential units, staff group hierarchies are formed around skill areas. These include the abilities to establish good rapport with certain types of children; to give children enthusiasm about the outside world; to deal with external agencies and authorities; to establish good fostering relationships; and to promote the discussion of problems with families. Conflict can occur in units if members of the group attempt to establish the superiority of one area of expertise at the expense of another.

Power contests between staff members usually involve attempts to validate one type of expertise as being the only type relevant to the unit's work. This can cause problems for the therapist, in joining with a staff group, since her status and power is invested in a particular area of skill. If a therapist is to attempt to work with a certain member of staff, then that staff member acquires some status and power from the therapist, and it is possible that his or her position in the group may be enhanced. It is necessary to ensure that the skills of other members of staff, from which they claim their status, are valued, while at the same time reinforcing and maintaining the skills and conceptions of change that family therapy stresses. In some circumstances it may be appropriate to include in any treatment programme some activity that the child may be involved in which includes the skills of other staff members. This would be a strategy designed to offer the child a range of experiences and to allow therapy to progress without sabotage from individuals with other skills.

In attempting to collaborate with any staff member, the therapist needs to be aware of their relative position within the group, since this helps the therapist to assess the standing that the therapy process has within the unit. The therapist will then be able to anticipate some of the undermining mechanisms that are likely to be encountered. For example, the collaborating individual of low status may have elected to work with the therapist in order to elevate his or her status. Alternatively, such a person may have been 'given' to the therapist by the group to demonstrate that therapy is of low status and hence likely to be ineffective. Such individuals could attempt to draw the therapist unwittingly into a coalition against something that is valued within the on-going ethos of the staff group. Another undermining mechanism is for a person with considerable status within the group to be assigned as the co-worker in order to 'prove' that the approach will not work. Therapists will therefore encounter strategies by staff group members which aim to change the group's hierarchical structure, and also strategies that are designed to shore up these same structures. All the usual family therapy procedures and tactics used with families need to be adopted with the staff group in order to circumvent and overcome these problems within the group.

Dominating the other hierarchies within the unit is the formal authority hierarchy which has been created by the unit's employing agency. The head of the unit holds considerable power, and the therapist needs to be aware both of the central position which he occupies, and the way in which he performs his job. However, the formal hierarchy is extended out into the realms of the wider agency. Within Social Service Departments, for example, a usual organizational structure is for each unit to be 'supervised' by a residential care adviser, who, although external to the unit (in the sense of playing little or no part in daily care routines), plays some role with regard to the procedures, ethics and atmosphere that the unit embraces.

The therapist must be mindful of the nature of the boundary between internal and external authority, for its permeability will vary in different situations. Within a family the therapist should be able to deal with any hierarchical issues from either a peer, a superior or an inferior position. When working with an organization the therapist must also be able to demonstrate that he or she is meta to the system by being able to move freely within the organization's hierarchies. Thus, the therapist should be able to converse with the 'outside' formal authority in a way which both validates the individual's position and at the same time respects and validates the boundary that the unit and the residential care adviser have established. Contact with the external authority should preferably occur in the early stages of work with a unit, with the aim of outlining the general goals and methods that will be employed. By this means it may be possible to prevent any homeostatic manoeuvres caused either by the direct intervention of the external authority or by attempts by the head of the unit to call in the external authority in order to form a strong coalition against the therapist.

The replication of family patterns in staff groups

It is important that the therapist is aware that the child she is concerned with is not the only child with which the unit will be dealing. The 'target' child needs to be seen in relation to the other children in the unit. It is a typical feature of residential establishments that some children adopt the same role in the unit as they were assigned by their family. So, one finds 'jokers', 'victims', 'bullies', 'bosses' and 'babies' amongst the children in any group. There are some children who appear particularly able to hold on to their assigned family role even when it involves having other children change theirs. Borowitz (1970) has noted this process and commented on how staff in units for disturbed children can tend to take up responses to children under their care and reflect processes in the children's family of origin, such as being punitive towards a particular child. Reder and Kraemer (1980) have commented on a similar process which they label as 'systems counter-transference' where care-givers, because of their position in a professional network (and to a lesser extent because of their personalities) are often cast in, and act out, the roles of members of their client's families. Consequently, one can for example see the male head of the unit being cast in the role of father, not only by the child but also by other professionals who have contact with that child. The replication of family patterns seems to appear more frequently and with greater force, in those units where there is little organized contact with families, and in units in which the fundamental task encompasses notions of change which stress the residential experience as being the central experience. Once again it is in the early stages of therapeutic collaboration that these processes come to the fore, although it can happen that the process will make an appearance as a homeostatic mechanism when the therapy is making progress. Typically, it is family members who attempt to initiate this homeostatic mode. The therapist, therefore, needs to be aware of the possibility of the system adopting the interactional patterns of the family system (as Hugh Jenkins points out in chapter 4).

Intervening with staff groups

The possibility that features of the staff group will affect the process of therapy raises the question of whether the staff group should be dealt with as a distinct entity. Staff in residential establishments are rarely given the experience of being approached as a self-contained unit involved in the management of any one particular child. The most common practice is for non-residential staff to conduct their business in a fragmented and informal way with one or occasionally two staff members. The only situation where the staff may all be involved in decision-making about children is the 'case review', but such reviews are usually attended by a number of non-residential staff who may carry considerable powers of decision because of the formal authority which is vested in them. Given that this is the typical experience of staff groups, a therapist, who is collaborating with a unit, needs to appreciate that staff meetings about one particular child are threatening experiences — care and sensitivity are required in the convening and running of such meetings since staff reactions to the child may be discussed.

Clearly when a therapist becomes involved in a children's residential unit for the first time, the unit is inexperienced as far as this type of work is concerned. However the process of therapy will touch upon many issues pertinent to the staff group itself. The threat to the group may well be so great that it proves very difficult to conduct work on a collaborative basis. In such circumstances it may be necessary to choose other methods of therapeutic work, or even to move the child to a unit more amenable to involvement with family work. The latter is quite naturally a very difficult decision to take as it involves considerable upheaval for a child, who is in all probability undergoing more than his or her fair share of upheavals.

On the other hand, some staff groups meet the challenge of ongoing therapeutic work with enthusiasm and frankness. Their openness allows their own internal problems to be presented to the

therapist as a focus for discussion. At this point the therapist will
naturally be seeking to facilitate those aspects of group interaction
and functioning that allow for the smooth progress of work with the
family. However, this may only represent a minimal amount of
change for the group itself, who will continue to seek some solution
to what they perceive as major dysfunctions themselves. The question
of a consultant for the staff group is therefore raised at this juncture.
The therapist will need to decide whether or not she is capable of
playing the two roles of therapist and consultant within one unit.
Experience suggests that this, in fact, is not a viable proposition as
the consultant is often brought issues which would require her to be
'meta' to the therapist. It is of course impossible to be meta to
oneself! The solution is for the therapist to suggest to the staff
group that another person be recruited as a consultant. It is debatable
as to whether or not it aids the development of a service for children
in care if the consultant comes from the same agency with the same
ideology as the therapist, but certainly the danger to avoid is the
creation of a coalition between therapist and consultant to change a
staff group for the better.

FAMILY THERAPY INITIATED BY A RESIDENTIAL
STAFF MEMBER

When a residential unit provides the therapist, the therapeutic task
still remains the same. The family needs to be assisted in remaining
'open', the parenting functions need to be shared. The therapist
needs to be allowed to adopt a meta-position to other professionals
involved with the family because she may need to intervene in the
relationships between the family and the supervising social worker.
This situation creates considerable problems for the traditional
relationship between residential and non-residential staff since it
reverses the usually perceived hierarchical relationship between
field social workers and their counterparts in residential establishments.

When a residential worker plays the principal coordinating and
therapeutic role for a particular family, then the field social worker's
activities are reduced to monitoring, supporting and reporting. Such
activities and roles tend to be disliked by social workers because they
are usually forced into them as a result of their relationships with

other more powerful professionals, such as psychiatrists. The therapist from the residential unit therefore needs to be mindful of these issues when discussing with supervising social workers; once again the need to validate the involvement of any professional is essential. Some supervising social workers are only too happy to play a collaborative role with residential staff — for others, however, this can pose major problems of role identity.

Should a unit choose to operate in such a way that family therapy work is undertaken consistently, then the unit needs to exert greater control over the case than the supervising social worker, in order to safeguard the residential worker's role as family therapist. A unit is able to achieve this position by clearly setting out its table of wares and methods of working even before placements of children are made. In order to have a child placed at a particular unit, a social worker would therefore have to accept the rules which the unit lays down in accordance with its conceptualization of its fundamental task. The supervising social worker, however, constantly carries a responsibility for the child, regardless of the therapeutic strategies that are pursued, and in this sense the child always 'belongs' to the social worker. But residential units can, and do, have the choice of sharing some of that responsibility with the social worker. The social worker has power over certain issues but not over others and the unit needs to respect this fact.

The therapist also needs to be aware of the difficulties that the social worker faces within the social services system. Such difficulties have been explored by David Dungworth and Sigurd Reimers, in chapter 5, but it is obvious that the central issue revolves around where professional autonomy ends and departmental policy begins. The therapist must therefore clarify whether an individual social worker has freedom of action or whether her decisions have to be referred to someone in higher authority. It is axiomatic that the therapist should have access to the social worker's superiors. In practice this may amount to little more than the ability to invite the person senior to the supervising social worker to join in one of the initial planning meetings. It is the ability to move freely within systems that allow therapists to be optimally efficient, since it enables them to overcome obstacles and mobilise those resources that are conducive to therapeutic movement. Freedom and flexibility are aspects of the therapist's role which have to be safeguarded at all times.

At this point it is worth summarizing the principles that determine the successful utilization of family therapy by a residential unit.

1   The goals of therapy for a family need to be clearly specified not only to the family but also to the professional carers.
2   The methods of effecting change need to be clearly established by the therapist and his or her professional colleagues.
3   The expectations to be placed on all parties with regard to attendance, visiting the unit, weekend visits for the child, etc., need to be established at the outset of therapy. Many of these expectations will focus on the need to maintain family contact.
4   The place, the time, and the composition of the group involved in decision-making needs to be clearly stated.
5   Initial meetings of the relevant individuals should be organized prior to the start of active work.
6   The therapist should realize that any part of the target system will attempt to form coalitions, or engage in undermining strategies or change-evading strategies.

In the remainder of this chapter, I will describe a project which incorporates the principles which I have outlined. I hope the more concrete description of this work will provide some flesh to the bones of the discussion so far.

THE NANSEN PROJECT

Since the summer of 1981 I have been involved in the creation of a family-orientated unit within a community home. The unit was developed in order to provide residential care for boys who came from families who could be involved in therapy.

Nansen House is a ten-bed unit within Headlands School, Penarth, which is a community home run by National Children's Homes (NCH). Boys from the unit attend the school which is an integral part of the home. In order to describe, as economically as possible, the functioning of the unit, I will concentrate on outlining the organizational procedures which have been adopted to enable the unit to function in a family-orientated way.

In essence the first step in the procedure concerns the method of advertising the unit's approach as far as 'client' agencies are concerned. Interested agencies are sent a letter which stresses that the unit has places for boys who have been placed in care, but with whom it is believed that some family work is possible. The letter emphasizes that the main therapeutic role will be undertaken by the unit staff, though they expect to collaborate fully with the supervising social workers. It also stresses that major decisions may only be taken with the consent of all parties involved; the Nansen staff, the supervising social worker and the family.

Applications received by the unit are invariably accompanied by a substantial social service department file on the boy in question. On the basis of initial information about the boy and his family, it is decided whether or not to offer an interview. If an interview takes place the boy, his parents, other family members and the social worker involved are all invited to undertake a tour of the facilities. Some separate discussions may be held with the social worker, but the initial plan is to conduct the preliminary interviews with the family and the social worker jointly. In some circumstances it may well be that two interviews are held, perhaps to involve other family members (usually siblings) who are difficult to convene initially, or to allow for some time to elapse so that certain issues can be clarified. For example, a concurrent application for the boy to attend another establishment may have been made, the family might be contemplating moving, or a court appearance might be impending. However, a firm rule has been established that no interviews take place without both parents being present. (If the family is a single-parent family then obviously this rule is waived.) Usually the child is already in care, and placed in an assessment and observation centre. The aim of the interview is to see the family together in order to establish the willingness of them to cooperate with the unit's programme, and to estimate the extent of the family's rejection. The formal offer of a place is made in a letter sent several days later. This procedure has been adopted because experience has shown that families tend to say 'yes' immediately an offer is made. This may be because they consider that they have no other option and feel under pressure from the authorities.

The family therefore leaves the initial interview with full information about the unit's programme and it is hoped that they will come to their decision in their own way. With the type of families that present it is not expected that they will necessarily make their decision in a clear, logical manner, but it may be important at a later stage of therapy to refer back to the non-pressurized way they decided to join in the unit's programme.

At the initial interview the fundamental principle of the unit is fully explained to the family and social worker. Originally the unit believed that the returning of the boy to his home was an essential part of its fundamental task. However, many families were resistant to this idea and the staff group also expressed some anxieties about its feasibility. The goal was so obvious and yet so difficult to envisage at the initial meeting that it was merely a utopian ideal which hindered the progress of change. Consequently, it was decided that the fundamental task should be modified. It was agreed that the aim of the unit was to create an environment for the boy and his family so that they could develop in as healthy a way as possible — the issue of the return home was left to be discussed later. This stated aim has removed an over-optimistic expectation on the part of referring agencies, and reduced the pressure on the staff to achieve goals which may have turned out to be impossible. The revised aim allows a specific definition of what constitutes change and progress to be negotiated with each family. This then prevents professionals from imposing their version of progress on the family.

If the parents and the social worker agree to join in the programme than a number of initial contracts are signed. The parents sign a contract to agree to take part in the programme activities that have been outlined to them. The social worker signs a contract to agree to be involved in the way specified by the unit's programme, and to keep the unit staff informed of any developments that may occur. The boy signs a contract to say that he will take part in family meetings, that he will keep to the rules that will be set for him regarding weekend visits, holidays, school, etc., and that he will take part in all the activities of the unit. The Nansen staff then also sign a contract which states that they will use their skill to help the family in whatever way is thought appropriate, that they will not change any of the programme without discussing it with the family and the social worker, and that they will keep the social worker informed of all aspects of progress. The social worker signs the contract on behalf of the local authority, and the Nansen staff sign on behalf of Headlands School. These contracts are therefore on an agency-to-agency basis, but the family and the boy are clearly contracted as well.

During the initial period of the programme, which lasts

approximately 12 weeks, it is planned that the boy will return home for weekends on Friday night and return on Sunday afternoon. The parents are expected to fill in some forms on these visits so that they can be monitored. The parents are also told that they may be given some simple tasks to perform relevant to their daily routine whilst the boy is home for the weekend. These tasks can include such things as sending the boy to bed at a certain time, waking him up at a certain time, or preparing a meal for him. During this period a member of the Nansen staff makes a scheduled visit to the family home at least once a fortnight in order to discuss the weekends with both parents and other family members. It is always specified beforehand by letter when such visits will take place and who should be present. Care is naturally taken in selecting times that are convenient for working families. Two or three visits by family members to the unit are also scheduled. Again, these are worked out at mutually convenient times and those who should attend are specified in advance. It is agreed that reports of all the family visits will be made in writing to the social worker. It is also agreed that a number of visits to the home will be carried out by the social worker. It is hoped that several of these visits will occur following weekends, so that the social worker can receive a first-hand report of them. It is also planned that the social worker will send reports of these visits to the unit. An invitation is also made to the social worker to attend all the family/unit meetings, if he or she wishes.

An interim review meeting is scheduled with the social worker some six to eight weeks into the programme, so that the unit staff can discuss progress. The family does not attend this meeting as its principal aim is to discuss the social worker/Nansen relationship. However, the family are informed of any aspect that may affect them. Finally, at the end of the programmed period a review session is held with all concerned (the boy, the family, the social worker and the Nansen staff) so that progress can be assessed and new contracts prepared.

It is during the initial phase that much valuable information is acquired. For example, it was discovered (in what seemed to be a single-parent family) that there was a paternal uncle who exerted considerable influence over a boy who had been sent to the school. There was also a slightly older sister, upon whom the mother refused to put pressure to attend sessions, and a younger brother who had an involvement with an educational welfare officer for non-attendance at school. The family's social worker tended to 'pop in' on the family on the day the social security giro cheque arrived, to help plan the budget, and the mother left all the organizing of the boy to the elder sister. This important information was gained at a preliminary interview and was not seen by the staff as information gained as a result of attempting therapy. For the therapist concerned, the information was construed as very valuable and was not seen as constituting evidence for the idea that either the family or the social worker would be unwilling or unable to cooperate in achieving change.

At the review sessions, issues such as those described above would be fully discussed, and efforts made to include suitable clauses in the contracts to be drawn up. Within the example given, it was decided that budgeting for the family was a priority and that the therapist, in conjunction with the social worker, should assist the parent in working out a plan, and that this plan would be monitored fortnightly by the social worker. It was also agreed that some special arrangements would be made for including both the sister and the paternal uncle in the sessions. At this stage in our involvement with the family, the principle therapeutic aims involved establishing the mother's authority over her own children, and the creation of appropriate boundaries both between the parents and the children and between the family and the other groups with which they interact.

Following the review, work with the families then continues with the therapeutic effort being geared along structural family therapy lines, but with some discussion of transgenerational family themes being included. At the review session, specific indices of progress are laid down. Continuing with the above example, one element of progress was defined as the sibling attending school regularly. If such changes occur, then the aim is to have the boy return home for longer periods of time and this would again be monitored. The return of a boy to his home takes place in a planned way, and Nansen staff continue to play the leading therapeutic role. Naturally changes of this order have to be fully discussed with the schools concerned and for each boy a different pattern of school and home attendance needs to be established.

In the early stages of the project some failures were encountered. These failures were due to the unit and the supervising social worker not sharing the same expectations and goals. However, by being very open about the way in which the unit operates, and by ensuring that a continuous flow of information takes place, this type of failure has almost been eliminated. However, other types of difficulties have been experienced for there are some families who seem unable to keep to the demands of the programme in the first instance, and who show an inability or unwillingness to participate fully, even though they made an initial agreement to do so. These are also those families who agree and cooperate in the initial period but who then become less cooperative when the programme becomes more specific in its goal setting. These two types of 'failures' are seen as involving technical problems of therapy rather than involving insurmountable problems brought to therapy by the family.

However, with some families the programme is not for them since rejection has become a fixed feature of their behaviour. Decisions then need to be taken concerning the nature of provision for the boy, and whether or not this may include his return to the family home. The type of 'failure' does not mean that good work has not been done, or that the boy and his family are consigned to the 'no-hoper' category. At the end of the initial period in the unit an exceptionally comprehensive assessment of the family system has been made. When this is placed in conjunction with the assessment of the boy's needs then it becomes clear what type of facility is required. Often some change of unit within the school complex is made, whilst in other circumstances it is conceivable that a boy may be transferred to another establishment. With one boy a substitute family was found within the family network and some therapy was carried out with them to enable them to admit the boy into their family home.

The Nansen project continues to progress and is making minor changes to its programme. Essentially, however, it is felt that the structure and programme that has been developed by the unit is an appropriate one for the situation in which residential staff are the family therapists.

CONCLUSION

Children who are placed in residential care need the best professional care available. Their families also need skilled help, since there is a grave danger that such families will become disconnected from their children. I have argued in this chapter that a family-systems perspective has much to offer professionals who are attempting to work with these families. I have also stressed that many of the difficulties of working with such families cannot and should not be explained solely by the nature of the families themselves. It is the context that has been established to deal with such children that presents the initial, and possibly the greatest problem, for the would-be therapist. I hope this chapter will have demonstrated that professionals can help rather than hinder and that, regardless of whether or not the therapist is a member of the residential staff, therapy can take place efficiently and effectively.

5

Family Therapy in Social Services Departments

DAVID DUNGWORTH AND SIGURD REIMERS

At the fifth Annual Conference of the Association for Family Therapy, Bill Jordan threw down a challenge to family therapists in general and to those working in Social Services Departments in particular. He pointed out that, compared with the great interest generated by family therapy, its application within the social services was very limited:

> An indication of this for me — looking at family therapy's impact on social work, and particularly on Social Services Departments — is the apparent gap between the very evident devotion and enthusiasm for the method among many social workers, and the relatively narrow bank of families who actually receive family therapy. Considering the number of keen and convinced family therapy converts in Social Services Departments, relatively little is done in practice; and above all, it has had no apparent influence on the direction of policy in relation to statutory work with families. The training is there, the enthusiasm is there, and the support groups are there, but the impact is rather disappointing. (Jordan, 1981)

First, it is striking that in the USA, and this country, family therapy has been largely carried out within clinical settings where the role of the therapist is unambiguous compared with the many roles occupied by social services social workers. The field worker in a social services office may occupy a number of varying and sometimes conflicting roles, of which a therapeutic role is but one amongst many. Social services clients rarely think of their social workers as therapists. More often they refer to us as 'the welfare', and see us as the gatekeepers of physical or financial resources. In the past, too much family therapy training has assumed that adopting a therapeutic role is both easy and appropriate. It has not considered ways of helping social workers to adopt other roles in order to achieve a clear contract and understanding with the family.

Second, it is apparent from most of the current family therapy literature that most problems are seen as taking place *within* the family. We feel that other systems outside the family play a crucial part in the problems families experience, and should be given greater emphasis. Systems theory seems to us to be applicable to interventions with these systems as well because the relationships involved are essentially similar.

Social workers are not employed by their agencies as family therapists. It is therefore the purpose of this chapter to illustrate how a family therapy perspective can be used within a social services department in a way that is consistent with the various tasks that field social workers are required by law to carry out. These duties mainly deal with the protection of vulnerable people and the delivery of welfare services, but social workers may also carry out social control functions. At the same time we also hope to show that family therapy can provide an effective means of working, not only with the family, but with the wider range of clients that find their way through the doors of their local office.

ROLES

At first sight it might appear that family therapy skills are irrelevant to the fulfilment of many of the roles which local authority social workers are expected to carry out.

The Barclay Report (1982) draws a broad distinction between 'social care planning' and 'counselling' but recognize that there are difficulties in defining social work roles and tasks exactly. The more common roles can be listed as follows:

investigator
provider of resources
controller, monitor and supervisor
liaison officer with other agencies
negotiator and advocate
nurturer and supporter
therapist
referrer to other agencies

Although only one of these roles is specifically therapeutic, family therapy has a good deal to offer because the theory can be applied to the understanding and practice of the other roles. Three common examples, two from long-term child care, and one from an application for material aid, will be used to illustrate this point.

EXAMPLES OF INTERVENTIONS IN STATUTORY SOCIAL WORK

Clearly, long-term work is particularly difficult because of the wearing down of the social worker by chronic demands, lack of positive feed-back, and the flattening effect of time. Family therapy has always maintained that the effectiveness and dignity of the family depend on adequate hierarchy and boundaries. This may be difficult for the social worker to support in cases of long-term child care, especially where separation of family members will create its own problems of familiarity breeding contempt. Family therapy ideas do not have to stop once a child has come into care, even though such a move may be an apparent example of its failure. At least the absent child's position in the family can still be kept open in the minds of the family by the social worker being the bringer of news or acting as a minor irritant. Her very visiting every month or so for a few minutes may help prevent the sense of 'closure' described by Scott and Starr (1981) in their work on mental health admissions. Boundaries can be kept supple and the family hierarchy can be respected by the invitation of parents to in-care reviews and joint decision-making as the following case illustrates.

Simon had been in care for two and a half years since the age of fifteen, because of a life-long conflict between himself and his parents. His parents would have nothing to do with him in care and prevented his brothers and sisters from writing. Simon himself never willingly spoke of his parents. The social worker kept the subject of his parents open by bringing back bits of news about births, marriages and deaths within the extended family, to a silent Simon. News of Simon's successes at work and increasing maturity (duly defined as rewards for good early parenting on the part of the parents) were periodically reported to uninterested parents. The parents never attended a boarding-out review, but the review papers were taken home to the parents every six months. (These reviews are laid down in law by the Boarding-Out of Children Regulations, 1955.) Eventually Simon suddenly decided to repay his father £20 for money he had once stolen from his school, and which his father had had to pay as compensation to the juvenile court. The parents had maintained that Simon had for years been resentful towards them and silently sat in judgement on them. His total lack of communication with them while he was in care had embittered them further. It seems likely that he had had similar feelings about the parents but never spoke of them. The return of the money appears to have broken that spell dramatically, and his parents made a bid for Simon's return, to which Simon responded immediately. Following a period at home under supervision (home on trial), he was discharged from care. In this case a minimum amount of formal visiting had kept Simon's place open enough for him to return when the circumstances were right.

Theories of family therapy can also help us clarify the confusions we experience in our relationship with foster families. Foster families have variously been regarded as clients, volunteers, and colleagues (Holman 1975; Short and Gray 1982). They are sometimes addressed by first names, sometimes by surnames. Further dilemmas can be caused by a Department's demand that foster parents who are involved in long-term placements should treat the foster children as their own, but at the same time help the children keep a place in their hearts for their natural parents — a dilemma described by Satir (1972). The requirement to give unconditional affection may clash with the department's right to hold regular boarding-out reviews, to inspect the child's bedroom, and even to remove the child from the foster home if necessary.

Minuchin and Fishman (1981) refer to the conflict between being asked to incorporate children into foster families as naturally as possible, on the one hand, and the artificial over-protection offered through emotional and financial cushioning by Social Services Departments on the other. The power implied in the Department's legal right to remove a child from a foster family is countered by that of the foster parents who demand instant removal of a child when they feel they can no longer cope. It is interesting that the foster parents' right to offer or withhold services, according to some research by Blau and Scott (1963), accounts for their relatively high status and that of the child welfare agencies they serve. This high status was assumed to be derived from the relationship of equality which was established between the social workers and the foster parents. With such a degree of equality, it is hardly surprising if social workers frequently become embedded in the family structure of the foster family, as the following case history illustrates.

The Whites became enthusiastic foster parents after their own children had grown up and left home. Mr White was a plumber, and Mrs White worked at home. They were both very dry, methodical, and serious, but had successfully fostered Sharon, Shirley, and Sheila (aged thirteen, eleven and nine years) for 18 months, when they suddenly gave written notice asking for the immediate removal of the children. The girls had come from a deprived background where the father was dead and their mother had neglected them badly. Although Sharon had crossed the 'culture gap' between her own family and the foster family, the intense secrecy between the girls had made the foster parents feel excluded. By lobbying the departmental managers, the social worker was able to ensure that the department resisted the pressure from the foster parents. The managers pointed out to the foster parents the disastrous effect removal would have on the children, but accepted the feelings of inadequacy the foster parents had expressed. They were at pains to stress the confidence they had in the foster parents, and offered an intensive period of working at the problem with the additional help of another social worker who did not have as informal a relationship with the family as did the original social worker. Both workers agreed to work on the presented problem of the girls' lack of communication with their foster parents, and it was found desirable to treat the foster parents as colleagues requiring a consultation rather than clients needing therapy. Time was spent on helping the foster parents to see the girls as separate individuals, by repeatedly using their names, and identifying differences and similarities between them. The foster parents were also given the professional task of helping each girl complete a life-story book. Mr White was encouraged to take photographs of places known to the girls in the past, but the greatest change came when the foster parents were challenged to stop Sharon, their favourite, from constantly being over-helpful in interpreting all the remarks made to her sisters. She in turn found the loss of her main role as interpreter distressing; when she later stole money from her foster parents, Shirley and Sheila began to be seen in a more favourable light.

Other features (described by Satir (1972) and commonly also

found in step-families) became apparent. There was a clear tendency to want to create an instant family overnight, coupled with a denial of the child's past (which had the effect of creating a ghost family). Ultimately the suspicion of 'bad blood' was mooted when everything else failed. Asking the foster parents to experiment with doing something different was felt to be less offensive than pointing out their mistakes and difficulties.

In some cases family therapy can be used to go beyond the immediate terms of referral and deal with the interactional problems which contribute to maintaining the problem for which a family was referred.

George was a mentally-handicapped three year-old child. His parents, Mr and Mrs Smith, were encouraged to apply for help in providing a garden fence because of George's 'hyperactive' behaviour. This request was seen by the social worker to fall within the terms of the Chronically Sick and Disabled Persons Act (1970), but she also felt that George's restless behaviour might be dealt with in other ways.

Mrs Smith had great difficulty in controlling George, which was not helped by the fact that her husband always discussed George's behaviour with his mother rather than with her. Mr Smith worked long hours for an insurance company, and did not have much time to spend at home. When he did, he had little trouble in handling George. Needless to say, his discussions with his mother had the effect of reinforcing his wife's incompetence, since his mother thought that George should be handled by Mrs Smith in a more disciplined way. This strengthened Mrs Smith's existing resentment of the amount of time her husband spent with his mother. Mr Smith was torn between his wife and his mother, because while he was sorry for his wife he felt a fair degree of loyalty to his mother who was a widow with time and energy which no one else seemed to need.

A fence was provided out of the department's aids and adaptations budget, but help was also given to the parents to work together and become more effective, while at the same time encouraging the grandmother to take on a different helping role which made her feel worthwhile, and which relieved Mrs Smith of some of the day-to-day pressures. In this case it was not a question of whether to deal with the 'presenting' or the 'underlying' problem, but of bringing together two roles in social work — provider of resources and therapist.

These three case histories show that whether one adopts an overtly therapeutic role or not, family therapy can promote change and a better use of roles. What is more difficult is the consideration of roles which are not always seen as helpful. It is necessary to clarify a number of important questions about the nature of our roles. When we act on behalf of our Social Services Department, using a family-systems approach, we must be clear from the outset why our agency is involved. What is the function of our agency that we are being asked to carry out? How does this impinge on our client and our client's system? How does the client view our intervention in their family, and what does he or she expect of the agency?

'Clients' are not necessarily clients

Referrals are frequently made in unclear and ambiguous ways. Individuals and families may not be aware that they are being referred, and they may not wish to be referred. A study of a year's intake to an area team by Goldberg et al. (1977), showed that only 32 per cent of cases were self-referred. In cases where compulsory action is being sought by an outside agent, it may not be clear on whose behalf the referral is being made.

In a situation, for example, when a child is deemed to be 'at risk', the law makes it quite clear that the child's interests are paramount. Although we are expected to work with the child's parents, and may even refer to them as 'clients', we are reminded that our overriding responsibility is to the child, and this may make the state, acting on the child's behalf, the real client.

The hazards of multiple roles have been explored by our colleague Brian Dimmock (Dimmock and Dungworth 1983):

> Unfortunately, we . . . [confuse] . . . these roles, trying to persuade the family that we are there to help them with 'their problem' of abusing their child. The family may not accept that they do have this problem, let alone that a social worker can help. The family may believe that the social worker is their problem (see Cade 1978) and that being constantly under suspicion may bring about the very problem that it is designed to prevent. The confusion brought about by such practice may lead to behaviour which is

construed as evidence of uncooperativeness and reinforces the need to be suspicious. Thus the solution becomes the problem.

The difficulty becomes one of moving between roles in a way that is overtly recognized as being legitimate by all concerned. A social worker may occupy a number of roles, sometimes uneasily and often unwittingly. For example, in a case of child abuse the social worker can act as policeman, provider of resources, and even therapist. As often as not social workers themselves are unsure about how and when to change their roles. Mayer and Timms (1970) have clearly illustrated how clients perceive social workers, often viewing them as two-faced when they combine roles without either being clear themselves or making it clear to the clients (or other professionals) when they move between roles.

It is often difficult to clarify our roles in complex situations, but we have had some success with requests for reception into care by recognizing that families who make such requests are certainly not asking for a therapist to intervene. The social worker's initial stance should be 'Yes, I do receive children into care, but first of all the law requires me to assess whether it is in your child's best interests that I do this.' This may appear to be a 'linear' explanation but the effect is to bring the family together. When acting as a gatekeeper for a particular resource, we are obliged to use it within a legal framework, and to the best possible advantage in relation to the client and the wider community. In order to do this, a number of meetings with all those concerned can be arranged.

It is explained to the family that the purpose of these meetings is to establish whether the statutory requirements for reception into care are being met in accordance with the Child Care Act (1980), Section 2. We may decide, after a thorough assessment, that the request for reception into care is not appropriate, but we may also recognize that the family circumstances contain relationship problems and then go on to offer the use of our therapeutic skills. This need not mean that we see therapeutic help as a substitute for the lack of much-needed financial and physical resources, but rather that the two often need to be offered together. We would go so far as to say that having a number of roles to choose from may actually give the social worker a flexibility of service denied to many who work in clinical settings.

The following case history may serve to illustrate the point that there is a variety of roles open to the social worker in dealing with problematic behaviour, but that some roles will be more useful than others and may require therapeutic skills.

Norman (aged thirteen) was referred to one of the authors shortly before he was made the subject of a Supervision Order for approximately 20 incidents of theft. These thefts involved either bicycles or parts from bicycles, all of which were immediately dumped or given to friends. He had a brother of twelve and a sister of fourteen who attended the same school, but were academically more able. Norman's father (Mr Thompson) was a heavy goods vehicle driver, who worked long and unsocial hours, although he was only occasionally absent overnight. Mr Thompson had also experienced periods of residential care as a child. Mrs Thompson worked part-time and was grossly overweight, a problem shared by Norman.

The social worker was faced with two immediate problems. Firstly, the process of the court hearing had clearly identified Norman as the problem, thereby strengthening the family's rigid view of him. This in turn conferred a particular role (controller and monitor) on the social worker. Although it seemed that the family structure and history suggested that there might be problematic relationships, it was unlikely that an early focus on these problems would be helpful or acceptable. The social worker also had to consider whether the family was necessarily the most effective group to work with, or whether working outside the family system might be more appropriate. If a role is to be adopted which allows more flexibility in using family therapy skills, it is necessary that the existing role is not too quickly abandoned, as this is likely to cause anxiety, confusion, and hostility.

On the question of role conflict, Davies (1981) has commented:

Can the social worker fulfil the policing role firmly, even aggressively if he also has to gain the family's confidence, and to convey the personal warmth and genuineness in his professional role? The answer is that it has to be done; and the evidence from earlier models of child care and probation suggests that it is by no means impossible to achieve — providing the social worker is crystal clear about the nature of his job and the quality of his roles. He may even need to warn the family at the beginning about trusting him on the grounds that he is there in an inspectorial role — paradoxical though this may seem.

One way of being crystal clear is by bringing in a second worker. In the case of Norman, the social worker used the family's perception of their difficulties, i.e. Norman's behaviour, as the means of bringing them together for the 'overt' purpose of 'assessment'. The family's position had been clearly stated. It was Norman who had the 'problem' and who needed to change if he was to fit into their family. This created difficulties for the social worker. First, he needed their cooperation if a family meeting was to be arranged; second, society, through a Statutory Order which had named Norman, had strengthened the family's arguments. The social worker could not simply ignore the implications of the Supervision Order on the family or himself. The social worker needed to find a means of stressing to the family that their family meetings were something different, and of avoiding the linear trap of being constantly drawn into seeing Norman as the problem.

Both these changes were achieved by introducing a consultant (see chapter 11) which clearly marked a change for the social worker and the family. From this position it was possible, legitimately, to ask the family to perform certain tasks that would help the social workers to understand more clearly how the 'problem behaviour' affected the whole family. In this way the social worker's original role was broadened to include other roles that included the possibility of using therapeutic skills in relation to the family system.

It may seem a small battle to win to bring the family together for assessment, but already some purpose and structure have been placed on the social worker—family relationship which defines the positive role of the family in helping its 'problem' member. Depending on the structure of the family and the pattern of its functioning, the act of coming together can in itself trigger new forms of coping, particularly if the family pattern was one of disorganization. This illustrates the point that assessment cannot be neutral but is always part of the therapeutic process. With Norman and his family it became possible to involve the whole family, but other factors outside the immediate family were also seen to be important, and in this case, as in most social services cases, it was essential to consider the wider systems which impinge on the family.

INTERVENING IN WIDER SYSTEMS

Most social workers recognize the importance of the effect of outside agencies on the family. Unfortunately, this recognition seems largely expressed in terms of frustration at not being able to manipulate these agencies to help the family in ways acceptable to the social worker. But it is not simply a 'resource' question. Families are constantly involved with other systems. Umbarger (1972) describes the way the relationship between the individual and society is mediated by the role of the family:

> In an ecological view of individual health and illness, the family is the basic transactional unit within which one develops a base for dealing with the realities of internal feelings and external stresses with regard to extra-familial society. What transpires and is learned within the family is a microcosm of the inter-personal negotiations carried on, at another time, between the family and other subsystems such as school, job, neighbourhood, courts and welfare agencies.

Family therapy can be criticized for too often opting to work on the internal structure of the family when an intervention at the linkage between the family and other agencies (or systems) could be more appropriate. Tucker and Dyson (1976) and Aponte (1976) have illustrated attempts to bring together child, family, school and therapist to create change at the interface between family and school. What we are describing is a boundary of the type cited by Minuchin (1974), and if such a boundary ceases to exist or is too rigid then we can expect inappropriate relationships and responses to difficulties. For an example of this kind of approach we should return to the case history of Norman.

Norman was seen by his teachers as a difficult child who was involved in petty misbehaviour on a daily basis. It was obviously essential to examine this area, to understand how the family and school related, and to explore what part this inter-relationship played in the maintenance of Norman's difficulties. The staff had tried their usual strategy in attempting to help Norman conform to school life, but without success. At one stage the year tutor had attempted to discuss the difficulties with Norman's parents, but had only met Mrs Thompson, who was already involved with the school through the parent—teacher association, and was therefore well known to the teacher concerned. Norman's father had never been to the school and the teacher had formed the impression that he had little interest in his son; she felt sorry for both Norman and his mother. The meetings between the teacher and Norman's mother usually ended with little positive achievement, and with the teacher reassuring Mrs Thompson that they would carry on trying. Mr Thompson had a somewhat different view of the process. He felt angry with the teacher for regularly talking to his wife about what he saw as his son's minor difficulties. Consequently he felt there was little to be gained from contact with the school, since he would only vent his anger and annoyance. The teacher guessed the situation through talking to Mrs Thompson, and this served to increase her perception of him as an uncaring self-centred father.

From the social worker's meetings with the family, it had become apparent that the parents differed in their relationship with the children. Mrs Thompson was somewhat over-involved and often acted more like a sister than a parent. Mr Thompson was indeed somewhat disengaged, preferring to leave the children's welfare to his wife, but often finding himself drawn in to administer discipline when the children misbehaved with their mother. The children were confused as a result of the lack of a clear parental boundary, with Norman seeming least able to cope with the situation.

The social worker could have decided to intervene solely within the family, but the family—school relationship would have continued to undermine any early steps towards change within the family, particularly as the teaching staff were losing patience with Norman's behaviour. It seemed more appropriate to work at the linkage between family and school in the form of a joint family—school interview.

This approach can be difficult, particularly since the school or other agency will not necessarily see itself as the target of change, especially if it is also the referring agent. However, as Aponte (1976) has suggested, if the interview is used principally as a way of finding solutions rather than of digging for the causes of trouble, then this difficulty can be overcome. He stresses that the therapist must attempt to make the interview a practical experience in which the family and school staff will recognize the relevance of their roles as agents of positive change.

In other words, concentrating on the need to find solutions, and acknowledging the primacy of school staff and parents in their respective contexts, leads away from resentment at being treated as inferior. In the case of Norman, the meeting between his parents, year tutor, and social worker resulted in a major change of attitudes. Norman's father became more positive about the teaching staff, and he and his wife maintained regular contact with the school. The year tutor altered his perception of Norman's parents and sought their help in solving Norman's school problems, rather than ignoring them because of a long-held negative impression of the family.

SOCIAL WORK AS PART OF THE PROBLEM: FAMILIES AND AGENCIES

It is easy to assume that agencies can work together as if they were neutral in relation to their clients' problems. What has become increasingly obvious to us is that the difficulties in the relationship between agencies can play an important part in maintaining family problems. Reder (1983), referring to work with disorganized families, stresses how important it is, in the face of chaotic family relationships, for all agencies to be clear about their respective roles, and to make these roles clear to the family.

Case conferences are to be particularly important, in that they can make use of family therapy skills directly at the linkage between the family and its wider network. Case conferences bear some point of resemblance to the method called network assembly, which involves bringing together in one place as many friends, relatives, neighbours, and professionals as are involved with a person who is in need of help. Speck and Attneave (1973) suggest that such meetings can provide the opportunity to move to new sets of relationships and therefore new solutions to existing problems. Such problem-solving is not simply at the emotional level, but is also carried out in terms of creating practical resources that help the individual, or family, cope more effectively.

Although case conferences are common, network assemblies are rare. The difference between the two is that, with case conferences, agencies share their knowledge about a particular individual or family — usually without the client being present — and seek to combine their various skills and resources to plan effectively for the protection or future development of that individual or family. Network assemblies, on the other hand, seek to use this process *together with* the family in the present to bring about change. Case conferences often give more information about inter-agency relations than they do about the family system, and it is usually preferable to have family members present. Problems can arise when the family is not directly involved in case conferences. For example, if the family is absent who should then take on the responsibility of representing their views? Social workers may try to do this, but in practice the pressures and confusions of working within a wide network seem so often to prevent them from acting in the client's best interest. They easily succumb to their own doubts about what constitutes their best interests, and to the influence of professionals who may be less confused and enjoy higher status than themselves.

In some authorities it may be against agency policy to involve family members in formal case conferences, at least for the time being. Nevertheless, case conferences do give a good opportunity to estimate the demands that different agencies place on a family. In particular, it is easy for social workers to omit to observe and respect the family's own boundaries, with the result that they can intrude on the family's social life. As Janzen and Harris (1980) observe:

> Agencies which require the family to conform to agency policy, operate as though the family is an extension of the agency and subject to its bidding. Instead of providing support to the family's own problem-solving efforts, the policies of agencies and the action of workers often serve to inhibit the capacity for independent thought and action. In conceptual terms the family loses its boundaries as a separate system and becomes incorporated as part of the agency system, thus increasing rather than decreasing its dependency.

The position of various agencies towards the client family and towards each other is not always clear. Roberts (1979) warns of what may happen if there is not sufficient clarity:

> The family may find themselves caught between agencies. They will probably have learned the game of playing off one agency against another. Thus if communication between workers is difficult — or even non-existent (and this is more commonplace than one might suppose!) — the family may become trapped in a system being maintained by the agencies for their own interests.

Mattinson and Sinclair (1979) describe how a problem relationship between marital partners can be reflected down the line between client, student, social worker, team leader, area manager, and outside agencies with great accuracy.

In practice, we find that the processes described are likely to involve repetitive cycles — similar to those in which family members can find themselves trapped. Figure 5.1 gives a simplified view of how a problem tends to repeat itself.

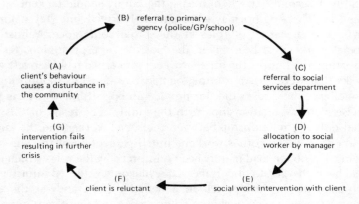

FIGURE 5.1 Problem repetition

If a social worker becomes aware of such a process, then there are a number of ways in which she can try to intervene. She may focus on the client (E) and try to find a different and more acceptable role. Alternatively, she may seek to have the referral re-defined at (C) — by asking the referring agent to gain more information, or at (B) — by encouraging the referring agent to try and influence the community's response to the client's behaviour.

She may also try and influence her manager to adopt a different policy at (D). It should be noted that any attempt to break such repetitive cycles may result in pressure and criticism from others inside or outside our agency. Nowhere is this more clear than in case conferences, where the pressures are brought together in one room.

Using the child abuse case conference as an example, we should not be surprised when other agencies, who may not have the same potentially active role with the family as ourselves, are not as enthusiastic about the change we perceive following our involvement. Much has been written about cooperation in multi-disciplinary settings (Hallet and Stevenson 1980), particularly from the perspective of sharing one's understanding of the family and improving cooperation with other agencies. In a case conference (in which one of us was involved) called to consider the possible discharge of a family from the child abuse register, two of the agencies concerned argued that because the children spoke 'freely' and had 'seconds' at school meals, the family should be kept on the register. These points may seem extremely trivial, but they stemmed from the allocation of roles at the initial conference. Whilst the social worker had been given the 'positive' and prestigious task of 'treating' the family, the other workers concerned had been left with tasks that were either routine, or negative (such as monitoring or policing). These tasks did not provide an opportunity for changing these workers' relationships with the family. The result of this was that only the relationship between the social worker and the family had changed. The other workers' initial perception of the family as being a 'problem' had merely been reinforced by the roles which they had been charged to undertake. They had only gathered information which could be interpreted in a negative light and, at the case conference, had been unable to acknowledge any significant improvement in the family.

This kind of process will be familiar to many workers who, in their dealings with families, have inadvertently excluded important members of a family system from participating in achieving change. In allocating roles at case conferences, as in allocating tasks to members of a family in therapy, it is essential to include everybody so that they have an investment in change taking place. When it does, all can share in the satisfaction.

Cade (1978) in an article on family violence, has argued that professional involvement can increase the likelihood of even more serious violence if we do not help the family break the existing pattern of transactions. This serves to remind us that case conferences have important implications for the family, particularly if the result is a continuation of the existing set of relationships between family and agency. The difficulty with case conferences is that they may tell us more about the agencies than about the family. If we are serious in arguing that the relationship between the family and the wider systems is a legitimate area of work, then we must consider how agencies like our own can hinder as well as help families. Clients of Social Services Departments are often involved with a number of agencies, both voluntary and statutory, who may have conflicting policies and priorities. This process may inadvertently divide family members (rather than bring them together), and hence prevent them from either using or enhancing their existing capacities to solve problems. It is our responsibility as family system workers to identify and prevent such a pernicious process.

Network assembly

Within family therapy there have been attempts to work directly with the family and its wider network. As a method, network assembly involves bringing together in one place as many friends, relatives, neighbours and professionals as are involved with the family. It aims to achieve what Speck and Attneave (1973) call the 'network effect'. This is the opportunity to move to new sets of relationships and therefore provide new solutions to existing problems. The initial meeting is organized by the family and social workers concerned, and it seems that one meeting is very often sufficient to start the process of change. Social workers lead and direct the meeting to enable the participants to move into new relationships. In many respects the network is an enlarged case conference; it aims, however, not only to draw up a plan, but also to see that it is implemented immediately.

A network meeting can be most appropriate in situations where family boundaries and competence are being eroded by the action of powerful subsystems within the larger network. Looking at the files in any social services office we will find families that have virtually become part of the Department. These files testify to the more destructive part of our work. In these cases, social workers are not sufficiently neutral, and it is essential to have an outside consultant who will be responsible for the actual network meeting. The aim of such a meeting will be to help both social workers and family form a relationship which can be more positive, and which can lead to the family increasing its problem-solving abilities.

Our experience has taught us that such meetings can be extremely helpful, but should be used strictly according to need. Social workers must either recognize the potential of the wider network in relation to a particular problem, or their own part in the maintenance of the problem.

Intervening or not intervening

An early decision which has to be made in relation to referrals is whether the involvement of the social services department is likely to be helpful to the 'client'. In many long term cases the 'welfare' has become part of the family homeostasis which prevents change from taking place. At the same time we need to assess whether the involvement of other agencies is likely to undermine our work, and whether other agencies would be able, possibly with extra support, to make a better contribution by themselves.

GETTING STARTED WITH A FAMILY SYSTEMS APPROACH

Adams and Hill (1983) issue a warning about the dangers of applying family therapy within a statutory agency. The main problems are: the routine nature of much of the work; organizational rigidity; and the defensiveness created by having to take risks.

One could approach this dilemma in two ways. The first would be to make space for referrals of a 'clinical' kind. Here the social worker's role would be straightforwardly therapeutic and other agencies are not likely to be involved. Although this approach may have some limited use, we have argued that it misses the potential of family therapy as a total systems approach. This alternative approach requires the social worker to combine the role of a family therapist with whatever other roles prove necessary in attempting to produce change. In practice this may mean that as much time is devoted to working with other agencies as is devoted to working with the family and its community network. This may be easier said than done, but if a discreet, well-planned approach is adopted the results can be rewarding for everybody involved.

Involving managers

Whether a family systems approach is to involve the use of family therapy with certain families, or methods involving other agencies, it is essential that social workers accept that, like family members, they work within a hierarchy. Managers are likely to respond to a well-argued case, particularly if one avoids using technical terms. Managers have their own skills which are important to them in the execution of their management role — accordingly they must be treated with respect. Indeed, because of their knowledge and longer experience of dealing with other agencies and the law, they can play an essential role in establishing a wider systems approach, and help social workers not to overfocus on the family system.

It must be explained that family work need not be more time

consuming in the long run. On the contrary, its focused and contractual nature should make it a competitive approach within a busy statutory setting. This is particularly so where family casework has been used as a standard approach.

Some recent work by Adams and Hill (1983) has explored some of the deficiencies in family casework which were discovered as a result of research work carried out by Sainsbury (1980). Sainsbury was surprised to find that a large number of long-term cases involved work that lacked operationally defined goals. Too much time was spent on discussing the quality of relationships without discussing the purpose for which these relationships existed. Interestingly, since clients were also wholly dependent upon the limited expertise and vision of an individual worker, there was a real danger of ineffective work being carried out. A further error was caused by the method of case assignment — each client was wholly dependent upon the limited expertise and vision of the individual worker who worked with her. Since these workers generally had inadequate skills and too little time to devote to their case-loads it was not surprising that much of the work was ineffective. Sainsbury's remedy for these difficulties was to suggest that there should be a switch from 'need and dependency' to 'task and purpose'. In practice this would mean that social workers should shift from being supportive to being the agents of change.

These deficiencies are important and most managers will be sensitive to them. A family-orientated social worker needs to keep them in mind as she approaches her manager in order to gain permission to undertake family work. Obviously she needs to avoid an 'holier-than-thou' attitude but, at the same time, it is important to remember that the pragmatic, problem-solving forms of family therapy are specifically designed to meet the type of deficiencies that Sainsbury outlines.

Obviously it is not just managers who will be aware of the deficiencies in the work of Social Services Departments — our fieldwork colleagues will also be aware of them. We need to build a bridge to them because without their support our work will be isolated and vulnerable to criticism. In the long run, the best way to build support is to run a support group (see chapter 11).

Working with colleagues

Family therapy emphasizes the context in which change takes place. If social workers are to use family therapy skills, they are likely to be more effective if they can create the right overall context for their work. It is therefore essential to find like-minded colleagues with whom to form a support group. The process of finding allies takes time, and it is necessary to avoid preaching the gospel of family therapy and gaining a reputation of being narrow-minded.

Colleagues can support each other by discussion of cases and 'brainstorming' in order to develop some new angles on particularly difficult cases. Gradually, joint work and live consultation can be introduced as trust develops. When statutory work is involved, colleagues can learn to split roles, as we described earlier in this chapter when we reviewed the example of Norman and his family. If a support group is to be formed it pays to involve only those who are interested in practice and not just talking about practising. It is also not wise to attract large numbers — those who have a real interest will come, and a small group may be more effective anyway. Eventually a support group can gain enough confidence to act as a 'live consultation' group. The establishment of regular family therapy sessions with the use of such a group can quickly help practitioners develop technical skills. Fernandez has described a good example of this type of work in a statutory setting (Fernandez et al. 1983).

CONCLUSION

This chapter began with a quotation from Bill Jordan. His statement may be correct, to some degree, in that the method of family therapy by itself has a limited usefulness within a social service setting. However, we would agree with Adams and Hill (1983) that Jordan has overlooked the wider implications of family therapy and the radical influence that genuine systems theory can have. We hope that our chapter has demonstrated that family therapy can be adapted and modified in order to suit the type of work that is generated by a statutory setting. Of necessity this requires fieldwork practitioners to abandon the rather pure form of family therapy that is practised in clinical settings, such as Child Guidance Clinics. The form of practice that emerges from this approach involves the best use of systems theory which is an extraordinarily flexible and pragmatic framework for working in such complicated settings as Social Services Departments.

Some of our readers may feel that our approach has not gone far enough — they may well wish to see changes in both the philosophy and the policies of such settings. That, however, is another subject and requires another sort of book.

6

Family Therapy in Probation Practice

MARJORIE AINLEY

This chapter looks at the implications of adopting a family therapy approach in the Probation Service. It describes simple yet effective ways of engaging with families and overcoming the difficulties inherent in having a statutory responsibility for the supervision of only one individual in the family. It would be impossible to cover the entire scope of probation practice, so examples are confined to working with juvenile offenders on Supervision Orders and adult probationers. I do not wish to imply, by concentrating on only two aspects of a probation officer's work, that it is inappropriate or impossible to practice family therapy with those clients such as parolees, or young prisoners who have been prematurely released from penal establishments on licence, but lack of space precludes the necessary examination of issues relating to control, public safety and agency accountability. Similarly, the growing use of family therapy models by probation officers working as Divorce Court Welfare Officers requires a chapter to itself. The trend by Divorce Court Welfare Officers away from an adversarial model in favour of conciliation is beginning to be the subject of discussion in the Probation Service, as can be seen by recent articles featured in *Probation Journal.* Howard and Shepherd (1982) describe successful attempts to conciliate between divorcing couples who were in dispute over access arrangements or custody of children, and Davis (1982) highlights some of the problems which can arise from the attempt to impose a 'therapeutic' model onto the 'justice' model.

There is practically no literature relating specifically to probation officers functioning as family therapists, with the exception of the interesting example described by Broder and Sloman (1982). However, there are a number of publications describing how practitioners from other disciplines work with families which have a delinquent member. Particularly useful is Johnson's (1974) succinct account of the work of a family intervention service operating within the Probation Service as an arm of the juvenile court. The family intervention service accepts referrals from judges and probation staff, but probation officers do not themselves practice as therapists. Wendorf (1978) presents an interesting theoretical discussion and case study on a family therapy approach to the rehabilitation of adult offenders. Again, the scheme functions under the auspices of the local Probation Department, but the therapists are specially recruited clinical psychologists and not probation officers. The comprehensive counselling programme for severely delinquent adolescents and their families which is described by Chase et al. (1979) is closely linked to the Probation Service, but the counsellors are social workers. These papers, like most on the subject, are American. In England and Wales probation officers provide a social work service to the courts, so such literature should not be interpreted as an indication that the probation officer in this country must of necessity refer potential family therapy cases to another agency.

There have been a number of different attempts to provide a conceptual understanding of the origins of delinquency in families (Shapiro 1967; Cheek 1966; Ferreira 1960; Friedman 1969; Harms 1962; Serrano, et al. 1962). However, because all offenders are in conflict with authority, and the parents of juvenile clients often indicate that they cannot or will not control their child's behaviour, the writings of Haley (1976; 1980) and his focus upon hierarchy are particularly relevant to probation practice. Dedicated probation officers may flinch at his chapter on social control and therapy (1980), but they ought not to ignore it. He summarizes his argument as follows:

> . . . agents of social control represent the community, and their primary job is to do something to quiet troublemakers and other social deviants. Only secondarily is it their task to help the deviant. They tend to identify one person rather than a social situation as the problem and they ignore the family or consider it a noxious influence. These premises, and the institutions which develop from them, handicap a therapist who seeks to bring about change.

Madanes' (1980) descriptions of the power struggles between family members relate directly to problems experienced by probation officers in working with the families of individuals who persistently fight against the rules laid down by society. Minuchin's (1974) classic combination of an over-involved mother and an opting-out father is frequently encountered when working with the families of juvenile offenders. Parents may present as overwhelmed and unable to manage an out-of-control child, and it will not be fruitful to try immediately to persuade them to act otherwise. For tactical reasons the probation officer may therefore need to take responsibility for the child for a short period of time. This manoeuvre is well recognized in the structural family therapy literature and is helpfully described by Minuchin et al. (1978) who took over the feeding of a low-weight anorexic in order to remove the issue of eating as an ingredient in the power struggle operating within the family.

Wilson (1980), whilst not describing or advocating family intervention in cases of juvenile delinquency, nonetheless makes out a good case for considering family therapy when a child has appeared before the court. Through a British research project conducted in the Midlands, she demonstrated that lack of parental supervision is the crucial factor which seems to determine whether children living in high-risk crime areas become delinquent. Her paper needs to be considered in conjunction with the findings of Power et al. (1974) who conducted a long-term study of juveniles resident in Tower Hamlets. They claim that in their sample of delinquent boys aged between eleven and fourteen, those coming from broken homes or intact homes with serious problems were significantly more likely to become persistent offenders. However, they do go on to warn that it might be unhelpful to focus entirely on the family life of the delinquent. They advocate that a 'recognition by magistrates, teachers and social workers that the cause [of frequent court appearances] may frequently lay outside the family, would permit all concerned, including the parents, to work together in a more genuine partnership to act jointly on the "outside" influence.' I believe that probation officers do consider neighbourhood, schools, finance and employment problems when determining where and how to intervene on behalf of their clients.

However, the expectations of the courts, coupled with the way work is allocated and supervised in the Probation Service, result in a concentration on either the individual client *or* the wider systems. It is interesting to note that, unless an entire family is overtly delinquent, the probation officer may not so readily consider the influence of the family system on the delinquent behaviour of an individual. (Broder and Sloman (1982) make identical observations about the way in which Canadian probation officers work with their clients.)

ISSUES

Whilst I shall argue that family therapy can be a very effective approach in the probation setting, a number of important constraints must be taken into account. The individual client is publically and legally labelled as the problem. The making of a Probation Order (or a Supervision Order in the case of juveniles) is an acknowledgment by the court that the client needs and is entitled to help, but as an offender he also has to be supervised. Whether or not he gains any benefit, he is required to cooperate with his probation officer, who in turn is responsible to the court. There is no legal requirement on the probation officer to work with the members of his family and they are not under any obligation to participate in the supervisory process. However, an adult offender must give clear agreement before he can be placed on probation and the probation officer usually has an opportunity to negotiate a working contract prior to the court appearance.

In contrast, it is legally possible for a juvenile to be supervised without the consent of his parents. Although probation officers work with clients placed on supervision by the Domestic or Divorce Courts, most of their clients are subject to Supervision Orders made under the Children and Young Persons Act (1969), following criminal proceedings, and it is these to whom I refer throughout this chapter.

To work full-time in the penal system, and to be employed by a Probation Committee composed of magistrates, poses unique problems. The following example illustrates some of the issues which arise.

A probation officer wrote a social inquiry report on a fourteen year-old girl who had been taken before the juvenile court by the police. They had made an application for a Care Order on the grounds that 'she is exposed to moral danger and also that she is in need of care and control which she is unlikely to receive unless the court makes an order in respect of her' (Children and Young

Persons Act, 1969). There was evidence of the girl having had sexual intercourse with four youths and two men. The distressed parents, who had successfully reared four older children, seemed to have no control over their daughter.

The probation officer was able to negotiate a promising contract with the parents, which in her opinion justified the recommendation in her report that the girl be made subject to a Supervision Order. Expressing considerable reservation, the bench followed the recommendation. The parents were told that in such cases the court usually made a Care Order to the local authority in the expectation that the girl be removed from home, but on this occasion had been persuaded otherwise by the probation officer whose opinion they respected. The magistrates further stated that they expected the officer to return to court with the girl if there was any suspicion of sexual activity. The Supervision Order would then be considered to have failed and a Care Order would be substituted. Although such an instruction is not legally binding on a probation officer, realistically it could not be ignored. The girl was below the age of consent and any officer appearing to collude with her promiscuity would lose all credibility with the court.

This case illustrates how the probation officer's actions and freedom to plan a therapeutic intervention are constantly influenced by others, such as magistrates and the police, who directly implement the law. Haley (1980) argues that the therapist must either be in control of admission to, and release from, institutions or, alternatively, the start of therapy should be delayed until there is no risk of the therapist being over-ruled by a worker with more power. Probation officers often influence decisions, but they can never have full control over their client when dealing with courts. Even if therapy is proceeding to the satisfaction of the probation officer, if the client re-offends, the court may choose to ignore a recommendation to allow the defendant his liberty. The departure of the client into a prison or the care of the local authority is a fairly frequent occurrence.

Throughout this chapter, I describe the individual who is on probation or subject to a Supervision Order as the 'client', which is normal conversational usage, but the Probation Service has never really identified its 'client'. Using the Pincus and Minahan (1973) model, it is clear that the person on a statutory order is the 'target' for intervention; his family, peer group, school or place of work may be part of the 'target system', but there is no consensus that he is the client. Some argue that 'society' is the client, because probation officers are public servants, whereas others insist that the court is the 'client' because it recruits the services of the probation officer. Probation Committees, composed of magistrates, appoint probation officers to a specific area to supervise offenders at the direction of the court. For over 70 years, successive Acts of Parliament have acknowledged that a probation officer's role is to 'advise, assist and befriend' offenders, but each probationer and supervisee receives a copy of a court order 'instructing' him to 'report to the probation officer'. Probation officers, seeing themselves as social workers or therapists who just happen to work in the probation service, may find that the two roles are in conflict. The conflict is more easily resolved when probation officers see themselves primarily as officers of the court who have therapeutic skills which can be made available to those clients who both need and desire them. In this way, the court remains the 'client', but the person under supervision is the 'target' with the potential to become the 'client'.

The difficulties are real, but not insurmountable. Indeed, with practice, the constraints of statutory supervision can often be defined within the working relationship in such a way that they facilitate rather than inhibit the therapeutic process. This is especially so when working with juveniles, and I will return to this point later on.

The probation officer is in an advantageous position when liaising with other agencies. Social workers, teachers and medical personnel usually acknowledge the probation officer as a specialist in his or her field. There is unlikely to be competition for clients, as once an offence has been committed it is usual for people to be referred without question to the Probation Service. In my experience, probation officers feel that they enjoy high status in relation to the other professions, and where workers from two or more agencies do need to work together, the views of the probation officer are likely to command considerable weight.

Within his or her own agency, the probation officer functions with a high degree of autonomy. The officer may not have any control over the volume of work allocated, but it is usually possible to exercise choice over the type of work. Provided the officer displays an adequate level of professional competence, no one will place restrictions on how the work is done. Unlike some methods of working with clients (for example, group work), family therapy is not actively encouraged within the service, but no obstacles would impede the keen individual who regarded family therapy as a suitable way of working with clients.

FAMILY THERAPY WITH JUVENILE OFFENDERS

The Probation Service places high priority on work with juvenile offenders, and this is as it should be, for the consequences of failure are severe. Repeat offenders and those who commit serious offences are sent to a Detention Centre or to Youth Custody. Fortunately, however, juvenile courts are reluctant to sentence without the benefit of a social inquiry report and a recommendation from a probation officer.

Arriving at the appropriate recommendation for a particular child requires careful consideration of the options. In 1981, 11,580 children were placed under the supervision of the Probation Service. Over 50 per cent of these children had no previous convictions. Thomas (1982) quotes these figures as evidence of a prevailing ethic amongst probation officers and magistrates that 'juveniles can be treated out of delinquency by social work intervention.' He goes on to explain that many juvenile courts operate, albeit informally, a sentencing tariff scale. A Supervision Order comes well up the tariff and if the child re-offends whilst on supervision, the magistrates may be reluctant to impose a 'lesser' sentence, such as a conditional discharge or a fine. There is also the danger that supervision will be perceived to have failed. Thus, if a Supervision Order is made too early in the career of a juvenile offender there is the risk that he will by-pass certain rungs on the tariff ladder which leads ultimately to a Care Order or a custodial sentence. The reasoning is valid, but causes a dilemma for the probation officer. Some children may come before the court for very minor offences, but routine investigations by the probation officer may reveal severe problems at home or school. If the child, parents and teachers display an inability or disinclination to tackle difficulties effectively, the probation officer may feel a responsibility to recommend a Supervision Order as the only means of introducing the child and his family to a source of help. A delicate balance must be maintained. It is essential that assessment of juvenile offenders and recommendations to courts should take into account not only the child's circumstances and immediate needs, but also the criminal justice system and his long-term prospects should he re-offend.

As with the majority of Probation Service clients, children on supervision are required to 'report' at regular intervals to their officer in the probation office. Officers are expected to visit the home for the purpose of sharing information with the parents and in order to offer advice on any difficulties that they are experiencing with their child. It is interesting that there is no legal obligation on the officer to meet with the parents, although it is clearly stated in the Criminal Justice Act (1948) that the probation officer must visit the child's school. Since I started supervising the work of probation officers I have learned that some parents are not contacted by their child's probation officer through the entire life of a two-year Supervision Order. Probation officers seem to accept all responsibility for influencing the child's behaviour, including the prevention of further offences. If parents are ineffectual or absent they try to fill the gap. It is not unusual in case discussion for probation officers to suggest that if a father has deserted or is incompetent, the child can be compensated by contact with a male officer, and if there is no mother it will be argued that the supervisor should be a woman.

This approach is often not effective in bringing about change. The well-intentioned probation officer is faced in the office with a reluctant, monosyllabic young person. Further he suspects, or even knows, that the parents are subverting the requirements of the Supervision Order, which are that the child report to the office, attend school and behave in a way which minimizes the risk of further offences being committed, i.e. 'lives a good and industrious life'.

It is not hard to understand parental 'resistance'. They have not voluntarily sought advice or assistance, but have been identified by the courts as failed parents. The court has decreed that someone else is better equipped than they to supervise their child's behaviour and that person may be single, childless and young — nearer in age perhaps to the child than to the parents. The parents may feel that they cannot cope and need help, but it is difficult for them to welcome such help under the terms of a Supervision Order. An improvement in the child's behaviour following intervention by the supervisor would confirm that they had been inadequate in their parenting. In order to preserve their already demeaned status, they may feel that they have to undermine the probation officer. Similarly,

the child out of loyalty to his parents cannot wholeheartedly respond
to the probation officer's efforts on his behalf. Seeing the child in a
family setting goes a long way towards disarming parental resistance,
especially if their cooperation has been enlisted before the making of
the Supervision Order, and because of this a family therapy
orientation is the one I use when supervising juvenile clients.

Once family therapy is decided upon as the method of intervention,
the probation officer needs to devise strategies for functioning as a
therapist within the requirements of statutory supervision. Although
it is both conceptually and operationally difficult to integrate the
roles of therapist and supervisor, this must be achieved. Nonetheless,
on occasions the two roles will be mutually exclusive. It is impossible
to resolve contradictions if the probation officer perceives him or
herself solely as a therapist. A logical and manageable way of
marrying the roles is for the practitioners to see themselves primarily
as probation officers who are using family therapy as a way of
understanding and working with the client. The client only becomes
a candidate for a family therapy approach after committing an
offence and being placed on supervision. Family therapy literature is
sparse on this subject, but Johnson (1974) has some useful ideas,
both on convening families and in assessing suitability for therapy
when the presenting problem is a child who has appeared before the
court.

The first contact — the social inquiry report

The first contact with a family occurs when the child is referred by
the Police Juvenile Bureau (after an offence has allegedly been
committed, but before the court appearance) or by the Juvenile
Court (after one court appearance and a finding of guilt, but before
sentence). The probation officer is required to see the child, his
parents, and other significant people, such as teachers, in order to
prepare a social inquiry report. As well as giving a comprehensive
social history, the report will contain a recommendation as to
sentence. An adult offender can only be placed on probation if he
gives his consent, but a juvenile can be placed under supervision
without the consent of either child or parents. Probation officers are
in a position of considerable power at this stage in the proceedings.
If this is fully comprehended by the parents it may induce in them

feelings of anger and helplessness. The success of therapy can therefore depend on work done before the Supervision Order is made, and even before the decision to recommend supervision.

In order to deal with the difficult engagement phase of therapy, it is necessary to interview the parents alone. This first lengthy interview allows them to express their concern over the child and fears surrounding the pending court appearance. During this interview they should be fully briefed on the role and the powers of the probation officer. It is courteous and tactically important to take the family history at this stage as parents may find it distressing to be asked intimate questions about family relationships in the presence of their children. If such ground has been explored with them first they will not be taken by surprise in subsequent interviews with the children present. A joint session follows with parents and child. It is helpful to also see other family members, but the wishes of the parents should be respected. If they are ashamed of their offspring's misdemeanours they may have tried to keep things from younger children or other relatives; there is nothing to be gained by questioning their judgement at this stage. The parents' permission is sought for a separate interview with the offender. Their rights are being respected, but at the same time the child is defined as having a separate existence and individual responsibility for aspects of his own behaviour. Both the child and his parents should understand that the purpose of the separate interview is to discuss school, sport, friendships, etc., and not family habits or relationships.

It should be explained to the parents that the probation officer is required to make enquiries of school staff, and that information obtained from the school will be incorporated into the social inquiry report. If they are to trust the probation officer, the family must be given an honest picture of what is happening, and this means that an open approach is essential. If the school has important relevant information then this must be shared with the parents. This can cause problems if teachers insist on the confidential nature of their communications. It is sensible to explain to teachers from the outset that there is a legal requirement that parents or guardians who attend court with a child 'must be told the substance of any part of the information in the report which the court considers to be material and which has reference to his own character or conduct or to the character, conduct, home surroundings or health of the child or young person concerned' (Jarvis 1980).

The probation officer must decide the recommendation which is to be made to the court. Prior discussion with the parents is not an abdication of this responsibility. If the recommendation is for supervision, the parents should be introduced to the idea of joining with the probation officer to form a working team which will collaborate to ensure the welfare of the child. They need to know that they are a necessary part of supervision because they are the experts on their family and their child. The probation officer is equally important as an authority on juvenile offenders, the penal system and helping parents to regain control over their child. Parents recruited in this way at this stage are likely to make a commitment to therapy.

The Supervision Order: the first interview

There is a delay of anything from a few days to several weeks between the social inquiry interview and the making of the Supervision Order. This is a period of uncertainty as neither the family nor the officer know whether they are going to work together after the child has been sentenced.

If a Supervision Order is made, the working contract negotiated with the parents should be restated, as family members are sometimes unclear about discussions which took place in the panicky period before court. The parents can choose whether to participate in therapy, but the child has no choice about contact with his probation officer and must report when requested to do so. The possible consequences of failure to comply with the requirements of supervision must be spelled out to both child and parents. Although parents are not obliged to cooperate, they should carry the onus of knowing that if their child opts out of supervision or re-offends, the court could make a care order or send the child to a penal establishment.

Stages of therapy

Initially, interviews should focus on the child's behaviour, in particular those aspects associated with the court appearance. The family did not seek help, and the fact that the child offended is the therapist's authority for working with them. When the child's behaviour has stabilized enough to avert the threat of immediate incarceration, it may then be appropriate to work on other issues which trouble the family. Sometimes it is apparent from the outset that the child's behaviour is functional for the stability of the family by deflecting from more distressing and painful areas of family life (Haley 1980). This makes 'resistance' more understandable, and if, for example, marital work is attempted immediately and directly the parents may be put on the defensive. However, once the therapist is perceived by the couple as helpful in connection with the child's behaviour and their parenting function, it is then possible to lead on, where necessary, to working with their partnership. In my experience, both natural and step-parents are often quick to make a link between the child's problem behaviour and unresolved conflicts in their own relationship. Whether or not they give permission for this to become a focus for work, they can be helped to separate the role of parent from that of spouse. It may be possible eventually to do marital work, but the essential first stage of therapy is to break the cycle of deviant behaviour by the child (Haley 1980).

The ultimate aim of supervision is to get the parents to take charge of their child. Whilst allowing him freedom commensurate with his age and their own value system, they ought to be able to influence his behaviour to the extent of stopping illegal activities and modifying the more extreme manifestations of adolescent rebellion. Parents may seem unable or unwilling to take on this responsibility. When a child is wild and difficult, the parents show little confidence in taking charge. They collude in order to avoid painful scenes or swing from extremes of harsh discipline to casual permissiveness. They may behave in a contradictory manner, insisting that the child go to school, but refusing to comply with uniform requirements so that the child is sent home. If parents claim they cannot cope it is tactically sound for the probation officer to temporarily accept responsibility for the child's behaviour (Minuchin et al. 1978). It is important to avoid being pressurized by the parents into focusing on less important aspects of the child's behaviour, such as never being in for meals. The probation officer's concern should be directed towards aspects of the child's behaviour (such as buying alcohol if he is under age, or staying out all night) which may lead to the child committing further offences. The immediate need is to contain the child, but the long-term therapeutic goal is the resumption of parental authority.

Securing an initial commitment from the family is probably the most difficult stage for the probation officer embarking on family therapy. This is because courts, offenders, and the Probation Service itself, are all geared to the expectation that clients will be supervised on an individual basis. Once this obstacle has been overcome, the therapeutic process is unlikely to differ from normal practice in any other setting. My own experience, once I had acquired competence as a family therapist, was that once families are successfully recruited into therapy they tend to make a full commitment and stick to the working contract. Early in my career I made the mistake of trying to practice family therapy with extremely delinquent families. I assumed that if several members of a family were committing offences they must be unhappy and in need of help. This is not necessarily the case. Families need to be carefully assessed for suitability. Some do not need and therefore will not respond to therapy. However, they may be prepared to enter into a verbal agreement with the probation officer, knowing that their compliance may lead to the probation officer making a less punitive recommendation in the social inquiry report.

The main barrier to effective work is probably a failure by the probation officer to devote sufficient time to engaging the family. Another possibility is that the probation officer will not always treat family therapy sessions as a priority. Commitments to the courts or high-risk clients may be given precedence, leaving no time for pre-planning interviews or the management of co-worker relationships. The ability to organize a complex work load is just as necessary as therapeutic skills if family therapy is to be a successful way of working with probation clients.

I will now give an illustration of the use of family therapy in the context of Supervision Orders for juvenile offenders.

Fifteen year-old Peter was placed under supervision following a series of violent offences, including criminal damage and assault on the police. He sniffed glue, drank to excess and was described by his parents as totally out of their control. Although it was Peter's first court appearance, the offences were so numerous and serious that he was lucky not to receive a custodial sentence.

Both Peter and his parents were frightened by his aggressive behaviour. His parents welcomed the making of the Supervision Order and, although Peter expressed contempt at having to report to a probation officer, he indicated his acceptance by keeping all the appointments.

The probation officer's objective was to get the parents to take charge of Peter and impose controls on his behaviour. However, they were unable to withstand his aggression and they admitted that he openly defied them when their rules or wishes conflicted with his ambitions. Father behaved towards Peter in a critical, disciplinarian manner and yet was ineffectual in dealing with him. Mother was permissive and over-indulgent. It seemed likely that Peter would be back in court long before his parents learned how to combine their efforts and put a halt to his excesses. In these circumstances the probation officer told the parents that she would take on the responsibility of restraining Peter. She said she thought she ought to do so as they had made it clear that they could not. However, she also emphasized that in contrast to parental authority, the court order was a crude and unwieldy tool. She explained at length how the court was likely to react if supervision broke down, describing in graphic detail what would happen if Peter was sent to a Detention Centre or Borstal. The parents voiced their appreciation of the probation officer's offer, reiterating that they themselves had no control over Peter.

To start with, the probation officer persuaded Peter's parents to work out a set of rules which they wanted him to abide by. This took time as they needed help in reconciling the repressive regime favoured by father with the easy-going one acceptable to mother. Eventually they decided that Peter should not stay out all night, sniff glue, get drunk, or start smashing up the house whenever he felt thwarted. Although the parents agreed over what the rules should be, it was evident that they had little faith in their own ability to enforce them. The probation officer added a rule that Peter should not do anything illegal. Towards the end of this session, Peter was invited to contribute; he said that whether or not he smashed up the house was dependent to a large extent on the way he was treated by his parents. After discussion, the parents conceded to be less critical of annoyances like loud music, provided Peter kept the important rules which they had compiled.

The probation officer then instructed Peter's mother to telephone every morning with a detailed account of Peter's behaviour over the preceding 24 hours. When the probation officer was not available she was to dictate a report to the secretary. Her initial enthusiasm for this daily conversation soon palled, and instead of being a pleasure the task became a chore. For six weeks she reported daily, and was closely questioned on Mondays, following the risky weekend period.

At the same time, family sessions continued fortnightly; they, and the tasks between meetings, were designed to achieve the goal of handing over control to the parents. They made progress in reconciling their own differences as to how Peter should be managed, and also began to acquire confidence more generally in their joint ability to be effective parents. At intervals, the probation officer reminded them all of the likely consequences should Peter re-offend, pointing out that the exercise of parental authority is always preferable to the intervention of the law. They were given examples of the more subtle, but equally appropriate and effective sanctions which can be applied by parents.

Gradually, power was transferred from the probation officer to the parents. There were signs that his mother was either summarily disciplining Peter herself, or joining with her husband in his management. She seemed to find this course of action easier than being subject to persistent questioning on the telephone, especially when there had been problems which she and her husband could not solve.

Peter desperately wanted a moped for his sixteenth birthday, and the probation officer used this to show the parents the extent of their control over their son. With the probation officer's support, they told him that getting the moped was dependent on his good behaviour. During the intervening months there were times when they wavered, but they gained in confidence and determination as they discovered that they could affect Peter's behaviour on all sorts of things by the granting or withdrawing of privileges and pocket money. Originally sceptical, they learned that once they jointly became firm in their demands, but generous in their concessions, Peter would barter and keep his side of a bargain. When Peter finally got his moped he had earned it. His parents enjoyed donating the gift and did not, as on past occasions, feel they had been browbeaten into submission.

Therapy continued for nine months and Peter was seen individually for a further three months until the expiry of the Order. Three years after the making of the Supervision Order Peter had not re-offended, and conflicts at home remained within bounds which the family found acceptable. There was no glue-sniffing and only an occasional drinking bout. The probation officer took charge for only six months. Thereafter rules of behaviour were made and administered by the parents.

The early stages of this Supervision Order were very difficult for the probation officer. Peter's violence and frequent bouts of intoxication raised anxieties about his safety and the risks incurred by anyone who antagonized him. Teachers, the school welfare officer and the Child and Family Guidance social worker had all suggested confinement (for example, in a closed unit in a community home). The court was thinking of a Detention Centre and only agreed to try supervision in the community because of the well-argued social inquiry report submitted by the probation officer. In Peter's case a family approach was successful. The probation officer, by using her power and authority, stabilized Peter's behaviour enough for the long-term goals of therapy to be achieved. If she had failed and someone had been hurt, Peter would not have been the only loser. Any doubts which the magistrates felt about supervision in the community would have been confirmed, and they would themselves have felt some responsibility had further violence occurred. Thus the failure of therapy affects not only one family, but has implications for other children who appear before the courts having committed serious offences. Magistrates have to take into account public safety as well as the needs of the individual.

Contra-indications to family therapy as a method of working with juvenile clients

Not all juvenile clients come from unhappy, disturbed homes where the family needs help with its problems. Children commit offences for a variety of reasons, including lack of judgement due to immaturity, childish greed, or peer group pressures. Family intervention may be unnecessary. Instead the child can be required to report to the office or be involved in a group project with other youngsters. Although parents need not participate fully in the working relationship between probation officer and child, they should be included in the planning stage at the beginning of supervision. As well as being informed at intervals about progress, or lack of it, they should be aware that their involvement will be welcomed if they choose to initiate contact with their child's supervising officer.

The Supervision Order with an Intermediate
Treatment Order

An Intermediate Treatment Order enables the probation officer to
direct a child into approved activities, and in order for this to be
achieved he may be removed from home for up to 90 days. The
intention is admirable. Since the introduction of Intermediate
Treatment Orders in the Children and Young Persons Act (1969),
funds and staff have been made available and children from materially
and intellectually deprived backgrounds become involved in a wide
variety of activities. It is impossible to list more than a few of these
which include social skills groups, psychodrama, craftwork and
adventure training. However, it is insensitive and probably tactically
inadvisable to place a child in an Intermediate Treatment project
unless this has first been negotiated with the parents. If they have
punished their child for committing an offence, they may feel angry
and undermined if the probation officer then appears to reward the
miscreant by taking him off on holiday. Poor parents often cannot
afford similar outings for other children of the family. They may
experience a loss of authority and status with their children when
one child is receiving from the probation officer privileges which
they cannot themselves afford. Even when there are reasons for
working with the child outside the family, it is important for the
probation officer to retain a family perspective and not do anything
which could threaten the integrity of the family.

FAMILY THERAPY WITH ADULT PROBATIONERS

A clear need for family therapy is not always immediately obvious
when working with adult offenders. Some offenders have become
career criminals with records extending back years, if not decades.
They have learned how to supplement their incomes or enhance
their status amongst family and friends through the commission of
offences. In the course of interviewing such offenders it becomes
apparent that they have more to lose than to gain by changing their
ways.

With many clients the family's problems appear at first sight, and
after more prolonged assessment, to be linked with poverty. Offences

of theft by shoplifting, DHSS frauds and dishonest use of electricity are common. Kingston (1979) warns against the danger of family therapists minimizing the importance of the complex relationships which exist between the family and other social institutions.

It is hard to escape the conclusion that dysfunctional family relationships are often the effect and not the cause of an inability to get work and find a purposeful role in society. A family consisting of two parents and three teenage children functioned satisfactorily until the father was made redundant. In the space of 18 months they came into conflict with the law, the children became out of control, and the marriage deteriorated. The husband said he no longer felt like a man. He was unable to give his wife sufficient housekeeping money, could not buy decent clothes for the children and dare not join his mates in the pub for fear of spending too much money when it was his turn to buy a round. He was ashamed. The wife felt diminished in her role as housewife and mother. She could not afford to feed her family as she wanted, or redecorate her home when it needed doing. She became resentful towards her husband because his lack of work meant she could no longer do her job properly.

The case is not without scope for a family therapist, provided the probation officer intervenes in a way which acknowledges the predominant part played by other systems in the problems experienced by the family. The family needed help in adapting to their changed circumstances, and in renegotiating roles. They also needed to be relieved of their feelings of guilt deriving from a tendency to blame themselves for their misfortune. Their own coping mechanisms only faltered when they were caught up in economic and political processes which are adversely affecting millions of other people. In these circumstances, useful adjuncts to family therapy can be groups run by colleagues or specialist services (such as help with education or employment) offered by probation ancillaries.

As with juveniles, the probation officer may decide at an early stage (possibly whilst writing the pre-court social inquiry report, and therefore prior to the defendant becoming a client) that family therapy is the most appropriate method of work. However, different techniques may be needed to engage such families.

It is the probation officer's job to supervise the offender, but with an adult, family members should only be approached if the client gives permission. A professional, highly successful man of forty-six was convicted of an indecent assault against a fourteen year-old boy, and placed on probation for a period of two years. The man, a bachelor, was an only child, still living in the parental home. He described an extremely interdependent relationship with his mother. It seemed probable that the parents had been aware of the closeness developing between their son and the victim of the offence. The probation officer attempted to gain access to the family, but this was forbidden by the client. As far as he was concerned, being on probation was the punishment of the court. He was prepared to cooperate fully with the supervisory requirements of the Probation Order, but regarded anything else as an intrusion and an impertinence.

Such a blank refusal even to discuss family circumstances is the exception rather than the rule. Meetings with the probation officer are generally acceptable to other family members. In fact, officers are usually welcomed into the home and treated with friendliness and respect. It may, however, prove more difficult to recruit the family for a planned programme of therapy as engagement strategies designed for juveniles are not appropriate when the client is adult. Whereas the officer's status with the court can be mobilized when the offender is a juvenile, in order to recruit the family of an adult client the officer must rely entirely on his credibility as a therapist. This will carry no weight at all if the client and the family do not want the services of a therapist.

If the client admits to having problems and the desire to tackle them, but refuses to involve his family, or the family are not prepared to participate, the idea of family therapy need not be abandoned. Circumstances may not be ideal, but the probation officer must devise ways of working within the context of the agency structure and task. This means that the officer must not be circumscribed by some of the techniques which are taught and practised by the clinical therapists. For example, it may prove possible when working with the individual to involve the family, for various reasons, in occasional sessions, or to get their agreement to a short course of, say, three sessions. A few sessions with the family provide a better basis for individual therapy than do no sessions. They may also trigger motivation for the family to participate more fully in therapy. Haley (1976) makes this point — he suggests that the important issue is not how many members of the family are seen by the therapist. What is crucial is the way in which the therapist perceives the client's situation. The essential ingredient is an interactional and systems approach to the client's problems.

An example of work with an adult offender

Mrs Morrison, aged thirty-two, was married with two children. She was placed on probation for stealing a large sum of money from a friend of her husband's. A similar offence, committed six months previously, had been dealt with by means of a fine. Her husband agreed to meet the probation officer immediately following the court appearance. He was most courteous and expressed concern about his wife, said he was pleased she was on probation and would receive help, but insisted that he would not be involved in the process. There were financial reasons for this. He was a roofer and, after enduring a disastrously cold winter with very low take home pay, he was now enjoying a warm, dry summer which provided long hours of overtime and a much needed boost to the family income. He also admitted there were 'personal problems' which his wife needed to discuss, but was adamant that he could not bear to talk about them himself. He was so insistent that the probation officer decided to work with Mrs Morrison individually, whilst maintaining a family perspective in the hope that the husband could be included at a later stage.

Mrs Morrison said she had been very depressed for about two years. She did not know why she was depressed, nor could she explain why she had stolen money. Since becoming depressed she had been unable to talk to her husband. They now only communicated essential items of information. There was no sexual activity. About seven months ago — just prior to the commission of the first offence — Mr Morrison left home to live with another woman, but returned after five days. This was never mentioned between the couple. Mrs Morrison was worried because, after committing the second offence, her two small children witnessed her removal from home in police custody and she did not return for five hours. They had been extremely distressed and Mrs Morrison wondered how much they understood of the incident. She had not discussed it with them, nor had her husband. Since committing the first offence, Mrs Morrison had been too ashamed to visit her elderly house-bound mother who lived nearby. She had no friends. She said she loved her husband, children and mother, and wished for things to be different. She saw all her other problems as peripheral to the breakdown in her marriage. Her husband had suggested that 'personal problems' ought to be worked on and, although he had opted out of therapy, had indicated that the marriage was important to him. The probation officer decided to concentrate on the marital relationship.

The therapist decided it was necessary to re-establish communications between the couple immediately, but thought it unlikely this could be directly achieved through speech. Mrs Morrison, who expressed horror at the thought of trying to talk to her husband, appeared cautiously intrigued at the idea of passing messages without using words. The therapist pointed out that her husband supported the family financially, spent his leisure time improving the home and had voluntarily returned to the marriage after a painful, but very brief abandonment; in these ways he was communicating some of his feelings about his wife and children and the level of his commitment to the marriage. Mrs Morrison was asked how she could similarly communicate to him that he was a person of value to her, and that she too was committed to the marriage. She decided that one Friday evening she would have the house immaculate, dress in her best clothes and cook her husband's favourite meal. She was warned by the therapist not to expect any response as this was only a first, tentative practice step.

When Mrs Morrison arrived for the next session, she burst into tears when greeted in the waiting area and could hardly wait to begin talking. She had carried out the plan, although she had felt extremely anxious and, to her amazement, her husband had simply started chatting. The family had a happy evening with everybody behaving in a pleasant and relaxed manner, since when Mrs Morrison and her husband had continued conversing normally.

Therapy continued for six months. Mrs Morrison was helped to devise ways of behaving differently towards her husband, but she was never sent away with a task which required her to talk. By the end of six months, she and her husband had initiated discussion about his desertion of her for another woman, and her two court appearances. She also talked to her children about the commission of the offences and responded to her husband's moves to effect a reconciliation with her mother. She got a part-time job and enjoyed both the companionship and the income.

At the end of nine months, meetings were discontinued and Mrs Morrison did not take up the offer to renew contact should she feel the need. There was no detailed follow-up, but two years after the end of therapy she had not re-offended.

Mrs Morrison's situation is not untypical. Her husband cared about his family and wanted his wife 'sorted out', but was not prepared to inconvenience himself financially or emotionally. He was well disposed towards a therapeutic intervention, provided he was not on the receiving end. The probation officer was seen as an expert who could 'talk some sense' into his wife. There is the temptation for the probation officer to decide at this stage that family therapy is impossible. Unfortunately, some of the best teaching on family therapy is transmitted or received in a way that confirms probation officers in the belief that with the majority of probation clients family therapy will not be acceptable to the family and so is not worth the effort. As already conceded, with some clients family therapy is an impossibility, but with many where family therapy is the appropriate mode of intervention it is also a successful one. Adaptations and modifications to techniques practised by clinical family therapists are not necessarily compromises leading to a second-rate service. They are an acknowledgment that the job is not only about therapeutic skills. It is also about the ability to accommodate the route by which the client and his family have become available for therapy.

OPPORTUNITIES FOR PROFESSIONAL SUPERVISION
AND TRAINING

There are ample training opportunities for staff employed in the Probation Service; research into provision by one county showed there were no restrictions whatsoever (Ainley 1979). The Probation Service Regional Staff Development Units are agents of the probation areas and they mount residential courses on a variety of subjects. In addition, officers can often negotiate time off and funding to attend courses at any reputable teaching establishment. 'On the job' training opportunities are scarce.

Because the practice of family therapy is a minority interest amongst probation officers, it may be difficult for the family therapist to receive supervision or find a consultant from his or her normal professional support system. This need not necessarily be a barrier to good practice as the Probation Service willingly accommodates co-workers from other agencies, provided their professional reputation is vouchsafed. The officer will also be allowed to reciprocate and work in another agency if that is the only source of supervision. The onus is on the individual practitioner to ensure the necessary degree of support, going outside his or her own agency if necessary.

Working conditions may not be ideal. Few probation officers are equipped with video equipment and one-way screens are unheard of. These deficiencies can be readily overcome by having the supervisor or consultant in the room with the therapist and family. This method of work is described in detail by Ainley and Kingston (1981) and by John Carpenter in chapter 11.

CONCLUSION

Family therapy is a valid way of working with Probation clients; especially so in relation to juveniles who have committed offences. The methods by which cases are usually referred to probation officers mean that there may be difficulties in engaging with families, but these can often be overcome by simple adjustments to technique. Interviews which take place at social inquiry stage with juvenile offenders can often be adapted to serve the dual purposes of collecting information and securing from parents a commitment to participate fully in the supervisory process. Thereafter, the obvious constraints of probation practice cannot be ignored and they sometimes restrict the therapeutic goals of the officer. However, the reverse can also be true, especially when the identified client is a child, where the requirements of the Supervision Order, or the threat of custody where it exists, can be used constructively when integrated with the power and authority of the probation officer's role.

Because most adult clients have never requested therapy, but have had it almost thrust upon them as part of their sentence, consideration must be given to tailoring therapy to fit the client. In those cases where a family are unable or unwilling to be involved in therapy they can still be worked with through the identified client, provided the probation officer retains a family perspective and gives directives or sets tasks which includes them, albeit at second-hand, in the therapeutic process.

Models described by Minuchin (1974), Haley (1980) and Madanes (1981) seem most helpful to work in the probation setting where the client is in conflict with the rules of society. These models seem particularly relevant when working with juvenile clients because the child, as well as committing offences, may also be successfully challenging school rules, in addition to the authority of his parents.

Family therapy is neither appropriate nor necessary with all probation clients. Probation officers carry demanding, diverse case loads. The very heavy time commitment necessary for the effective practice of family therapy techniques can only be justified in those cases which have been reliably assessed as suitable for this method of work. When family therapy is identified as the appropriate way of working with a client it may also be necessary simultaneously to intervene in other systems, such as schools or employment agencies.

The enthusiasm and persistence of individual officers are the factors most likely to influence success in initiating and implementing family therapy techniques in probation practice. This method of working with clients is somewhat outside mainstream practice, but the great advantage of working for the probation service is that officers have choice. They can choose how they work, with whom they work and where to go for consultation. The likelihood that they will not be actively encouraged to function as family therapists is more than offset by the excellent opportunities for training, and it is likely that failure to establish oneself as a family therapist will be intra-personal rather than institutional. It is up to each probation officer to determine whether this autonomy shall be exhilaratingly enabling or worryingly inhibitive.

7

Developing Family Counselling in General Practice Settings

BRIAN DIMMOCK

Historically it is puzzling that family therapy has not been more closely associated with general practice. However, the development of group practices and the opening of health centres has created a potentially interesting new arena in which family therapists can work. Some social workers and clinical psychologists have been quick to capitalize on these developments and have formed close working relationships with GPs. Their work, which tends to be individually orientated, has proved very successful, but the case for using a family-orientated approach scarcely needs arguing in a setting which is so intrinsically family-orientated.

In this chapter I will review an experimental attachment of four local authority social workers as 'family counsellors' to a busy group general medical practice in Gloucester. The Gloucester Project is not a research project, but an attempt to establish family counselling in a new setting. It started with a conviction that counselling using family therapy techniques is an effective treatment method for a wide variety of family problems, and that the day-to-day work of the general practitioners could be enhanced by having access to the skills of such counsellors. The fact that we are social workers has influenced the development of the project, but our experiences are of general relevance to any practitioner who wishes to develop this type of work.

The case for using the skills of social workers in primary health care has been well argued by Williams and Clare (1982), and Harwin et al. (1970), but the problems of ill-health presented within this context cannot easily be separated from the broader social needs of the community. The steady trend toward multi-disciplinary working within group practices and health centres is a recognition of the importance of 'social problems' in the delivery of primary health care (Clare and Corney, 1982), although there is no consensus about how to deal with such problems (Cartwright and Anderson, 1981).

Evaluations of experimental attachments of social workers to general practitioners (Goldberg et al. 1977) have emphasized their 'preventive' function, since social workers have been able to take referrals before crises arise. However, bringing about a shift towards genuinely preventive work is not easy. Any professional worker is likely to experience resistance from her own agency and her own colleagues when she attempts to work in new ways or in different settings. This is entirely understandable since change is experienced as being threatening within agency systems. A common response to such changes, when they occur, is the questioning of whether the social worker is really doing the job she is being paid for. Obviously such objections must be taken seriously. We were aware that our agency acknowledged the importance of preventive work with families, at a theoretical level, though such work was not given a high priority as far as the day-to-day running of the agency was concerned. We were also aware that preventive work is clearly within the permissive framework governing the activities of social workers as outlined in the Children's Act (1980). In addition, both academic research and DHSS policy emphasize the need for greater inter-professional communication and cooperation (Hallett and Stevenson 1980; DHSS, 1968, 1974). Such policies and interventions within an agency system require determination, clear strategies and a belief in the objectives. With the Gloucester Project, commitment to preventive work with families, and the interest and enjoyment in doing this work, were major factors in the project's successful establishment.

Primary care attachments offer social workers the chance to use 'counselling' techniques if they have the necessary skills and credibility, although there is no clear indication in the literature about which model of counselling is the most suitable for this type of setting. Doctors are likely to refer clients who require practical help, rather than those who ask for counselling, at least until the social workers have established their credibility (Corney, 1980). Butler et al. (1982) argue that both 'task centred' counselling and behavioural approaches are appropriate in general practice settings, as clients are usually well motivated to take part in planned, limited programmes of counselling, especially if encouraged to do so by their GP.

Our experience in running the Gloucester Project suggests that family therapy is particularly appropriate to general practice since it emphasizes not only the interaction between the client and his or her family, but also the interaction between the client, the family and the therapist. However, it is important to stress that there is potentially a great deal of common ground between general practice and family therapy. For example, Hunt, in giving the Lloyd Roberts Lecture: 'The Renaissance of General Practice', emphasized a tradition in medicine which sees the patient in his family context (Hunt, 1972). This tradition seeks to reverse the erosion of the role of the GP which is being caused by the development of specialized services in hospitals. In fact, as Hunt argues, the GP is in a unique position to focus on health rather than on disease, and on normality rather than abnormality.

It is also important, in this context, to acknowledge the influence of Michael Balint. As a psychoanalyst and GP he drew attention to important interactional issues between doctors and patients. These interactions became a focus for study as a result of his work, but within his model they also became a focus for therapeutic inter-vention. (Balint 1957; Balint et al. 1970). Some of his thinking has been absorbed into the designing of GP training programmes. For example, the Leeunhorst Conference Working Party on General Practice (1972) recently recommended that:

> At the conclusion of the training programme the doctor should be able to demonstrate . . . his understanding of the way in which interpersonal relationships within the family can cause health problems or alter their presentation, course and management, just as illness can influence family relationships.

Such thinking clearly forms a bridge to family-systems theory but it is central to the main argument of this book that we should extend our thinking beyond family systems in order to include the wider contexts in which we work. These contexts involve complex professional and agency systems as well as the interaction between these systems. Most of the descriptions of developing counselling services in general practice published so far, have not focused on the important initial stages which involve important intra-agency and inter-agency negotiations. I will, therefore, begin my discussion by exploring the negotiations that occurred at the start of the Gloucester Project, before moving on to review the further steps taken to establish the project over a two-year period.

CONVINCING THE DEPARTMENT

Once the project members had explored the possibilities of working with local general practices it became clear that there was one particular general practice which would respond favourably to an approach. However, a number of difficulties arose because of the administrative organization of the Gloucester office. In 1977 the Gloucester Area Social Services Office had been re-organized into two specialized divisions: 'child care' and 'social welfare'. The four project members came from one of the child care teams, but the remaining four members of this team were not involved in the project. Obviously this division within the team could have been the source of great friction, particularly if the non-project members of the team had felt that they would have been forced to take on additional work because of the time that the project members were devoting to the family therapy project. Fortunately, the team leader was a project member and he was therefore able to offer his assistance and support if they wished to develop projects of their own. Team members were also given the opportunity to raise reservations about the venture in team meetings. The project members agreed to keep the social work team informed of progress in establishing the project; its implications for the team were discussed regularly at team meetings.

Since the geographical area covered by the local general practice did not overlap neatly with the social work team's area, it was also necessary to carry out detailed negotiations with colleagues in the neighbouring team. They proved to be extremely cooperative but the situation was undoubtedly helped by agreeing that only new cases would be taken on by the project team. This meant that any existing cases with social services involvement would continue to be dealt with in the normal way.

The functional division of labour within the Gloucester office proved not to be an obstacle. Team leaders covering social welfare work (with the 'mentally ill', the elderly and other client groups) whose areas overlapped those of the local general practice chosen by the project, were consulted about the implications for their work. Once assured that the project members would not get involved in existing open cases, or in cases involving the use of agency resources (such as occupational therapy, or Part III accommodation) these team leaders were able to agree to the project going ahead. Fortunately, the involvement of our middle-manager (i.e. the team leader) made this intervention easier as he was well placed to discuss 'management' issues with fellow managers. Having gained agreement with team leaders and the members of their teams, it was necessary to approach the area management in order to gain permission for the project. It was anticipated that management would be sympathetic to the project, but all the necessary homework was completed first so that the management's time would not be wasted in debating whether the project would be feasible or not. Since all major objections to the project had been dealt with in advance, and provisional agreement for the project had already been gained from the local general practice, the team leader member of the project was able to present a viable and attractive project to the management team of which he was part. Once this official agreement had been achieved the project was able to start. The organization of Gloucester social services is flexible and allows innovation; both teams and groups within the teams are given a great deal of autonomy to organize their work in ways that they feel are necessary. Project members were therefore able to conduct negotiations within and outside the agency with a minimum of friction. If the agency had been unable to tolerate such autonomy then different tactics would have been necessary.

APPROACHING THE GENERAL PRACTICE

Project members found the initial approach to the general practice problematic; they feared that their overtures would be misunderstood by the GPs. It was thought that GPs would use the opportunity to overload the project with intractable cases which would not respond well to the family therapy approach. In addition, there was the danger that GPs would attempt to use the services of the project members in ways that were limited by their previous experience of the functions of social workers. These fears have been shared by other social workers in similar positions. For example, Huntingdon's research, exploring the relationship between social work and general practice, led her to conclude:

> In the secondary setting, the social worker does not provide the major service for which the organisation is called into being, but rather a support service to the organisation . . . Even when doctors became convinced of the value of the medical social worker . . . they assumed that social workers offered an extension of their own service rather than an independent service to patients in its own right (Huntington 1981).

Whether these fears were groundless in relation to the particular general practice approached is difficult to decide. The response of the practice was much more positive than had been anticipated, but clearly the response could have been partly determined by the firmness with which GPs were approached. The project members made it clear from the outset that they wished to offer GPs an independent service which would be based in the group practice but organized by the project members themselves. The team offering these skills were mutually supportive and confident that they had the necessary knowledge and skills to provide the general practice with a worthwhile service. (The average age of the project members was thirty-seven, and none had less than seven years experience in social work.) With hindsight, it is probable that all these factors, coupled with the clarity and confidence with which the original proposal was put forward, helped to create a favourable impression. However, it is clear that other factors also intervened to determine the favourable initial response. The team was especially sensitive to the different occupational cultures in which social workers and GPs work. Huntington (1981) has summarized these differences:

> marked cultural differences of knowledge, technology, technique, work orientation, terminology, ideology, identity and relational orientations between social work and general medical practice exist, in part because the underlying structure, particularly with regard to sex, age of occupation and of membership, work setting, income size and type of clientele, are so radically different.

Group general medical practices are clearly very different from social services departments. Any professional, whether social worker, community nurse, psychologist or psychiatrist must recognize the differences between the large bureaucratic organizations (of which they are a part) and the highly autonomous nature of general practice. For example, in social work the occupational structure is highly graded with at least three grades at practitioner level and several more at managerial level. Progression through this hierarchy requires geographical mobility and has been, until recently, relatively rapid. In contrast, general practitioners are independent contractors and seniority is based largely on length of practice in one area, with little occupational hierarchy.

From a theoretical point of view, these differences may seem daunting, but it was clear to project members that since the two professions worked on different time scales it was necessary to think of the project as a fairly long-term commitment which would take time and patience to build into a success. Paradoxically, although the project members were prepared to make a long-term commitment to the project, it was decided that the service would at first be offered on the basis of a six-month trial. It was hoped that this offer would enable both sides to take the risk of starting something new, but would enable either side to withdraw if the experiment proved unsuccessful.

The project members also found it necessary to pay careful attention to the GPs' existing relationships with other helping professions and 'outside' agencies. In addition to other professions already attached to general practice, such as health visitors, district nurses and midwives, the GPs already referred patients to agencies such as child guidance clinics, psychiatric out-patient departments, social services departments, and departments of clinical psychology.

With considerable overlap between the functions of these professions, a new service, such as family and marital counselling, is likely to create important repercussions. Examples of friction between professions are common, and warrant careful study (see Dingwall 1979). The project members attempted to overcome such difficulties by underselling their skills. They were careful to ask the GPs to refer relatively straightforward cases and to avoid referring people who had either chronic neurotic problems or serious psychiatric illness. Any attempt to evangelize by providing an alternative view of 'psychological' or 'psychiatric' problems would have created confusion. In the same way, too much enthusiasm to prove the efficacy of family therapy techniques by taking on extreme problems would have jeopardized the chances of success.

Attention to the 'pace' of developing the project and the use of language was reflected in deciding what professional title should be used whilst working at the group practice (which was popularly called the surgery). 'Family therapist' was too new and potentially controversial a label; 'social worker' was too much identified with the bureaucratic and legal functions of social services departments. The term 'counsellor' was agreed upon, since it was sufficiently vague not to evoke prejudice, and different enough from doctor and social worker to suggest that something new was on offer. Thus, in the Gloucester project, social workers are referred to as counsellors, and it is left to the counsellor to explain to the patient that he or she is also a social worker. Experience has shown that if clients expressed any concern at the prospect of seeing a 'counsellor' it is due to their concern about the issue of confidentiality and the use of files in the Social Services Department. This concern is also shared by the GPs, and merits further discussion. Clearly any professional interested in establishing the use of family therapy techniques in general practice, needs a sound understanding of the GP—patient relationship. GPs see the other helping professions and the specialist medical services (medical and para-medical) as 'spokes' radiating from the 'hub' of the GP—patient relationship. This view is put forward by Hunt (1972):

> The family doctor of today has to work on his patients' behalf, in close and friendly cooperation with many different people, who include his general practitioner colleagues . . . and all those ancillary services which are essential for his own task . . . (maternity, child welfare, and school health with their personnel — health visitors, midwives, district nurses, home helps). . . . This is a long list and it could easily be made longer still; its length underlines the point I wish to make, which is that the activities of all these different people must be coordinated and correlated by the general practitioner to ensure that all his patients' particular needs are met.

GPs are therefore unlikely to entrust their patients to a counsellor if their view of the centrality of the GP—patient relationship is threatened. Special care has to be taken when the counsellor wishes to engage in any tactics which undermine this relationship. For example, if the counsellor is already seeing a patient (or a patient and his wife) but wishes to convene other family members, then the GP's permission must be obtained before this step is undertaken, as they may not all be his patients.

A further complication arises from the fact that the counsellor is also accountable to her employing agency and professional system. This accountability has to be 'dovetailed' with the GP's sense of responsibility for his patient's contacts with other professionals in the surgery setting. In the Gloucester Project it has proved possible to reconcile these demands. The Social Services Department requires that a file is opened with minimal details (name and address) and that some record of social work time used is available. The letters from the counsellor to the GP outlining the problems encountered and progress made can also be added to the file, although some patients may object. If this is the case, the letters are not put on file. The Social Services Department has been willing to accept this arrangement because the work undertaken has fallen clearly within the role of the counsellors based at the surgery. However, if the needs of the client change, so that the involvement of other social services resources (e.g. reception into care) are required, then the accountability for those resources and the handling of their use reverts to the Social Services Department. The change of relationship could be handled by involving a different social worker, but so far there have been few instances of this.

The problems outlined above illustrate the importance of defining 'boundaries' between the different systems involved; nevertheless, it is also important to consider the more practical problems concerning the use and availability of resources within a general practice. Anybody wishing to practice family therapy skills in general practice needs to tailor their requirements to the range of resources that are available. The Gloucester Project was fortunate in finding a well organized practice whose secretarial and reception facilities were excellent. The use of these resources was negotiated from the outset and reviewed regularly, in order to avoid mistakes and misunderstandings. Obviously, great care has to be taken in establishing good working relations with members of the general practice staff because the project members were initially intruders into an organization which had developed its own codes and rules of behaviour. Members quickly discovered that close scrutiny of the GP/patient/receptionist system provided a useful guide as to how to behave in the early stages of establishing the project. Who is called by their first name; who makes the tea for whom, and how often; and the level of noise in the reception area, are all indicators which a sensitive practitioner should consider as she decides how to make her initial approaches to staff members.

Issues of pace and style of working emerged very rapidly as the project got under way. It was assumed that good communication between project members and GPs would be vital but there was little understanding of how much time should be devoted to sharing ideas with the GP. Given the normal GP pace of working, it became clear that any communication had to be brief and to the point. The desire to feed back news of successes with cases also had to be curbed. While project members may well have felt the need for validation by reporting progress to the GPs, it was clear that this would be a drain on their limited time. In practice, the relationship with the GP developed not so much through a process of feedback concerning the progress of cases, but rather through seeking to make changes in referral and convening processes. It is a respected fact in family therapy that a well-organized first interview, either with a whole family, or with some members of a family, or even with a single client, is of prime importance in determining the subsequent development of the therapeutic process. The experience in developing the Gloucester Project certainly confirmed this proposition since it was the development of better referral procedures and convening strategies which proved so important in determining the project's success.

THE DEVELOPMENT OF REFERRAL PROCEDURES AND CONVENING STRATEGIES

In the case of the Gloucester Project, the development of a referral and convening system proved to be an accurate guide to the 'health' of the project. In the early stages referrals were made by letter from the GP and were left with the receptionists for the counsellors to read. All letters were addressed to the senior member of the counselling team (the team leader). Patients were invited to attend for an assessment interview, which took place at the surgery during an afternoon set aside for taking new counselling referrals. At the assessment interview, counsellor and patient would meet and a decision would be made about further sessions. If no further sessions were thought desirable by either party, the patient would be referred back to the GP. Where necessary, the convening of other family members was organized by the counsellor, usually by letter (but occasionally by telephone), and further meetings were arranged on the afternoon set aside for work. Formal communication with the GP was confined to two letters: one sent after the first interview, and another at the end of counselling. Informal contact took place through chance meetings, in the corridor, between GPs and counsellors.

In the early stages of the project there were difficulties with certain patients who attended the assessment for the wrong reasons. These patients were apparently not customers for family or marital counselling — they attended the session because the doctor suggested that they did so. They therefore proved very difficult to engage in counselling because they were not ready to see their problems in ways which could lead them to contract to work with a counsellor. The first review meeting with the GPs, which took place after the six months trial period, proved very valuable in dealing with such problems, since it was agreed that a new procedure was necessary in order to solve problems concerning whether or not patients were customers. Counsellors were now able to book into the GP's ordinary surgery time for fifteen-minute consultations about referrals, progress in counselling, or convening problems. This enabled more detailed discussion of how the problem referred by the GP could be broadened into an interpersonal approach with a marital or family focus. It also started the vital first step in coordinating the counsellor's and the GP's contact with the patient during the period of counselling. Inappropriate referrals ceased very quickly and GP involvement in convening other family members began to increase. The evidence from the Gloucester Project indicates that the best way to disengage overinvolved patients from their GP, so that counselling can take place, is through holding a joint session with the GP and the patient.

However, it took another year to develop a satisfactory new system which could cope with this problem. This new system now provides GPs and counsellors with an opportunity to hold a referral meeting either with the patient alone or with the patient and other family members. Each week, one half-hour session is set aside for such joint meetings which involve the more problematic referrals. At the meeting the GP will explain his reasons for asking for counselling help to both the patient and the counsellor. In addition, problems of medication and GP—patient contact during counselling are discussed with the patient, and the counsellor is able to outline to the patient what is involved in counselling and how it might proceed. Convening other family members is discussed, and a decision will be made about who should approach these people. In practice it is often the GP who is the most appropriate person. A further joint meeting can be arranged to deal with issues at the end of counselling. The patient is made aware that the counsellor and GP are in open communication during counselling, as the following case example demonstrates.

CASE EXAMPLE

Mrs Harris was a regular attender at the surgery, usually coming weekly or even more often. A married woman in her thirties, with two children (aged nine and seven), she was a housewife who worked occasionally and whose husband worked long hours as a brick layer. They owned their own house, a car, and were financially committed to the limit of their income. Mrs Harris's ailments were many and varied, ranging from panic attacks to vomiting, ulcerative colitis, and even physical injuries caused during marital violence. Despite the obvious marital problems, she believed that she was ill and regularly demanded hospital tests. No conclusive results were ever reported and the pattern repeated itself. Mrs Harris's GP was quite open with her — he believed her ailments were due to 'stress' (and not 'physical' causes) although on occasions he felt obliged to do tests because of her persistent demands. When he decided to refer her for counselling he realized that there could be difficulties, and after two unsuccessful referrals by letter, he arranged for a joint referral meeting with the patient and one of the counsellors. At this meeting he made it clear to Mrs Harris why he felt an alternative approach was appropriate and that whilst he couldn't refuse to see her he would much prefer that she and her husband tried to do some work on their obvious marital difficulties. Mrs Harris duly agreed; the therapist convened her husband by letter and a first appointment was made.

At this first meeting the male therapist worked unsupervised and received a distinctly frosty response particularly from Mr Harris. They agreed to a contract of four sessions of marital work, and the date for the next appointment was made. The following day, the counsellor received an urgent telephone call from the GP to say that Mrs Harris had appeared at morning surgery in a seriously disturbed state, which was so bad in fact that he felt almost obliged to seek a psychiatric opinion. In addition, Mr Harris had complained that the first session with the counsellor was 'forcing him and his wife together', and that he had expected to be seen alone. At the counsellor's request, the GP agreed to delay the psychiatric consultation until the counsellor had had a chance to present some thoughts about the case and how they might proceed. The counsellor then wrote to the GP outlining his hypothesis about the processes taking place both in the marital system and the referring system. He pointed out that Mrs Harris believed that referral to the counsellor effectively shut the door on her relationship with her doctor since it undermined the validity of her 'illness'. This shift in emphasis was clearly very important to her, and had important, and as yet unknown, repercussions within the marital system. She clearly needed to continue her role as being sick, and had therefore escalated her physical symptoms. Understandably, Mr Harris saw this as the consequence of the marital counselling.

The counsellor proposed an amendment to the agreement between the parties. If the GP would agree to maintain or marginally increase his contacts with Mrs Harris, the counsellor would agree to arrange separate meetings with her, and Mr Harris, and engage the help of a female member of the counselling team. The purpose and possible outcome of the separate meetings would be negotiated between the counsellors and Mr and Mrs Harris. The GP agreed to this, and to the counsellor contacting Mrs Harris with the message that the counsellor and GP had made a mistake; they now realized that she would need very close attention during the counselling to monitor its effect on her physical symptoms — it was therefore essential for her to see her GP regularly, at least weekly, even if she felt well. Negotiations then took place to reconvene Mr Harris, and counselling proceeded initially with separate meetings between the male counsellor and Mr Harris and the female counsellor and Mrs Harris. After four sessions of separate meetings, further joint work took place and the focus broadened to deal with difficulties which involved the children's behaviour as well.

This example illustrates the complexity of the referral process and the need for very good communication between the counsellor and the GP. In order to establish family counselling in this setting, as much attention needs to be paid to interventions in the GP—patient system as to interventions in the family system. The evidence of the project is that such developments are possible, but they take time to develop as mutual trust and cooperation needs to be built gradually.

Some of the more mundane issues of convening family members are also worth considering in relation to the general practice context. Patients are used to accommodating themselves to the schedules of busy GPs and are quite prepared to put themselves out in order to be seen. This has been of great value to the counsellors as family members have proved willing to come during the day, even if this requires time off work, or absence from school. Early in the establishment of the project, the GPs agreed to the use of a pro forma letter on surgery notepaper stating that a patient was required to attend the surgery for treatment (unspecified). It has proved possible to keep the vast majority of new referrals and ongoing work within the consulting hours of the counsellors (i.e. 1.30—5.30 p.m.) on two specified afternoons per week. It has proved useful to keep communication with clients as far as possible to the surgery, using surgery notepaper and surgery receptionists. This has enabled potentially reluctant patients to be engaged in counselling and not to be scared off by the stigma of seeing a social worker. In practice, once family members are engaged in counselling, this stigma ceases and communication via the counsellor's other agency (i.e. the Social Services Department) can take place if convenient. Clearly, the cooperation of the GP's reception staff is vital if this system is to work. They take their lead from the GP and (in the Gloucester project) have handled patients' sensibilities with great tact. It is quite common for some families to announce to the receptionist, in front of other waiting patients, that they have an appointment with a counsellor. Similarly there have been a few examples of patients referring themselves for counselling after initial work has been completed and further difficulties have emerged. Clearly, reference to GPs should be made in the case of re-referrals, in order to re-establish the GP's consent.

ENGAGING PATIENTS IN FAMILY COUNSELLING

Since the engagement process is so crucial to the development of successful work in general practice it is worth exploring some of the issues involved in greater depth. Patients normally present themselves to GPs in a manner which they think the GP will find an appropriate use of his time and skills. When confronted with a 'counsellor' for the first time, (bearing in mind that it is in the familiar medical setting of the surgery) many patients tend to ask a number of questions which the counsellor needs to be able to answer. Patients' attitudes towards counselling seem to be of four different types:

1   'Am I ill/mad/normal?' (i.e. 'is there something wrong with me?')
   There are a number of ways of dealing with questions in this group but it is essential to avoid the trap of discussing 'medical' issues, and to help the patient experience counselling as different from a GP consultation. These questions provide the counsellor with a good opportunity to obtain information about the patient's view of their relationship with the GP and about the patient's perception of the problem. The best tactic to adopt when asked these questions is to reply with open-ended questions, or statements of the following sort: 'Your doctor has written to me telling me a little about your difficulties; what do you think he has said?'; or 'Your doctor has suggested that you have an initial talk with a counsellor and you have agreed to come along today — do you think talking would be helpful?'; or 'I'm not qualified to diagnose illness, but I can help people solve problems which may arise between them when someone feels ill.' All three replies, (and there are of course potentially many more of equal value) start the process of making the patient an active participant in discussing what to do. In the case of the first of these questions, the patient is given some responsibility for giving his or her view of their interaction with the GP, and an opportunity to give their opinion of the problem. The second question covers this latter ground in a slightly different way, but in the case of the third response, matters of illness, madness and normality are side-stepped by the counsellor taking a 'non-expert' position in relation to such matters but an 'expert' position in relation to interpersonal issues.

2   'I don't think I'll be able to cope without the drugs'; or 'I've been feeling worse because of the thought of seeing a counsellor and I've made another appointment to see my doctor.'
   The above examples indicate that the client is reluctant to disengage from the GP, or to contemplate the terrifying prospect of change. Any threat to the patient's view that they are 'ill' may

increase their fears and can only be dealt with, initially, by accepting their validity. The first attitude indicates that the referral may have been precipitated by either the GP's or the patient's concern about the use of medication. It can be dealt with by asking the patient how they find that medication helps, and what other family members think about it. It should be made clear that it is not the counsellor's job to stop the patient taking medication, but rather to help the patient look at the difficulties that he or she has with their symptoms, and to see how these may be eased, with the help of the people that are important to them.

With the second of the two attitudes the counsellor can utilize the patient's desire to see the GP to begin the engagement process. The patient should be praised for the normality of their response to talking about their difficulties with a stranger, and for their sensible suggestion of going back to the GP if they still feel ill. However, as their GP has asked that they see the counsellor, and for the counsellor's advice on whether counselling will be helpful, it is important to proceed with the assessment interview. If, at the end of the session, the patient is still feeling very nervous or 'ill', the counsellor will help them to make an appointment with the GP. Such a response helps the patient relax and reduces their fears about counselling.

One final point needs to be added: if patients display either of these attitudes at first contact with the counsellor it is essential to understand that they indicate that she needs continued support from the GP. This may well mean (as in the case of Mrs Harris) that the rate of consultation with the GP may have to be increased, at least in the initial stages of counselling.

3 'It's very nice of you to see me, but I don't think I'll ever get better'; or 'I don't know why I'm here really — there isn't anything that can be done to help me.'

Statements of this type are usually made by experienced patients with a long history of various illnesses. In common with adult psychiatric patients seen in other contexts, they are dutiful and obedient and can be relied on to do anything except change. In these cases, emphasis should be on being doubtful about the prospects of counselling, but dutiful in carrying out the GP's request for an 'assessment'. In common with other settings, dealing with experienced patients, the emphasis has to be on how to engage other family members without radically threatening the view that one of them is ill. It is crucial to be able to get the GP's help in such difficult cases in order to add authority to the request for the 'well' members to attend; such 'well' members then need to be treated with the greatest respect. Initially the prospect of helping the patient change should be played down, and efforts should be made to look at how the problems presented by the illness can be handled with the active cooperation of the 'well' members of the family.

4 'I don't mind coming but my husband/wife will never agree'; or 'What has my symptom got to do with my family (or children)?'
    In the case of the first of these examples a 'yes—but' approach is useful. The patient should be regarded as the expert on their partner's likely response, but the importance of engaging them means that all methods of achieving this goal must be examined. The patient should then be encouraged to explore what their partner might say to the prospect, and they can be invited to behave 'as if' their partner were in the room (perhaps using an empty-chair technique if the patient is well enough 'joined'). This will then provide the counsellor with accurate information about the patient's view of the marital or family interaction, and enable the counsellor to develop a strategy for engaging other family members. The patient can be asked which of several different approaches is least likely to fail, and from whom their partner is most likely to accept a request for his or her attendance. Thus, the patient's view of the reluctance of their partner to attend can be explored in a systemic way and the best strategy for convening them can be devised.
    The second of these two examples can be approached by exploring the GP's possible reasons for referring such a patient to a counsellor. For example, the counsellor can say that it would be helpful to learn as much about the patient as possible and to hear from the people that know them best. The counsellor's function at this stage can be explained as investigative (i.e. she is concerned to find out about the stresses and strains that may affect the patient's illness). Any threat of implicating 'innocent' parties in the patient's illness should be avoided. The counsellor can say that she has more time to look at this aspect of the patient's life than the GP.
    The above examples illustrate some ways of engaging and convening families in general practice settings. Counsellors from different professional backgrounds may well find that they are able

to mobilize their different knowledge and experience to find new ways of overcoming such difficulties. Care should always be taken to be respectful when dealing with the patient's relationship with their GP and the view they have of their complaint. All the above examples relate to those who believe that they are 'ill'. Not all referrals are so difficult; many patients present problems in their family relationships directly, or are quite willing to move to this focus when invited to do so. Most child-focused referrals do not present such complex convening problems, except where there is a 'peripheral' parent or step-parent. In such cases, great care should be taken in discussing with the active parent (and possibly the GP) the best way of approaching the other parent or step-parent.

SUMMARY AND CONCLUSION

This chapter has concentrated on the practical issues involved in establishing family counselling in general medical practice, drawing on the particular experience of the Gloucester Project, and generalizing, where possible, for other practitioners. There are likely to be some elements of the process of setting up such a service that are shared, even though different professional groups may be involved in taking the initiative. For example, it is crucial to consider one's own agency as a system and devise strategies to create sufficient flexibility to move into general practice. In addition, it is important to understand general practice as a system, and to be aware of its interaction and with one's own professional and agency system. This provides the potential for overcoming inter-agency and inter-professional disagreements and finding common ground, despite the many differences which may exist. Having started practising, great care is required to continue the process of 'joining' with the general practice system. Too much concern about the patient/family system may divert attention from the importance of the referral and convening process with its emphasis on the referring person (i.e. the GP). Finally, having respect for the GP's view of problem (or symptom) formation, and resolution is not the same as being subsumed within the medical profession as an appendage to medicine. For family counselling to grow *with* this setting requires a strong independent support system to maintain autonomy and explore interdependence.

The success of the Gloucester Project has rested largely upon two factors. The first of these is concerned with the GPs' views on therapeutic issues; we accepted the validity of their framework and did not seek to proselytize in favour of our own views. The second factor concerns the issue of mutual trust. We hoped our robust and open-handed approach to the general practice would enable the GPs to begin to trust our approach — in return we respected their skills and their concern to provide their patients with the best possible service. We are glad to say that our approach does seem to have influenced the practice of our GP colleagues. For example, it has been possible to detect that the interpersonal approach to change, characteristic of family therapy, has influenced the day-to-day practice of the GPs, who now convene other family members in order to make more sense of some of their patient's complaints.

The potential of a family/systems model of human behaviour to GPs reaches far beyond the use of family counsellors two afternoons each week. The context of the patient is not just the family, but the family as an open system interacting with many societal systems (which include General Practices and Social Services Departments). As the first point of contact for many people with a vast range of difficulties and problems, the GP needs to be aware of the implications of his actions on other members of the patient's family and other societal systems with which the family interacts. A family-systems model of human behaviour offers a potentially fruitful framework within which to practise medicine. In turn, the general practice context offers social workers and others the opportunity to give skilled family counselling to patients who would not otherwise consider using the skills of a social worker (Corney and Bowen 1982). In common with the other examples in this book, the Gloucester Project demonstrates the importance of applying the principles of general systems theory, not only to the families with which we work, but to the organizations within which we are employed.

8

Developing Family Therapy in the Day Hospital

HARRY PROCTER AND TRISH STEPHENS

Developing a Family Therapy Service in a psychiatric day hospital can be a difficult business, but our experience has been exciting and challenging and leads to many new fruitful ideas. Once the clinic system is established, even quite serious and complicated psychiatric problems can be tackled briefly. Also it provides a new type of working environment for the Day Hospital which people enjoy, perhaps because it can allow everyone to contribute to the work. Finally, it provides a very efficient way of training staff because they can see effective therapy from the start, they are involved in it and they get immediate feedback on their performance and developing ideas.

As far as we know Southwood House was the first Day Hospital to develop a comprehensive family therapy service using live supervision. There is very little published work in this area; Bennet et al. (1976) have been using a family approach based on group analytic principles in which a visiting psychotherapist meets with the staff in order to develop their awareness. More recently Olie (1982) describes work in the Netherlands in which family meetings are used in parallel with other therapeutic inputs such as group therapy, psychodrama, movement therapy, milieu therapy and so on. Asen et al. (1982) describe a day unit which treats up to ten families intensively. The families attend five days a week from 9.00 am to 3.00 pm.

In Southwood House nearly all the work is conducted on a sessional basis and only one therapeutic format is offered at a time. Family therapy allows a tremendous reduction in the need for 'day care', in the sense of having clients attend for one or more full days per week. Thus, it has value not just in acute work, but in the care of the chronic patients as well. Approximately 50 families are in treatment at any one time.

First we will describe in overall terms how the clinics are currently organized in Bridgwater and then move on to discuss how they may be established in various different types of Day Hospital environment. We will then look in more detail at some of the day-to-day procedures that we have found valuable.

ORGANIZATION

At present, in Southwood House we have seven small teams which are called *clinics*. Five of these work at the day hospital with a one-way screen and two visit people's homes. One of the latter specializes in geriatric problems and is described in detail in chapter 9 of this book. We have aimed to include in each clinic two more experienced therapists together with two or three trainees, but in practice this has to vary according to the number of available staff and the demand for training.

The staff are drawn from members of the Day Hospital team, together with some outsiders. For example, we have had workers from the local Social Service and Probation Offices, staff from the main psychiatric hospital and two therapists from the Open University. We train students from the Social Work courses at Bristol and Exeter, from the local GP training scheme, as well as psychology and nursing students. We have also had some lay counsellors train with us. There is a fine balance between the continuity provided by the more permanent staff and the fresh stimulation and challenge provided by the people who train with us, usually for between three and six months. Sometimes there has been the danger of losing the culture through too many staff changes.

Each clinic meets for a three-and-a-half-hour morning or afternoon session during which two families are seen. The time is divided up very much in the way outlined by the Milan team (Palazzoli et al. 1978) with a pre-session discussion (15 minutes), the family interview (approximately 45 minutes), team discussion (10—15 minutes), final intervention (5 minutes) and a summing up period (10 minutes). This process occurs twice, hopefully leaving 15 minutes for a tea break. Each clinic has about ten families assigned to it at any one time. Although each clinic is a separate entity and tends to develop its own culture and cohesiveness, there is some overlap because most of the staff are in more than one clinic in various permutations and combinations. We think this is an important factor in the stability and growth of the overall service. Ideas generated in one clinic will gradually permeate through to the others and the therapists learn much from comparing the different styles that each clinic develops.

Traditionally Day Hospitals seem to be organized in one of two ways. Either they are hierarchical, reflecting the typical organization of the medical and nursing professions, or they attempt to follow the democratic ideal of the therapeutic community. Day Hospitals often have some kind of staff group or sensitivity group to offer support and to deal with interpersonal conflicts. The clinic system, with its relatively autonomous but partially overlapping small clinics, offers a new way of organizing the day hospital team. The personal support required in working with psychiatric problems is now provided by the small team rather than a large sensitivity group. Perhaps the small clinic system works well because it mirrors and utilizes the way that people naturally organize and communicate. Another advantage is that it does not seem to conflict with the hierarchical demands placed on workers in the Health Service. However, this could be peculiar to our own experience in a relatively small Day Hospital with only one consultant. Of course all the staff in the Day Hospital still meet weekly, but this becomes more of a business meeting in which staff are assigned to clinics and the overall work is monitored.

SETTING UP A CLINIC

There are perhaps three types of situation which may face the reader who wants to set up a Family Therapy Service in a Day Hospital.

Situation One

The first situation is the most straight forward in which the developments are introduced 'from the top'. This will be of interest to consultant psychiatrists, or other people in an executive position who want to introduce this kind of service. This situation existed at

Edward Long Fox House, a psychiatric Day Hospital in Weston-Super-Mare. One of the authors (Harry Procter) was invited by one of the consultant psychiatrists to help set up a Family Therapy Service. This proved to be relatively straightforward. A clinic was established and was led by Harry Procter for six months. At the end of this time the members split up to form a number of clinics and at the time of writing (one year later) five clinics are running successfully.

Although this is the most straightforward situation there will of course still be teething problems. There will be the usual difficulties of learning anything new, mistakes will be made, you may fail to engage families and initially it will be tempting to go back to more familiar ways of working. Misgivings are likely to arise during this learning process from within the clinic, from elsewhere in the Day Hospital team, or even from non-clinical staff. These may not be expressed overtly, but can come out as criticisms of an administrative nature, for example the time of the tea break, or who is responsible for closing the windows. Forming a coalition at this point is tempting but we strongly advise people to take a 'one down' stance, to take criticism seriously, to be apologetic and understanding.

There will be external pressures too, particularly from referring agents. Best again to play down that any new approach is being applied and we do not use the term 'family therapy'. Explanations of why we want other people in the family to attend are usually framed in terms of *assessment* and wanting to get a clearer understanding of the problem, perhaps adding, incidentally, that we might be able to give them some guidance on how to deal with the patient. In general, we go along with the referrer's understanding of the problem. Occasionally, sharing the systemic view with the referrer (or any other interested party) can complicate matters if the family go back to them asking for explanations.

In general, the new approach should be framed as being experimental, something that might prove valuable and the approach should be left to earn its own reputation. Just as with clients themselves, one tends to avoid selling the approach or 'touting' for business.

Situation Two

All these points are even more important in the second situation where the reader is setting up family therapy in a day hospital where there is loyalty to an existing approach, such as traditional psychiatry, behaviour therapy, group psychotherapy or any other strong prevailing ideology. Systems theory, when properly applied, should not in fact invalidate any other approach since it is a method of utilizing people's positions. We hope that this will become clear as we proceed.

When the first author (Harry Procter) arrived in Southwood House in 1976 it was organized on therapeutic community lines. New approaches were added to the existing programme as opportunities arose. Family and marital therapy was conducted initially on cases other than those being dealt with in the existing Day Hospital programme. Co-therapy was employed as a working format and people worked together in different combinations. Co-therapy pairs often included people from other helping agencies in Bridgwater. This arrangement provided the basis for the later formation of the clinic teams; it would be a useful format in Day Hospitals which are not yet ready for full live supervision. Other useful experiences at this time were the exploration of the couples group format (Procter and Pottle 1980) and the use of 'Brief Therapy' in a relaxation group (Walker and Procter 1981). These provided useful bridges between group and family therapy ideologies.

It is possible to trace the development of the service by looking at the points at which different pieces of equipment became available. It should be said that in the caring environment people naturally tend to feel ambivalent about using machinery in therapy and it is best not to try and persuade or impose the technology on anybody. We found that once people satisfied themselves that the use of the equipment need not detract from the human side of therapy they tended to start using it as a matter of course. In Bridgwater this occurred naturally because the equipment only became available gradually. It may well be that the stages we went through could be used in other places as a planned way of gradually introducing a full clinic system. Over about a period of three years we went through five steps:

1   People worked mainly in co-therapy pairs, meeting in a weekly support group and bringing audio tapes to aid case discussion.
2   A one-way screen was installed, with equipment to carry

sound from the therapy room to the observation room. People were still working in pairs — one in front, one behind the screen. At this stage we were still only audio-taping.

3   With the increased interest generated by having the one-way screen it was possible to form four small working teams, each one led by a pair who had been accustomed to working in co-therapy.

4   The acquisition of a video tape recorder was another thing people had to get used to, with the necessity of explaining the video to the families and getting their consent, as well as learning to be confident in using the equipment.

5   After a while we realized that having the video allowed us to use the existing sound equipment for an ear phone or 'bug'. Up to this point the team could only intervene by knocking on the door. The bug proved to be another item we all had to learn how to use: we will return to this later in the chapter.

Situation Three

In an environment where there is an existing, but not necessarily hostile approach, it is important to work slowly and cautiously. This is even more true in the third situation where open resistance is anticipated or has already been experienced. Here great care is required. As in working with many of the families themselves it is important to accept and utilize the prevailing Day Hospital ideology. Perhaps the most common situation would be where a traditional medical view of psychiatric problems is exercised. Without challenging the existing model at all a great deal of useful work can be achieved using the systems approach.

Most resistance from the families themselves, as well as professional colleagues, is avoided if you start the work in the following way: you suggest that it would be useful to invite the patient's wife, husband, children, mother or whoever in order to get from them a detailed picture of how the problem manifests itself. It can be added, perhaps in a casual way, that it may be possible to give the relatives a bit of guidance on how best to manage the person as they recover from their illness. This approach will usually be maintained throughout treatment, relatives being invited to subsequent sessions on the basis of 'continued monitoring'.

Once you start to see the relatives in this way the systemic patterns and sequences that are maintaining the problem will become clear. It is all too tempting at this point to forget the medical, or whatever, position you are utilizing and to start making interactional interpretations of the problem to the rest of the Day Hospital team. This is nearly always a mistake.

The next difficulty to consider is when actions are taken with which you do not agree, by other members of the team. For example, blame may be attached arbitarily to certain members of the family system, the identified patient may be given drugs, group therapy and so on. In fact such interventions, though complications, are no different from interventions by people within the family system. They should therefore be accepted and utilized in the same way. For example, if your patient is put into a group you can be pleased with this, mentioning that it may well be helpful, perhaps we could meet again in six months time to review the situation and we will put a couple of these meetings 'in the bank', only to be used if problems remain at that time. In this way an overall contract is maintained.

You should trust the work you are initiating to gain its own momentum. One problem can occur when certain members of the team may be 'won over' and become very enthusiastic. This may be a bid to enter coalition against the prevailing methods. This of course should be avoided and may be met with a sympathetic, but non-committal approach. Coalition is an extremely common pitfall at this stage, it can happen before you even realize it, and may be indicated by nothing more than certain mischievous glint in the eye.

RUNNING A CLINIC

The rest of this chapter will be devoted to the day-to-day considerations of running a clinic. Clearly readers will have to find their own solutions to the many small problems that arise, but we hope that some of our experiences will prove helpful and act as guidelines.

Paperwork

Before the clinic starts its work, it is useful to get some of the basic administrative details sorted out. You will need a duplicated referral form which can be given to referring agents asking for basic details, including the reason for referral, the composition of the family, and the name of the GP and any other agents involved. We have a session sheet which is filled out after each interview. This has spaces for the hypothesis, the plan for the session, information gathered, observations, interventions during the session, the final intervention, the next appointment and the new hypothesis. You will need a consent form for the family to sign if they agree to be video taped. Our form contains three levels of consent which they can delete as appropriate:

1   taping for use by the team
2   for use by the therapist's supervisor
3   for teaching other professionals

We have also found it useful to have a special clinic diary separate from the main day hospital diary. The team members record their absences in this diary so that they can make appointments for their colleagues. Therapists are responsible for keeping the files of their families up to date and they also write the letters to the family, referrer, GP, etc., although of course such letters are carefully planned by the team as a whole.

We have a standard first-appointment letter, suggesting that it is helpful for us to see everybody currently living in the household, but leaving it up to them as to who it would be appropriate to bring. This letter is of course reworded to suit the particular family situation. For example, we may only invite the parents in the first instance if the problem concerns a difficult adolescent. We tend to follow the Brief Therapy model of inviting the 'customer for change' (Fisch et al. 1982) and if there are signs that someone would prefer not to come we ensure they are not invited to the first interview. For example, where a person has indicated that their husband or wife would be reluctant to come, we may send a standard letter as above, but add a qualifying sentence: 'perhaps it would be best, however, to come on your own in the first instance.' The same principle applies later on in therapy. Suppose, for example, that a couple display resistance to the team seeing the children, we might close a session by saying 'we think it would be useful to see your daughter, but just the two of you come next time.' This willingness to meet the clients half-way often leads to a relaxing of their conditions on the next occasion.

The pre-session discussion

This is a very important period and at least 15 minutes should be allowed for it. It is a time when the team members become 'tuned in' to the family. It is divided into two parts: first a hypothesis is generated, which takes into account all the information so far obtained (Palazzoli et al. 1980). For a first interview the referral form and medical notes, if available, are examined. The position of the particular family in the family life cycle is noted, and possible family structures (e.g. coalitions, conflict detouring, hierarchy and closeness/distance) are considered. The position of the referrer and those of any other people involved are examined carefully. After building this general picture, the symptom is considered together with possible attempted solutions that may be maintaining it. We therefore start with a wide lens and then narrow down to the possible specific process. Secondly, a plan is sketched out in the light of the hypothesis for the direction that the interview might take. Usually we use the first interview format of the Brief Therapy school as a starting point (careful definition of problems, attempted solutions, goal, smallest significant first step to the goal). Special lines of enquiry related to the particular case will be grafted on to this. For example, the attempted solution phase of the interview is a particularly useful place at which to begin an exploration of who is involved in the problem, because it implicitly labels everybody's involvement as positive. For example:

'Mrs Jones, are your parents still living?'
'How often do you see your mother?'
'What does she suggest in order to try and help
    you with your difficulties?'

As with the hypothesis much deviation from the plan will probably occur during the interview. Nevertheless, the pre-session has an important function in preparing the team and getting the correct mental set and is also a very useful training aid.

Introducing the family to the arrangements and seeking their consent for video-taping

The next thing to happen is that the team receive a phone call from the receptionist saying that the family has arrived and that they are in the waiting room. The therapist goes and greets them and leads them to the therapy room. The most important factor in getting the family to accept live supervision is the therapist's manner in her introduction — a relaxed, matter-of-fact air which quite naturally demonstrates that it is a good way to work. The introduction usually goes something like this:

> The way we work here is as a team. My colleagues are sitting in the next room and will watch the session through this screen, which is a one-way screen. They can speak to me on this [showing them the 'bug' and putting it in the ear]. They are there to help *me* help you, and they may give me suggestions or ask me to ask particular questions over the bug. We also like to video the session. This is extremely useful for us, but we need your consent to do this and will ask you to sign a form a little later on to give your consent if that is all right. Is that OK? [looking at each of the adults].

This works in nine cases out of ten, but people sometimes seek additional information or explanations. One question is, 'Why can't they sit in here?'. To this it is explained that the team are in a continual process of discussion. Sometimes people ask who is behind the screen. The answer can be given: 'We are a multi-disciplinary team and we find it useful to have a doctor, a social worker, a psychologist, a nurse and so on, so that your problems can be discussed from a variety of perspectives and so that we may come up with the best advice for you'. Occasionally clients will reject the set up outright. This will usually mean they are not 'customers for change' anyway, but often some solution can be found if they are willing to discuss the matter. We usually ask the families to sign the consent form when the therapist is with the team discussing the final intervention.

The investigation phase of the interview and the implicit contract

This is not the place to go into detail about the process of therapy itself, although it is probably worth mentioning that we have found the questioning methods of the Brief Therapy approach (Herr and Weakland, 1979; Fisch et al. 1982) and the Milan approach (Palazzoli et al. 1980) particularly valuable. We have found it important to make an implicit contract with the family about which problems are to be worked on. The following questions are valuable towards that end.

'If you come for a course of therapy with us, what would you see as the goal of the work?'
'Is it the panic attacks that you want us to help you with?'
'Do you *want* to be able to go out more often?'
'Do you *want* us to work together on these problems then?'

Getting clients to say yes to these 'want' questions is very valuable for motivation and clarification of the issues. Doubtful affirmation can be met with such measures as 'perhaps you would like to think carefully and discuss whether you want us to help over the next few days and let us know if you want an appointment.' But this kind of statement is best left until after careful discussion with the team has taken place.

The break for discussion and the final intervention

The therapist then explains to the family that she will take a break for a while and have a discussion with the team. She might well thank the family at this point for all the useful information they have given.

As with the pre-session, we conceive of the discussion period as falling into two phases. Firstly, a 'wind-down' phase where members of the team get things off their chests — mention for them what was the most important or amusing incident. All sorts or different comments may be made, often totally unrelated. It is important that a sufficient amount of time is allowed so that the creative process can unfold. Often after five or ten minutes a particularly good insight or 'reframe' will be suggested by someone apparently out of nowhere, and this leads to the formulation of the final intervention. We think it is important for the team to postpone suggestions as to what to do until some reasonable measure of agreement about what is happening in the family has occurred.

We will nearly always get the therapist to write out the

intervention. If necessary she can mention there has been an involved discussion and she has made some notes. The intervention should be read slowly and clearly. The family's response to it should be noted extremely carefully and handled with sensitivity. The family should not be rushed out of the room if there is a misunderstanding. On the other hand, academic discussions which dilute and weaken the impact of the final intervention should be avoided. A useful measure here is 'that's a good point, I think we should discuss that in detail next time.' We usually give the time and date of the appointment in a very straightforward manner: 'We would like to see you again on the 10th of May at 4.00 pm.' Reasons for difficulties in attendance should be taken seriously and at face value even if it is suspected that these represent resistance. A rather forlorn 'Hm, I wonder what we should do about that?' often stimulates the family to solve the problem spontaneously. After the family have gone it is very tempting to collapse with relief, but it will make for difficulties next time if the session sheet is not filled out properly.

Relating to other professionals

Even if the therapy is proceeding in a straightforward manner, a number of problems can arise in relation to other professionals. After the first interview or when the family have been engaged in therapy (sometimes more than one interview is labelled as assessment), a letter is written to the GP, to the referrer and any other relevant person such as a social worker, explaining that the family have been taken on for treatment and progress will be reported in due course. We indicate that we would be willing to provide further information if it is wished. If necessary a letter of this type may be sent after subsequent sessions as well, but we tend to keep these letters fairly brief. One issue that can arise is in relation to medication. In general we accept the GP's advice and urge people to follow it. For example: 'continue to take the medication; you will know when the right time arises for you to want to start reducing the tablets and you should do this in consultation with your GP.' It is very important to avoid siding with the family against the GP. If a patient insists on presenting a GP or anyone else for that matter in a negative light it may be countered with a comment such as 'that's strange, I've always heard well of Dr X.'

Admission to psychiatric hospital

Sometimes it will be necessary, or people will request that, the identified patient be admitted to the psychiatric hospital. Although you may feel disappointed with this it is best to adopt a positive, accepting attitude. It is often raised as a challenge to the therapy process itself and the request is often dropped when the therapist shows willingness to cooperate. We usually say that the admission to the psychiatric hospital can prove very valuable, as a break, in order to give the other members of the family a rest; that this can probably be arranged; and that an appointment will be fixed in three to four weeks time so that therapy can resume after the admission. In other words the admission is implicitly labelled as 'not therapy'. The danger is that cases will slip through the net after admission. This of course depends on the relationship the team has with the acute ward staff. We always get the staff to reinforce attendance at the next session, even if this is to renegotiate therapy. A letter giving the necessary details of the therapy should be sent to the ward for filing in the hospital notes.

Appearance of family members between sessions

Should family members either call in to the Day Hospital between sessions, or phone, this usually constitutes a challenge to the therapy. In general we advise a strategy of 'sweeping back' to the next therapy session. It is useful to tell GPs and other professionals about this. The problem brought should be listened to carefully, but unless something requiring urgent attention has occurred no advice or suggestions should be given. Rather it should be said that these things are very important and require detailed consideration and that they should be brought to the attention of the therapist at the next appointment. If this proves insufficient and some measure has to be offered it should be labelled as strictly temporary and the whole matter will be reviewed at the next session.

SUPERVISION AND TRAINING USING CONTINUOUS
INTERVENTION

As we said earlier, the live supervision clinic provides an extremely valuable setting in which to train staff members. Perhaps because we are a fairly small centre we have been able to maintain a generous attitude in this respect. Obviously, for people who can only stay with us for three months our objectives must remain fairly limited, but we believe even brief contact with interactional thinking will have a valuable impact on that person's working career.

In Bridgwater we have experimented with continuous intervention using the earphone. New therapists start off by being given *everything* that they have to say in the investigative part of the interview over the 'bug'. Then, as the trainee learns the ropes, the supervisor is able to allow her more and more autonomy according to her rate of progress. The model is rather like teaching someone to swim. To start with the swimmer is held in the water and her limbs are guided by the teacher. As the swimmer learns the motions the teacher can gradually relax her control, but if the swimmer begins to sink the teacher is there to rescue her. The most important advantage of this method of training is that the quality of the therapy is maintained. It also constitutes perhaps the most powerful method of training in therapy so far devised, although it is clearly most suited to a style of therapy based on questioning. However, there are pitfalls that need to be treated with sensitivity. This form of training involves going through a number of stages. First, the trainees should have the questions at their fingertips. A sheet of questions derived from the Brief Therapy model, the Milan school and various other sources has been compiled for this purpose. It is useful for the trainee to have the opportunity to become comfortable with repeating all the forms of question given to her over the bug. People often complain at this point that they cannot concentrate on what the family is saying to them. It can be pointed out that the supervisor 'has the ears' and that they 'have the mouth'. It obviously requires skill on the part of the supervisor and trust on the part of the trainee. The trainee should be urged not only to repeat the exact words, but also faithfully to reflect the analogical components, particularly the intonation and emphasis, which can change a question's meaning completely. People may think their individuality may be compromised, but this is only a means to an end, and all our students have found they begin to develop their own style. The supervisor of course soon learns to accommodate her input to the style of the trainee. The trainee, with the supervisor's assistance, should examine her first few sessions on the video tape.

As soon as the trainee shows a reasonable degree of competence, she can begin her training as a supervisor. This can be started by the new supervisor being handed the microphone during less crucial phases of the therapy, once the family has been engaged — the co-pilot model. Learning to supervise with the bug is a whole new area in itself. Timing is particularly crucial — obviously a message should not be given when the therapist is already talking. The supervisor needs to be extremely sensitive to feedback from the family. She needs to learn when to use covert interventions (where the family is unaware that the therapist has received a message), and when to suggest an overt intervention (where the therapist looks away and acknowledges that she is listening to the supervisor).

Continuous intervention with the earphone is an extremely fascinating tool with many alternative uses which we are continuing to explore. When it is going well, it becomes very clear what is meant in the family therapy literature by the term 'therapeutic system'. From the meta-position the supervisor is able to guide and nudge the progress of the therapy in an optimal way. Not just words, but the therapist's posture, mannerisms, tone of voice and mood can be influenced. This may sound very contrived, but the result is that the therapist is able to be much more sensitively attuned to each family member. Further, it has been a pleasure to see very 'green' therapy trainees conduct sophisticated therapy successfully. It goes a long way to validate Palazzoli's claim that 'if the method is correct no charisma whatsoever is needed' (Palazzoli et al. 1978).

PROBLEMS IN THE TEAM

Any small team has, of course, to negotiate a boundary and a hierarchy and each team will do so in its own way. Each of the clinics at Southwood House has evolved its own style and atmosphere. Some work more hierarchically and some prefer a more democratic mode of decision making. The work is very challenging and each clinic needs to be led by someone who can cope with steering the team through often highly emotionally charged situations. The clinic leaders need to be sensitive to the less experienced members of the clinic, in order to make sure that they are able to contribute and that their ideas are taken seriously. At the same time very rapid decision making is often necessary. It would clearly be inappropriate to have lengthy committee meetings at critical moments, but it is also important that the team has time to thrash out issues at length. However, all in all, our experience has been that surprisingly few enduring problems have been encountered.

An example of one of the issues that has arisen fairly regularly is allowing observers to sit in on the session. We have a steady stream of people requesting that they sit in, and we think it is important that each clinic team decide its own policy in this matter. There are occasions when a team will want to deny access to visitors, for example when a shy trainee is doing his first interview or when there are sensitive issues to be resolved. Enthusiastic visitors may be tempted to offer continuous comment and suggestions. It may be best to inform them immediately that it is important for quietness in the observation room to be maintained so that the supervisor can concentrate on the therapy. A period of time after the family have left can be set aside for the visitor to ask any questions.

CONCLUSION

We have now come to the end of our discussion of how to develop a Family Therapy Service in a psychiatric Day Hospital. We have described one way of setting up a service and some of the lessons and pitfalls that we have encountered. It is very much an ongoing venture and we fully expect to be doing things differently and we hope more effectively as time goes by.

We have focused on teamwork using live supervision because we believe that if people are going to get involved in the methods at all they should think big and go for a comprehensive service as a goal. We hope that this chapter will also be valuable for people wanting to develop family therapy in a more modest way in day hospitals. Some of the experiences we have had should be of interest to workers in other settings too.

It is too soon to assess rigorously the effectiveness of the service we have described. At present we are expecting to obtain a word-processing computer which will enable us to store and classify details of cases, interventions, outcomes and follow-up data. Not only will this allow us to accumulate a back-up store of therapeutic interventions, which should be invaluable for both therapy and training, but it should allow process and outcome research to be conducted with a minimum amount of administrative effort.

9

Developing a Network-orientated Service for Elderly People and their Carers

SUE POTTLE

The current population 'explosion' in the over sixty-five age group has been well recorded and documented. By 1991 there will be a million more people aged sixty-five and over, in England and Wales, than 20 years before (Ashley, 1971). The over sixty-fives were 4.7 per cent of the population in 1901; by the 1971 census the proportion was 13.3 per cent. However, it is the increase in the number of people over seventy-five which poses the biggest challenge to health and social services. This age group has increased nearly six-fold during this century and will continue to increase into the next (Arie and Isaacs 1978).

Alongside the increasing numbers of elderly people, there is naturally a corresponding increase in the number of people suffering from psychiatric disorders associated with old age. Mortimer and Schuman (1981) have summarized studies of the prevalence of dementia. They suggest that 22 per cent of the population over eighty show evidence of severe dementia. They bring home the importance of this statistic by stating that, at a personal level, each individual alive today has a 20 per cent risk of becoming severely demented.

They refer to dementia as a public health problem of enormous magnitude which is not, however, matched by resources to combat it. As Jack (1983) points out, the problem is circular. Psychogeriatric patients are doubly stigmatized, being both old and 'insane'. Those caring for elderly people have limited resources at their disposal, which means that excessive demands are made on the carers. Their response to such demands may well be abuse and neglect of the elderly people themselves. However, the limited resources available reflect, in their turn, the neglect and abuse of the elderly at a societal level. Levin and Levin (1980) point out that our society is prone to a form of discrimination they call 'ageism': 'Senior citizens are supposed to stay out of the way, sit in their rocking-chairs and enjoy the golden years. They are expected to be inactive, invisible and happy.'

Herr and Weakland (1979), pointed out the slow development of psychotherapy with elderly people compared with the range of therapeutic techniques used with younger age groups. In the American family therapy literature of the 1970s, there was a growing recognition that the inclusion of the grandparent generation often helped in solving problems developing within the first and second generations. Spark and Brody (1970) encourage the inclusion of elderly members in family sessions to prevent family problems repeating themselves generation after generation. They also recognize the impact of institutional placement of an elder family member on the whole family lifestyle since they argue that: 'the prospect of institutional placement may constitute a crucible in which family patterns are revealed in full strength.' In all these examples the therapy was not specifically to help the elderly people, but rather to include them in order to help the younger generations with their own problems. The family therapy literature, therefore, also reflects the relative neglect of services for elderly people.

Herr and Weakland's *Counselling Elders and their Families* (1979) is a refreshing exception to this general trend. They have used the brief therapy model developed at the Mental Research Institute in Palo Alto, California, with families which include an elderly member. Their book describes the virtues of eliciting specific problems, and stresses that as long as problems have no specific definition, they are by definition without a solution. Having determined from every family member present how they see the problem, the counsellor is then encouraged to move on to examine the solutions that the family system has already attempted. The writers point out that 'most of the problems you will encounter in your counselling with elders and their families will be problems created and perpetuated by inappropriate solutions.' A possible example of this is the move of an elderly family member from their own home into the home of one of their relatives. Short-term memory loss is aggravated by the change in surroundings, and further compounded by irritation displayed by younger family members, who find their territory invaded.

Kirschner (1979) describes clearly the simultaneous transitions which all family members are going through at a time when their aged member is needing support: 'The adult children are facing the problems of menopause, the climacteric and retirement; grandchildren are experiencing the difficulties of adolescence or new marriages; great-grandchildren are being born and claiming the attention of the family.' With all these pressures, it is perhaps not surprising that, as some American studies have shown, younger family members are responsive to being included in treatment programmes for their elderly member. For example, Reifler and Eisdorfer (1980) describe the establishment of a Geriatric and Family Services Outpatient Clinic. This clinic provides psychiatric, medical, social and nursing evaluations and recommendations for impaired older people, and also provides support and practical advice to the family. The whole family, including the elderly member, were asked to attend an outpatient clinic. Only 2 per cent of these families failed to attend or dropped out. It seems, therefore, that relatives who have problems with their elderly family members are keen to seek advice and help from professionals in the field; in therapy terminology, they are 'customers'.

The importance of wider community support for elderly people is increasingly recognized. Whitehead (1974) points out that not only are family and friends important — milkmen, postmen, home helps, all provide 'a web of support, interest and reason for living that can result in disaster if it is destroyed or interfered with.' Rowlings (1981), in her book *Social Work with Elderly People,* recognizes that a valid social work role with elderly people involves the creation and maintenance of supportive care networks, including volunteers and domiciliary care staff. Whitehead (1974) suggests that such networks should themselves become the focus for intervention 'since the old person who becomes a patient is so dependent on these community contacts and may in fact have become ill because of some disturbance in the network of physical and emotional support, effective treatment is only possible if the family and community are involved in this treatment.' Possible ways of convening and treating such networks are described by Speck and Attneave (1973), although they do not work specifically with the problem of elderly people. Since breakdown of these caring networks inevitably results in increased pressure on already over-burdened institutional care, it is surely not only humane, but also economically advantageous to support and shore up the networks wherever possible, especially in a climate of economic cutbacks.

In addition to academic literature on the subject, there is a growing national media coverage of problems with the elderly. A BBC 1 television play entitled 'Where's the Key?', broadcast in January 1983, showed vividly the stresses and strains of caring relatives trying to look after a demented elderly person, and the impact of this on the other generations. Documentaries have taken up the theme of granny battering, showing the mental and physical violence to which caring relatives are often driven through the lack of support given to them. So the present climate is ripe for change. We have a population explosion among the elderly which far exceeds existing resources, a growing media coverage of problems affecting the elderly, and a growing enthusiasm among professional staff groups for new approaches in the field of provision for elderly people. The approach I will describe shows how such enthusiasm can be channelled into changing existing caring systems, even when additional resources are not available. In the Bridgwater area of Somerset, our attempts to improve care for the elderly began, not unexpectedly, with moves to stimulate change within the hospital which formed the backbone of the psychogeriatric service.

ESTABLISHING A SYSTEMS APPROACH IN A HOSPITAL PSYCHOGERIATRIC WARD

When a new approach is introduced within an institutional setting, it is common for conflict to arise, since the new approach seems to challenge the existing treatment methods used by senior staff. However, confused elderly people are usually treated as a low-status client group; there is less competition to control their treatment and fewer existing treatment programmes. The field is therefore reasonably open to innovation.

Before 1981, the responsibility for the care of the elderly patients on the psychogeriatric wards in our local hospital was left largely with the nursing staff. The consultant assessed elderly people at home through a domiciliary visit and admitted them to the long-stay psychiatric wards, when he felt it was appropriate. In my role as social worker to the consultant's multi-disciplinary team, I was expected to seek out such patients for discharge back to the community. I found this a daunting prospect and neglected this part of my work. Hence the beds became blocked, leading to dissatisfaction on the part of the consultant who was, in turn, under pressure from general practitioners. The situation changed radically in 1981, when I was able to team up with a clinical assistant in psychiatry and community psychiatric nurse, who joined the consultant's team at the same time. Both had an active interest in work with the elderly, and together we formed what became known as the Psychogeriatric Team.

With full cooperation from the senior nursing staff on the psychogeriatric wards, who felt that they and their patients were neglected in comparison with the acute wards, we took the initial step towards change. This involved establishing a monthly ward round to review all patients on the psychogeriatric wards. The ward round took the form of a meeting between the clinical assistant in psychiatry, the two junior doctors responsible for the wards, the nurses in charge, two social workers and the community psychiatric nurse. At these ward rounds, we were able to identify the few patients who no longer needed long-term psychiatric hospital care. Most had been in hospital too long for a return to their own home to be possible, but we were able to discharge a few to Social Services and private elderly persons' homes. This initial success gave the team a sense of progress, and also created bed vacancies. At this stage, the consultant transferred the decision-making involved in the allocation of beds on the psychogeriatric wards to his clinical assistant. Thus, our psychogeriatric team was able to establish control over both admission and discharge procedures on these wards. This has enabled us to be flexible about the use of beds, in order to meet needs within the community.

Thanks to this control, we have now developed a procedure whereby a review of every patient takes place approximately three weeks after admission. The patient, the patient's relatives, nursing staff on the ward, the junior doctor responsible for the ward, community psychiatric nurse and social worker are all invited to this review. The pattern the review takes is as follows:

1   An outline is given by the nursing staff of any problems the patient may be having or causing in hospital and the steps being taken to overcome them.

2   A review is undertaken of the problems that the relatives are having at home.

3   Decisions about future plans are made — for example, whether the patient should remain in hospital, return to his or her own home or be transferred to an elderly persons' home.

Whatever decision is made, the team is at pains to put it in a positive light in the hope of alleviating the inevitable guilt feelings expressed by relatives at these reviews. The meetings also help to strengthen the relationship between nursing staff and visiting relatives. Hearing the detail of the problems relatives were having at home helps to prevent the staff feeling that the elderly person is being dumped on them for no good reason. Relatives may also feel less guilty if they hear that the staff too have problems in handling their elderly family member's behaviour. These reviews can be seen as the fusion of the two caring systems — the relatives at home and the staff in the hospital — so that a new system of shared care emerges. This helps to resolve the potential competition between the family and the staff about who is best at looking after the elderly person.

If the patient has been admitted from an elderly persons' home, we make a point of inviting the head of the home, and care assistant, as well as the relatives. Such options as a trial period in the elderly persons' home (with the bed being kept in hospital) can then be discussed realistically. We have also arranged reciprocal visits between the staff in elderly persons' homes and the nursing staff on the wards, so that both can compare their different settings and appreciate each other's difficulties. Behaviour, such as the spitting out of food at the dinner table or rifling other people's possessions, may be tolerated in a ward where the fellow patients are confused, but is certainly not acceptable amongst fellow residents in an elderly persons' home. We have found that such meetings have been accompanied by an increased willingness on the part of the officers in charge of homes to take some of the confused patients as residents in the knowledge that they will be re-admitted to hospital if the situation becomes impossible.

ESTABLISHING A DOMICILIARY PSYCHOGERIATRIC TEAM

Although establishing smooth running procedures in the hospital service for psychogeriatric patients is obviously important, we were equally keen to adopt a similar approach when tackling the problems of confused elderly people living within the community. We were fortunate in Bridgwater that family therapy had already been established as a method of intervention in the work of a very active psychiatric day hospital, as outlined by Harry Procter in chapter 8.

Local GPs were therefore already aware that family therapy was a possible option which would be offered to their patients when they made a referral to the consultant psychiatrist. It must be noted that our own service for elderly people was developed later than the other family therapy clinics, reflecting the universal tendency for services to this age group to lag behind. The service I will now describe is provided by a team of three who visit the patient's home. The team is multi-disciplinary and consists of a psychiatrist, community psychiatric nurse and psychiatric social worker. As a team we are able to mobilize a range of therapeutic skills and methods, but it is important to remember that we also act as gate-keepers to a considerable range of practical resources. These include both the allocation of acute and geriatric hospital beds, and access to permanent, short-stay and day-care places in Social Services homes for elderly people. Having such resources at our disposal is of course a positive advantage in our success rate in convening family and professional networks.

Working methods

The team meet weekly, from 9 am to 12.30 pm, and usually see two families; but they will fit in a third if a crisis has arisen. The emphasis is on brief problem-focused interventions, which are designed to encourage the family network to mobilize its own resources. We have chosen to see the elderly people in their own homes since the home setting itself may be part of the problem with which the family is struggling.

Referrals to our service come from the consultant psychiatrist, from the area office at the local Social Services Department, or direct from GPs. We ask them to complete a short referral form which stresses the importance of providing detailed information of known relatives, neighbours and agencies already involved. On the basis of this information, we decide who to invite for our assessment interview. We seek above all else to convene the person who actually

wants change to take place. It is crucial to recognize that this is very
rarely the old person. For example, having a poor memory may not
worry the old person, but it may be intolerable to a relative who is
asked the same question ten times in as many minutes.

Generally we find that there is a considerable existing support
system which has enabled the elderly person to carry on living in the
community thus far. We therefore consider it important to invite as
many of its members as possible. For example, the provision of a
home help may well be the key factor enabling someone to remain
within their own home. Through close liaison with the Home Help
Organizer, therefore, we always ensure that the home help is there
at the time of our visit. We also invite district nurses, health
visitors, relatives, friends, neighbours, in fact anyone who is known
to be involved in the old person's life. We always inform the
patient's GP of our intention to visit, and ask him to let us know if
he has any objections to our intervention. Because of the pressure of
work on GPs, we accept that he will not usually be able to be present
for our assessment, but as we see him as a vital member of the
community support team, we explain to him any recommendations
we have made by letter or by telephone on the day of our visit. If
immediate action, for example hospital admission is necessary, we
call at the surgery in person to arrange this with the GP. We have
found that careful planning of who to invite to our assessment is
absolutely essential. On the occasions when we have not invited the
support system in advance, the interview has been almost fruitless,
particularly if we have descended on an old person with simply an
introductory letter. This can be very unsettling and definitely not a
good way of finding out what the problems are. It may well be felt
that having three of us visit an old person is a fairly formidable
ordeal for him or her, but this threat is undoubtedly eased by the
presence of the family members and professional workers with
whom he or she are familiar.

Interviewing Methods

We allow an hour for each visit. When we enter the house, we
introduce ourselves, explaining who we are. One of us then conducts
the interview while the other two sit in a corner of the room taking
notes. If either wish to intervene, we usually pass a note to the
therapist. The format of our interview borrows heavily from the

brief therapy model as described by Herr and Weakland (1979). The first questions we ask are: 'What is the problem?'; 'To whom is it a problem?'; 'How is it a problem to them?'; 'What are the solutions offered so far?'; and 'How do the family members think that we, as a team, can help them?' Having gathered this information from every person in the room, the therapist explains that he would like to take a short break during which the team would like to go into an adjoining room to confer. We have never found anybody object to this — we usually find it provides a welcome coffee break, and it gives the family a chance to relax and talk amongst themselves. Often, when we return from our break, we find that the family themselves have come up with new ideas.

A question we always ask ourselves during this break (when considering the origins of a problem presented to us) is 'Why now?'; in other words, 'Why not six months ago or a week ago?' One might have thought that the 'Why now?' was due to some degeneration in the old person's physical or mental state. In fact, although this may be the case, we very often find that the most immediate precipitant is a breakdown in the existing support system, and if this system can be reconstructed, the situation may well return to normal.

A clear example of such a breakdown was the illness of a private domestic help. She was the only person who could get on with an old lady who lived next door to her daughter and son-in-law in a granny flat. Once the private home help became ill, the old lady became aggressive and violent and eventually had to be admitted to the psychiatric hospital under Section 25 of the Mental Health Act. It was clear that it was not her condition that had degenerated but rather that the illness of the private help had highlighted her poor relationship with her daughter, which became apparent when the buffer between them was removed. We sometimes find that cases are referred to us when the usual home help goes on holiday and the locum replacing her is perhaps either startled by what she finds or just finds it generally difficult to cope. On the return of the ordinary home help, the situation goes back to normal.

A sudden change in medication may be another possible precipitant which causes mental confusion. Here we face what is in effect an iatrogenic problem, since it is the presence of too many conflicting medications which is causing the mental confusion in the elderly person. This is why we ask the particular question: 'What are the other solutions that have been offered so far?' According to Herr and Weakland's brief therapy model, existing proffered solutions may in fact be perpetuating the problem. The GP may have been extremely helpful in prescribing medicines, but unfortunately the old person may not have necessarily taken them according to prescription, or there may have been a succession of doctors calling and prescribing different tablets. In this sort of case, a few tactful suggestions from our team or possibly a brief hospital admission to sort out the medication may be all that is necessary for the old person to return to a contented independent lifestyle.

Theoretical perspectives

We rely heavily on the concept of positive reframing used especially by Palazzoli and her co-workers (Palazzoli et al. 1978). The actions of all members of the system are always seen in a positive light and are therefore commended by us. We have found that, contrary to current assumptions, there is a great deal being done by families and neighbours and community services to support the elderly. One of the best services our clinic can provide is a positive affirmation of this fact, so that the existing supporters feel encouraged to carry on, perhaps with a little extra help. We also take care to reframe the behaviour of the elderly person, often praising them for their independence and the determination to cope within their own home, despite physical ailments. Being aware of the resistance to change inherent in all family systems, we make strong use of such resistance by suggesting that in many instances the elderly person may not wish to change at all. Change is particularly threatening to someone in later life who may have spent all their life in one place and may have a set routine which forms the basis for their security. Change may in fact precipitate an illness rather than relieve it. We all know that admission to a hospital or home is very often followed by death.

On the other hand, this resistance to change may sometimes be preventing old people from receiving the very services which would help them to maintain their independence. A clear example of this occurred when we became aware, as a result of one of our visits, that an elderly couple urgently needed the services of a home help if they were to stay out of hospital for any period. We were equally aware that they were fiercely independent and resented disclosing their financial circumstances. There was an unresolved conflict between husband and wife — the wife recognized her need for help but was over-ruled by her husband's rather unrealistic hopes that all would be well, and his tendency to postpone decisions.

After conferring, we said to the couple that everybody seemed to have been trying to persuade them that having a home help was a good idea, but that we quite appreciated that they wanted to remain independent and we thought that they were therefore very unlikely to accept anyone else's help in their home. They clearly had extremely high standards and no one else would be able to do the work to their satisfaction. We said, therefore, that we did not expect them to decide in favour of such a service. The wife immediately replied that she certainly needed help, that she simply did not have the strength to carry on. The husband countered this by saying that it was too soon to make up his mind. We said that they obviously needed a longer time to think it over so that we would ring back after the weekend to see if they had been able to make any decisions. Fortunately, the Home Help Organizer had already visited them twice in the past and was equally doubtful that they would accept help because they had refused it before. When she made a further visit with one of our team members, she was therefore very disinclined to push them into anything. Much to everyone's surprise and delight they accepted both the financial assessment and the services of the home help. They have been delighted with her services and have managed to remain within the community since the time she was introduced.

A SYSTEMS MODEL FOR ONGOING INTERVENTION

Although sometimes a single assessment interview is sufficient to mobilize or reassure the existing support system, we may also, at that interview, delegate specific tasks to one of our own team members, so that they carry out a task which is part of their ordinary professional role. The individual team member then temporarily becomes a member of the client's support system, which naturally means that she may become stuck or sucked in and therefore powerless if the system once more gets into difficulties. At such a point, the team member can once again call on the help of the whole psychogeriatric team to re-mobilize the system. The following case example (which involved my undertaking specific social work tasks and then calling in the team's help once again) illustrates the model I have described.

1   *Referral to Psychogeriatric Team*

The problem, according to the GP, was that Mr Barnes was wandering at night. The social work file revealed that Mr Barnes aged seventy-seven, lived alone. His wife, who was approximately 20 years younger, was living and working in a city many miles away, though she came to visit him from time to time. He had a son who lived nearby.

2   *Psychogeriatric Team visit Mr Barnes at home*

He was alone at the time of our visit. His account of the problem was as follows:

> I get lost; they tell me I have been wandering around at night but I don't remember it. It has got very difficult now to cope on my own. I don't know when my wife is coming home. She will soon be retiring on a pension. A house is never the same without a woman. I think I did something wrong at my wife's home and she won't have me there. I have been quite happy here until the last five years, but life is not worth living at the moment. It gets you down when you can't do something. Give me the tablets and I'll finish it off right now.

Since he maintained that his wife was due home very soon, we wrote a letter to her asking her to contact us because we were concerned about her husband.

We then visited a neighbour, who said that Mr Barnes had wandered to her house several times in the middle of the night and that she had let him in and then encouraged him to go home. It was obvious that she felt his wife should be at home looking after her husband. Two days later, we received an angry phone call from Mrs Barnes who had come down to see her husband. She had received our letter and complained that we were upsetting her husband to no purpose. However, she did agree to see us on the date suggested. It was clear at this point that in our anxiety to respond promptly to the referral from the doctor, we had visited without marshalling the whole support system. We had thereby incurred Mrs Barnes's anger, and had not gathered a full picture of the support system and how it functioned. When we next called to see both Mr and Mrs Barnes, we arranged for the home help, who was also a close neighbour, to be present. The problems identified were:

1 Mr Barnes leaves the gas on. Mrs Barnes offered to buy a small electric Belling cooker, and instruct her husband how to use it.
2 The fire risk from the open fire and paraffin. Mrs Barnes suggested that they might block up the open grate. The home help pointed out that Mr Barnes uses the calor gas heater safely.
3 Mr Barnes's lack of personal hygiene. It was agreed that a district nurse would be asked to call occasionally to wash him and encourage him to change his clothes. The team wrote to the doctor requesting this.
4 Mr Barnes is very depressed when alone. Mrs Barnes talked about taking early retirement and returning to care for her husband, but admitted that she had not yet been able to make up her mind about this. The team therefore recommended an anti-depressant, possibly to be given at night with the existing sleeping tablet, which was administered by the home help.

We did not arrange any further visit, but asked the home help or Mrs Barnes to contact me at the Social Services Department if they had any anxieties. We had no further contact for the next three months.

I then received a message from the home help saying that Mr Barnes had stuffed a taper down the gas heater and ruined it. Mrs Barnes had installed an electric fire, but when the home help called in, she found that Mr Barnes had stuffed a metal piece down into the fire which she could not pull out. He had also burnt the kettle out. The home help revealed that Mrs Barnes has been coming to see her husband much more frequently, in fact every weekend, and was now talking of coming for two months on unpaid leave. In response to this telephone message, I visited a week later on my own and saw the home help, and Mrs Barnes, to see if there was any further help we could offer. Mrs Barnes confirmed that she was taking two months unpaid leave. She was now fully aware of the problems her husband was having, rather than denying them. The home help had been talking a lot about one of the social services elderly persons' homes to Mr Barnes, and he was now willing to go and see the home with a view to a possible short stay there. Mrs Barnes was also in favour of

this plan so I arranged an afternoon visit. I took Mr and Mrs Barnes
to see round the home a few days later. Both seemed very impressed,
and we provisionally booked some short-stay dates. I asked Mrs
Barnes to confirm with me a few days later whether she wanted to
take these up. She rang me after the weekend to say that, although
Mr Barnes had seemed happy enough at the time, she had had a very
difficult weekend with him. She attributed this to his being upset at
the idea of going to a social services home, so she said she would like
to call off the idea.

A fortnight later, I received a phone call from the home help to
tell me that Mr Barnes had wandered down to her house in his
slippers complaining that his wife was treating him badly. Mrs
Barnes had also called in to see her and said that she had been sitting
crying all day and did not care if her husband was in or out. She just
felt she wanted to leave him again. The GP had already visited but
could not see what he could do to help. I felt similarly powerless, so
asked the home help to get Mrs Barnes's permission for a further
visit by the psychogeriatric team, to which she agreed. It was now
clear that the crisis over Mr Barnes's future care had re-opened the
issue of the couple's marital conflict.

3   *Further visit by Psychogeriatric Team*

Problems stated by Mrs Barnes: 'Mr Barnes is used to his own
muddled way and there is no use arguing. We argue because he
leaves the door open and then says he is cold. He goes out and
worries the neighbours.'

Mr Barnes denied that he had any problems or worries.

The Home Help pointed out that Mr Barnes does become verbally
aggressive at times, especially towards his wife, and occasionally
towards her.

The Barnes's son, Mike, pointed out that the friction between his
mother and father was contributing to the upset. He said that they
had not had a happy marriage when they were younger and he would
now be worried about both of them if they were to carry on living
together.

We asked those present what they thought would help.

Mrs Barnes: Any way of improving Mr Barnes's confusion by
   therapy, but if it can't be helped, I don't want him put in
   different places.

Mr Barnes: I don't remember going to the old people's home, but if it came up that I could go there, I would try it.

The Barnes's son, Mike: I don't see any resolution, but probably in an old people's home with the corridor and doors, he would get more confused and use the wrong doors; but he can't stay here on his own, it would be good some days and bad others and he would go out and fall over. Nor do I see my mother and father getting on together if they lived together again.

Home Help: He has been asking about the old people's home because another lady from the village has gone there. He can't cope in the house on his own because he can't dress or make tea or keep warm. He gets bored and then he fiddles and takes things apart, which is dangerous.

Our team then suggested that Mr Barnes should have a trial period at the elderly persons' home. I shared his son's reservations about the success of this venture, but could see that this solution was the only one that Mrs Barnes seemed likely to accept at this stage. She contacted us a few days later to say that she would like her husband to try day care at the elderly persons' home instead. When this was arranged, Mr Barnes wandered out from the house, and the staff said they would not be able to cope with him as a resident.

A week later the home help rang me to say that Mr Barnes had wandered away from his own home, even while his wife was staying there. As it was snowing at the time, he had had to be rescued by a neighbour. Mike rang me later to say that his mother had now decided to go back to her own home. She had now also realized that her husband could not be left alone, and was agreeing that he should be admitted to our local psychiatric hospital. I arranged this through the GP and consultant, so that Mr Barnes was admitted within a few days.

4 Case Review

Three weeks later, we arranged a case review on the psychogeriatric ward following a complaint letter from Mrs Barnes about the care of her husband there. The consultant agreed to be present as well as the ward staff and psychogeriatric team. Mr and Mrs Barnes and Mike also came. Mike was a little bewildered as he did not know about his mother's complaint. Mrs Barnes said that her husband had been incontinent on arrival and had seemed quite distressed. The ward staff agreed with her that he had taken some time to settle. As

Mr Barnes was at the meeting, the consultant asked him where he would like to live. Mr Barnes replied that the psychogeriatric ward was a home from home. He turned to his wife who looked upset and told her that she could come and see him there, but that he was quite all right and that she must take care of herself and not worry about him. Mrs Barnes was in tears through much of the meeting, and acknowledged that she was feeling guilty for not looking after her husband herself. The consultant told her that she was very wise as she had a good job and her life in front of her. The ward staff would always be glad to see her on visits. When asked for his opinion, Mike said if his father had not been admitted to hospital, they would have had two admissions, since his mother would have been admitted as well. All present agreed that permanent admission to the psychogeriatric ward was the best solution.

Initially, Mr Barnes's depression and loss of short-term memory appeared to be the problem referred to the psychogeriatric team. However, he was also the partner in an unresolved marital conflict. His wife had moved out, but not divorced her husband, and therefore naturally reacted strongly against someone else taking over his care. Her first attempted solution was to move in with her husband, but this led to conflict between them. She next suggested care in an elderly persons' home, until this proved impracticable. Eventually, it was her son's intervention which persuaded her to accept the idea of hospital admission. It was important that our team did not make a scapegoat of Mrs Barnes, but rather saw her as a wife very concerned for her husband's welfare; and torn between her own desire to continue an independent career and her sense of responsibility towards her husband. Through her inclusion in our sessions, the home help was able to move from a position of Mr Barnes's ally, to an active mediator between the couple. She also helped to reduce the tension between Mrs Barnes and the other neighbours. This situation also illustrates the fact that admission to a psychogeriatric ward may be seen by the elderly person himself as a positive move to relieve his depression and sense of isolation.

CONCLUSION

We hope that our network-orientated approach answers many of the criticisms that are levelled at family therapy for being too narrowly focused on family systems. Our work is truly systemic since it involves convening members of the family, the local community and professional agencies. Often we do little more than to act as go-betweens for renegotiating a system of care which is shared by all three of these groups. At other times we enter the situation more actively, mobilizing our own skills and elements of our own professional system which are not immediately available to help deal with the crisis that has triggered off the referral. The strength of our approach hinges around its lack of complexity and its ability to stimulate the very real caring skills which are present in the various communities which we serve.

Our overall aim is to mobilize and reactivate the elderly person's support system within the community. If this system has temporarily ground to a halt, we hope that our visits may provide the inch of traction which it needs to get going again. Although our particular experience lies with the problems associated with psychiatric disorder in elderly people, we hope that our model is applicable to all kinds of work with elderly people and their carers.

10

Family Therapy in Mental Hospitals

ANDY TREACHER

To many readers the title of this chapter will be in itself paradoxical. To hospitalize a patient and hence isolate him from his natural system (his family and other social networks) seems a retrograde step if, at the same time, a therapist is endeavouring to intervene to change the functioning of that system. I would hasten to agree with this position, but would nevertheless insist that since there are times when hospitalization is the only possible course of action in dealing with a community-based crisis, family therapists need to develop skills which enable them to treat families who are temporarily disconnected through one member being hospitalized.

Such a view is largely unfashionable in family therapy circles. For instance, Haley (1980) has placed great stress on the necessity for avoiding hospitalization if at all possible, while Madanes (1981) has explored tactics for preventing re-hospitalization. I agree with Haley and Madanes on these issues, but I believe that I am nevertheless correct in detecting a clear tendency in the family therapy literature to avoid a discussion of the *positive* features of hospital settings. Such an omission is perfectly understandable given the chequered history of mental hospitals and the problematic relationship that they have with their 'client' populations.

Mental hospitals are very challenging places as far as family therapists are concerned. In his recent book, *The Psychiatric Hospital and the Family,* Harbin (1982) points out some of the reasons for this:

> The basic assumption underlying the hospital treatment approach, has been an individually oriented (either biological or psychological) etiological model of madness. Yet most people are placed in the hospital because their family or community is unable to tolerate their disturbing behaviour, no matter what the etiology of the illness happens to be. Families have been excluded from the

hospital often because of their own wishes and the ignorance of the hospital staff.

Harbin's argument is important since it stresses the significance of social factors in determining hospitalization. Sociologists have, of course, documented such phenomena in great detail (Goffman 1968; Spitzer and Denzin 1968; Scheff 1966) but a number of pioneering psychiatrists such as Langsley in the USA and Scott in Britain, have successfully demonstrated that a remarkably high percentage of potential hospital admissions can, in fact, be prevented if skilful crisis intervention techniques are utilized. Such work has highlighted the role that families and networks play in determining hospitalization, but at the same time such results invite family therapists to rethink their attitudes towards the role that the family—mental hospital system plays in determining the outcome of therapy. If intervention to prevent hospitalization is not successful then it is still possible to involve the family in the admission, treatment and discharge of the patient.

It is unfortunate that this pioneer work (which concentrated on crisis intervention) tended to ignore the role that hospital-based workers could play as part of a coordinated service. This neglect has unfortunately been compounded by another process which concerns the development of family therapy. Family therapy has been largely developed by therapists who have had little or no involvement in hospital settings.

From an historical point of view this development is puzzling because, as Harbin again stresses, many of the earliest observations about problem families were made by professionals treating hospitalized schizophrenics (e.g. Fromm-Reichman 1948; Laing and Esterson 1964). In some cases early pioneering work actually involved hospitalizing whole families (e.g. Bowen, 1965, Brodey, 1959). Harbin suggests that most of this work was discontinued for economic and practical reasons, but he overlooks the self-evident fact that a thoroughgoing family therapy approach can run into considerable political opposition. For example, according to Broderick and Schrader (1981), Bowen's failure to develop his exciting project (which involved the concurrent hospitalization of two or three families) was due to lack of support from the National Institute of Mental Health. This lack of support apparently resulted from Bowen's ignoring the conventions of traditional psychiatric practice.

THE 'HOSPITAL FAMILY PSYCHOTHERAPY' MOVEMENT

Harbin's own work is representative of a growing movement in the USA which treats 'hospital family psychotherapy' (to use a term borrowed from Lansky 1981) as an area of study in its own right. However, Harbin is prepared to admit that at present there is considerable confusion concerning the development of such work. Some family therapists have become clear advocates of an independent speciality (Boyd 1981) while others have stressed the significant drawbacks of such an approach (Carter 1981). I do not want to enter into this particular controversy here since I believe it is a largely unproductive dispute. Instead I would like to outline my own position on this issue.

Unlike some other family therapists we do not assume that hospital treatment is a last resort form of treatment whose underlying philosophy is diametrically opposed to that of family therapy. The whole issue can be summarized as follows:

1 Family therapists need to understand that the present organization of the adult psychiatric services is unlikely to change radically in the foreseeable future.
2 Since these services are largely unchanging, family therapists need to develop approaches which enable them to work within services that have been designed with a different model in mind.
3 If family therapy is to be successful then family therapists need to be able to integrate their work with that of their colleagues, within the hospital. At all costs they must avoid taking up adversary positions which undermine the work of their colleagues.

Clearly, if the family therapy approach is to be influential at all it must avoid taking up a messianic position. Laing and Cooper's radical approach which contributed to the development of anti-psychiatry (Laing and Esterson 1964; Esterson et al. 1965; Sedgwick 1982) is of considerable theoretical and practical interest, but with hindsight it is clear that their most crucial failure concerned their inability to influence the thinking of the staff within mental hospitals. Some commentators would perhaps argue that such a criticism is inappropriate because the staff were incapable of responding, but I would see this as a counsel of despair which merely serves to preserve the status quo. If family therapy has failed to establish itself in mental hospitals, then we assume that there must be important reasons for its failure.

In the following section which is concerned with analysis of staff relationships within ward settings we shall discuss why family therapy has not been widely established in mental hospitals.

UNDERSTANDING THE STRUCTURE OF THE HOSPITAL

Since each ward has its own history and is unique, it is difficult to establish general principles that apply to every case, but it is nevertheless worth considering some general points. Recently Lieberman and Cooklin (1982) have explored the implications of adopting a system-orientated model within an institution such as a mental hospital. They argue:

> Family therapy unsettles the hierarchy (within the hospital) and may destabilize the organization since it deals with three non-traditional assumptions. First, causation — the family approach implies that the root of many problems resides in relationships, not in the psyche or soma of individuals. Secondly, the real world and real people are considered more important to psychiatric illness than intra-psychic fantasy or biology. Thirdly, the family therapist views himself as part of the family system rather than as an objective outsider.

Since these ideas inevitably collide with some of the accepted views that prevail within the institutions, the family therapist must be sensitive to the impact that such ideas have on other staff members. For example, Lieberman and Cooklin correctly point out that nurses and patients must at present accept that they perform reciprocal roles — the staff playing a caring or custodial role while the patients are basically dependent and in need of help. Obviously if a nurse were to change roles and become a family therapist, these role expectations would begin to change radically. As Lieberman and Cooklin have written:

> A nurse is a 'patient's person'; often the esteem of the nurse is highly dependent on the belief that he or she can be a helpful and supportive intimate 'other' for the patient. If the nurse . . . works with the whole family this automatically distances him or her

from the patient. This may be challenging the foundations on which his or her role is built . . . and may thus place the patient in the invidious position of having to choose between the nurse and his or her family.

Obviously nursing staff are reluctant to abandon their traditional role in favour of the much more challenging role of change agent. Their position needs to be respected if any progress is to be made. Nurses form the backbone of the hospital system but their caring and support for patients is too easily disregarded by members of the more elite professions (psychiatry, clinical psychology and social work) who tend to be on the wards for short periods of time and therefore do not bear the brunt of the day-to-day difficulties of ward life. The nursing staff's abilities to discharge what can be called the 'asylum' function of the mental hospital needs to be clearly recognized. Some patients undoubtedly benefit from being away from the normal stresses that burden them. Indeed, one of the major arguments in favour of recommending hospitalization for a particular patient may hinge around the ability of the hospital to provide this sort of care. However, it is part of the unfortunate heritage of mental hospitals that active treatments (medical or otherwise) are considered to be more status-giving, so the contribution that nurses make at a caring level is under-rated by everybody and even, at times, paradoxically by nurses themselves.

Many nurses are, of course, able to undertake group or individual psychotherapy, because these traditions have become established over a number of years, but it is important to realize that such forms of therapy can be easily subsumed under the heading of a 'caring' role. The problem with family therapy is precisely that it overtly challenges the role of the hospital *vis-à-vis* the patient and his family.

A family, in electing to 'extrude' a family member into the hospital system, expects the hospital staff to take over its caring role in relation to the patient. As Scott's careful work has demonstrated (Scott and Ashworth 1967; Scott 1973) the family does not expect that its role in the drama of hospitalization should be examined. For the hospital staff to adopt a family therapy approach is culturally unexpected — it is not cricket — it is to hospital that people go to be cured.

So, at the point at which a hospital unit starts to work in a family-orientated way, it works against the stream. For approximately a century and a half, psychiatrists insisted that the correct treatment for severe cases of 'mental illness' was medical treatment in a hospital. However, there is every sign that psychiatrists are able to show flexibility in relation to this issue. The medical model, as Clare (1980) has argued, is essentially very flexible and has the ability rapidly to absorb new frameworks as they arise. But it is the hospital-based nursing staff rather than the psychiatrists who are potentially most threatened by the growth of family therapy — because it is their caring role that is most challenged by the development of a highly interventionist form of therapy which often seeks to change the nature of the family system in a fundamental way. It is therefore important for family therapists to be aware of this threat when they seek to establish good working relationships with nurses.

It is obviously also very important that family therapists develop good working relations with consultants as well as nursing staff. Many consultants pride themselves on their flexibility and open-mindedness and are, therefore, willing to experiment with new approaches. However, given their crucial decision-making role and their medical responsibility for the patients, it is essential that they are involved in treatment decisions involving family therapy cases. Again such a proposal is anathema to many family therapists who require that their cases are 'clean' and without strings attached. If such a 'pure' approach is applied within the hospital, no family therapy will be undertaken, so it is best to start with the open-minded assumption that good working relationships can be established between consultants and family therapists. Trust needs to be built on both sides and this primarily involves family therapists inviting their consultant colleagues to view their work. If the consultant has insufficient time to do so, then other ways of sharing the method of working need to be devised. Psychiatrists are increasingly aware of the need for family therapy training for their staff and junior medical colleagues, so there is no need for pessimism about the long-term prospects for the introduction of family therapy.

The 'openness' of other professions to family therapy is difficult to gauge, especially as very rapid developments are occurring. However, clinical psychologists have traditionally not shown as much interest in family therapy as social workers and psychiatrists, although it is clear that some important bridges are currently being built between family therapy and behaviour therapy. For example, the programmes developed by Patterson and other workers (Patterson 1971; Gordon and Davidson 1981) for treating delinquents and their families are very influential in the USA, while the important related work by Herbert (1982) is now being recognized by many clinical psychologists in this country. The emphasis of this work is largely on parent training, but its similarity to structural family therapy (Minuchin 1974) is very striking.

Many clinical psychologists are currently coming under the influence of these ideas but it is important that family therapists are sympathetic to the intrinsic strengths of the clinical psychology tradition. As a result of their training clinical psychologists are generally sensitive to issues that concern the efficacy of different treatments. They, therefore, often take an interest in new therapies from a research angle, and it is possible that family therapy will appeal to them for the same reason.

Social workers' attitudes to family therapy are probably the most diverse, simply because their training is so disparate. If a social worker has been trained in a psychoanalytic casework tradition, then she is unlikely to be sympathetic to the pragmatism of family-orientated approaches. However, family therapy traditions in social work are growing so it is predictable that more recently trained social workers will be more sympathetic. It is the older, more experienced, social workers (with a specific psychiatric social work training) who often find it difficult to respond to staff who are trying to introduce family therapy.

One of the main reasons for this difficulty is the territorial issue of who should work with families. It is often the social worker who has been delegated to visit the family, hence forming the link between the hospital and the family. Such a role is often either information-seeking or supportive, or both, but does not involve the worker as a change agent. Obviously a would-be family therapist needs to approach such experienced workers with respect rather than arrogance. Trust can only be built up if work is shared and ideas of mutual interest are explored.

Finally, mention should be made of occupational therapists. This neglected group are also very important in hospitals, particularly in relation to chronic patients. Their approach has, of course, always been problem-focused and they have absorbed many important ideas from behaviour therapy. Much of their thinking is potentially sympathetic to family therapy approaches and it is clear from my own personal experiences in Bristol and elsewhere that they can make very significant contributions to the development of family therapy.

DEVELOPING FAMILY THERAPY IN MENTAL HOSPITALS — SOME ESSENTIAL STEPS

Forming a working alliance with ward staff

In practice it is difficult to discuss the development of family therapy without being clear who is the customer for change. Obviously different staff members may attempt to make the opening moves. For example, if a newly-appointed nurse takes the initiative then her approach will be different from that of a consultant. However, if she cannot create an interest in family therapy amongst her colleagues then any attempt to undertake family therapy will be abortive and prone to conscious or unconscious sabotage by other staff members. If a consultant wishes to initiate the introduction of family therapy the situation may appear more hopeful, but in practice this may not be so, since ability to exert formal power is not the same as the ability to exert informal power. As Palazzoli has recently pointed out (Palazzoli 1982) it is also hazardous for a family therapist to be aligned with a consultant psychiatrist who wishes to introduce change in a situation in which his staff is opposed to a family therapy approach. In the latter situation the family therapist is often trapped in the role of the 'fixer' who will attempt to persuade staff to work in a way that they have formerly resisted. It is at this point that the covert alliance between the family therapist and the consultant is the biggest drawback to progress, since its secretive nature prevents open discussion of the underlying issues involved in the therapist's attempts to engineer change. It is for this reason that Palazzoli insists a family therapist should never use an alliance with a consultant psychiatrist in order to gain leverage for change within an organization. Only an open-handed approach which explicitly explores avenues for changes can have any hope of succeeding.

If a discussion of the pros and cons of family therapy is to be initiated on a ward, it is important that the ward staff have a major say in deciding the pace of such an initiative. Ideally the invitation for such a discussion should come from the staff (perhaps as part of a usual seminar programme or as part of a case presentation). If such an invitation is received then the family therapist should adopt a low-key approach, presenting her ideas in a straightforward fashion which avoids proselytizing and making messianic claims. Whenever possible, technical terms should be avoided and the ideas should be presented in a way that does not distinguish the presentation from other presentations that are normally given on the ward. If video tapes are not used by the ward then video tape material should not be shown initially as this will only alienate staff who are not familiar with such material.

If the presentation is well received, then it is possible that the family therapist may be invited to start work with a particular patient. This apparently benign offer must be treated with great caution as the particular patient who is suggested may well prove to be so difficult to work with that the family therapist will inevitably fail. Sometimes staff are genuinely interested in whether the therapist can succeed or not, but on other occasions the move is clearly designed to put the therapist in her place (and hence carries the covert message 'you may think you're smart but we old hands know what's possible and what's not'). If the therapist is in doubt as to her ability to handle the case, then she should decline to do so — using the (perfectly correct) formula: 'This one is too tough for me. I can see that I'm going to be out of my depth, so I'd be glad if somebody more experienced took it on.' If the case is taken on for family therapy then it is important to involve the 'referrers' (i.e the staff members who made the suggestion that family therapy should be attempted in the management of the case). They can be cordially invited to attend the family therapy session and the therapist should be careful to use them as observers and discussants, so that their ideas can be discussed and incorporated, where possible, into therapeutic interventions. Even if the overall outcome of this work is unsuccessful, the staff attending the sessions may well become sympathetic to the approach as they will have experienced the genuine struggle of the family therapist to help the family change.

If some staff members become polarized by these developments, and are covertly or overtly critical of family therapy, it is important to avoid conflict with them. They too can be invited to sessions, on the basis that critical opinions are valuable when developing new ways of working. It is also important for the family therapist to avoid being 'different' from other ward staff — she should, therefore, always be very punctilious about attending meetings and take a genuine interest in all aspects of ward life, and ask to be invited to individual or group sessions if at all possible.

Most of these tactics can be framed under two overlapping rubrics:

1 'In mental hospitals family therapy is one treatment amongst many. It probably has an important contribution to make but it is not clear which clients benefit from it most.'

2 'In some cases family therapy is an important adjunct to other forms of treatment because we have all had the experience of our patients deteriorating when they return home from the hospital.'

To many family therapists these frameworks are anathema, but we would argue that they are the only workable frameworks within a system which espouses eclecticism as its predominant philosophy. Haley's well-known position on this issue, that the therapist should keep total control of all cases (Haley 1980), is, in our opinion, both inappropriate and misunderstood. Haley does not, as far as we understand it, work as an in-patient therapist — his stance is clearly defensible if it is understood as being appropriate to out-patient settings. In out-patient settings it is perfectly possible to gain control of a case in the way he suggests, but the challenge of in-patient therapy is precisely to develop methods of working which accept that multiple therapy will take place and that its effect can be beneficial.

The issue that emerges here is not *whether* multiple therapy will take place but *what sort of* multiple therapy will take place and who will monitor it. Glick and Kessler (1981) adopt a straightforward approach to the most crucial aspect of this problem — as the following passage reveals:

Who should do the family therapy? The primary hospital therapist is the one in the best position to do the family therapy, because he or she has the best overall grasp of the case. The advantages of one therapist doing both the individual and the family therapy far outweigh the disadvantages. Time constraints may not always make this possible, however, and alternative solutions may have to be devised.

From a theoretical point of view I would be among the first to agree with Glick and Kessler on this point but if a ward has not yet established a policy of combining these two roles then I would argue that it may be necessary for the family therapist to accept a compromise solution, i.e. of working in parallel with a therapist providing individual psychotherapy, but at the same time negotiating a contract with the therapist which enables both therapists to meet regularly to share their work.

Issues of confidentiality immediately arise in this type of situation. Glick and Kessler correctly insist that concepts of confidentiality need re-drawing when individual and family therapy are combined, but I see no reason why any insurmountable obstacle should arise from the parallel therapy situation that we have explored. Glick and Kessler argue their point as follows:

> How can the need for maximal communication among staff members be reconciled with the need for confidentiality of the patient and the therapist? Communication between staff seems crucial for effective treatment. The family should be told that the therapist will use all the material that is available in both the individual and family contacts to help the family function better.

If both the individual therapist and the family therapist make clear that they will be sharing material from their sessions so that the family and the individual can function better, then issues of confidentiality can be put to one side. If, of course, either the individual or the family refuses to accept this approach then they will create a major crisis for the therapists, but this can be used productively to create the next stage of therapy — provided the therapists are sufficiently skilful.

If the parallel method of working proves, in practice, to be problematic then the family therapist should avoid the trap of the 'told you so' stance and be prepared to sort out a new method of working. If this new method is not similar to the one that Glick and Kessler have proposed, then it is nevertheless essential for the family therapist to make renewed efforts to involve the individual therapists in this new type of package. An invitation to attend the family therapy sessions as an observer and adviser is probably the best solution since it will prevent the family therapy from being hived off and isolated from the therapeutic work of the ward.

It should be clear from what has been proposed so far, that we are really exploring the obvious fact that family therapy can only grow organically since it cannot be forced upon an unwilling staff group. Staff can and will respond positively if they feel free to develop their interest in family therapy. They will also respond if the family therapist is genuinely involved in the life of the ward, rather than being a shadowy figure who occasionally appears in order to undertake some sessions. However, it is equally true that a single unsupported family therapist will fail if he or she is not adequately supported. It is therefore essential that the worker involved is an active member of a support group which will be able to provide guidance and supervision when and if the need arises. Ideally the family therapist should have a colleague who acts as her consultant, and with whom she can swap roles. (See chapter 11 for a more detailed discussion of this subject.)

Deepening the family-orientated approach

If the initial tactics of the family therapist prove successful then the advantages of taking a family therapy approach will become apparent to the unit. It is then possible to move towards deepening the family-orientated approach, so that the ward policy concerning admission and discharge can be changed. Obviously such a move could only occur in the context of major changes in the attitudes of all the staff. I myself have no first-hand experiences of such changes, but it is clear, from a theoretical point of view, what steps need to be taken if such a programme is to be successful.

However, before discussing such a programme, it is essential that we draw attention to the obvious fact that many family therapists will never, in fact, work in units which adopt a predominantly family-orientated approach. This may at first appear to be a depressing statement but since the main philosophy of mental hospitals is one of eclecticism it is essential that family therapists do not become disheartened because their approach is not adopted as the major approach. Instead, family therapists need to remind themselves that the strength of the eclectic approach lies in its ability to allow experimentation, and the existence of different types of treatment. In practice this means that families and patients can and will receive the benefit of a family therapy approach.

Of course, not all units are eclectic in their approach, but even in non-eclectic units it is possible to make some headway. Staff are naturally worried by treatment failures, so it is possible for a would-be family therapist on a unit to raise issues concerning the best methods for dealing with such failures. Often the failure will be due to factors that are probably beyond any therapist's control — for example, the patient may have become hospital-centred and have no viable place to live in the community (Bott 1976) — but in other cases the treatment failure will hinge around the ward's failure to involve the patient's family adequately. Obviously there is a possibility that ward staff will take an interest in family work with such cases and the family therapist should endeavour to start working with such families, albeit on an experimental basis.

It is also possible to convince staff to experiment in more fundamental ways which can lead to the adoption of a more family and community-orientated approach. However, in order to make any moves in this direction it is necessary to develop a theoretical understanding of the relationship between the mental hospital and the community. Unfortunately, I do not have sufficient space to provide an in-depth analysis of these issues, but the following section of the chapter, coupled with a brief description of a project undertaken at Glenside Hospital in Bristol, is hopefully sufficient to give the reader some ideas of how an initiative can be developed.

A number of researchers, including Mechanic (1969), have suggested that admission to psychiatric hospital occurs primarily as a result of decisions taken by members of the community. Paradoxically, laymen believe the exact reverse — that it is 'medical' decisions taken in the light of expert knowledge that result in hospitalization. Research has clearly demonstrated that admission is not just a simple process dependent on diagnosis and severity of symptoms. The definitive work of Goldberg and Huxley (1980) has given us the clearest picture of the psychiatrist's role in admission procedures. In their study of the differing factors influencing the passage of individuals from the community via primary medical care to specialist psychiatric services, they have demonstrated that psychiatrists do not act as the main gatekeepers of in-patient beds. This surprising fact is true especially in relation to cases of severe disturbance. Psychiatrists thus do little more than vet lay decisions.

The paradoxical nature of admission procedures has been most usefully explored in this country by Scott and his colleagues at Napsbury Hospital (Scott and Ashworth 1967; Scott 1973). Scott has argued that most culturally prevalent views of mental illness stress the diminished responsibility and diminished rationality of sufferers. Such stereotyped views become operative at the point of breakdown — family members can no longer tolerate the disturbed behaviour of the identified patient who is treated as though he has no right to participate in any decisions concerning his future. He is now seen as mad and out of control, and it is assumed by the family that only medical intervention and hospitalization can solve the problem. Thus, they seek to abdicate responsibility for the patient's future, and to place him in other hands. If the complex interactions involved in the crisis leading to the admission are not examined by the staff who make initial contact with the patient and his family, then there is a very real risk that the family's tactics will go unchallenged. This has very important repercussions since, as Langsley and Kaplan (1968) have demonstrated, if a crisis is resolved by admission then admission will become the family's preferred solution in future crises.

Scott originally tackled this problem by initiating weekly meetings on his admission wards which involved both patients and their families. It proved possible to challenge the position taken up by both patients and their families in such a way that major changes could be established. The success of this approach led him to instigate a 24-hour crisis intervention service, which involved all potential admissions and their family being interviewed at home by members of his team (Scott and Starr 1981). The aim of this crucial meeting was to lower the tension within the family so that all the medical, psychological and social dimensions of the crisis could be explored. Only 25 per cent of cases were eventually admitted, although the majority of the remainder received some other form of short-term therapy.

Clearly there are benefits deriving from this approach: admissions and self-harm rates are decreased, and the admissions that do occur are of shorter duration. It is better too to start work with patients and their families when issues concern the needs of the patient and the family (and their mutual responsibility for the crisis surrounding the threatened admissions) have been brought into the open.

Scott's work has been substantially supported by related work by Bruggen and his colleagues, and by Cooklin. Bruggen et al. (1973) have described how issues involved in admission can be a very useful focus for work in a regional adolescent unit. Staff carefully examine issues of responsibility and the exact reasons for referral with referring agents, the family and the adolescent prior to admission being made. Cooklin (1974) has demonstrated how a formal written contract between staff and patient in an adult psychiatric in-patient unit can be used to clarify some of the issues, after admission. The

contract was agreed during a meeting between members of staff and
the patient and, often, members of the family. This meeting was
held within 48 hours of admission. Exact reasons for admission and
the stated needs of the family and the patient were carefully identified
and explored and then some estimation of appropriate therapy,
length of stay and degree of agreement between staff and patient
concerning these issues was recorded.

The reported success of this system was the inspiration for a
similar change in procedure in an acute admission ward serving the
District within which I worked. Here the emphasis on shared
responsibility for admission, therapy and discharge — established
when making the contract — was reinforced for both staff and
patients by small bi-weekly group meetings. The results of these
procedural changes were reported by Cook and Skeldon (1980).
They showed that although admission and readmission rates were
unaffected, average length of admission was significantly reduced.
Both studies stress the careful preparatory work required with all
staff members to get the changes off the ground, and the continued
intensive work necessary to maintain them. However, to balance
this they also report clear benefits in terms of staff morale and
clarity of subsequent therapy with patients. Despite these published
benefits, the contract admission system reported by Cook and Skeldon
did not survive several staff changes on the ward and no longer
existed within a year of publication of this paper. It is interesting to
note that a significant number of the enthusiastic staff who instigated
this system now work largely with families in a community-based
setting.

The lesson from the literature and my local experience seems to
be that significant useful changes can be made if admission issues
are tackled. Such work sets subsequent therapy, of whatever nature,
in a clear framework where issues of responsibility have been made
explicit and dealt with as honestly and appropriately as possible.
Such work is, however, innovative and may therefore meet opposition
from clients, families and other professionals (as Scott has shown).
It is also labour-intensive and so requires considerable commitment
from all team members to maintain it.

Obviously a family therapy-orientated ward would be expected to
introduce such a scheme to control its admission procedure, but it is
important to stress that Cooklin's important innovation took place
without a thorough-going family orientation being established. In

our experience, ward staff are very aware of the manipulative behaviour of patients and their families, and are therefore sympathetic to approaches which prevent staff from being caught up in such patterns of behaviour. Contract-making is, of course, ideal therapy for establishing boundaries, and can provide a link with the more interventionist techniques of family therapy. Needless to say, many other forms of therapy also adopt a contract-orientated approach, so it is clear that the introduction of contract-making is likely to be a very important area in which a family therapist can make progress in attempting to change a ward towards a more family- and network-orientated approach.

CLINICAL STRATEGIES FOR A FAMILY-ORIENTATED IN-PATIENT UNIT

Admission

Ideally a family interview should take place *prior* to admission, so that the family is clear that its responsibility for its 'sick' member does not terminate at the point of admission. (See Bruggen and O'Brian 1982, for an extended discussion of this issue.) If this interview has not taken place then it is advisable to conduct a family interview on the ward as soon as possible after admission. Prior to this interview, the family should be requested to come with the 'patient' to the ward. A well-organized reception procedure should be implemented so that the family tours the facilities of the ward. At the same time the ward's policy of family involvement is made clear and an appointment for the first family session is fixed.

Since nursing staff usually adopt the role of receiving patients on the ward, it is advisable that they should take on the role of receiving the family and the patient. Obviously the reception procedure itself may well generate important information which will be of value to the family therapist in beginning the first session. Before the first session takes place a family therapist will need to be assigned to the family but, given the likely complexity of the family, it is essential that this therapist has a co-worker who acts as a supervisor.

First family interview

Clearly the first interview with the family can be decisive in determining the success of the hospital phase of treatment. Often a family has not met together to discuss its problems and difficulties so there is likely to be considerable anxiety or hostility generated. The family may well feel that it is being blamed for the predicament of the identified patient, hence they may be on the defensive. Alternatively, they may insist that the hospital staff are solely responsible for getting the patient better.

Patterns of presentation are, in fact, very varied and difficult to predict, so it is essential that a considerable length of time (two and a half to three hours) is set aside for this interview, so that the therapist can take long consultation breaks during the course of the interview, should the need arise. A rushed first interview which does not result in a firm contract being negotiated between the ward, the patient and the family can lead to serious setbacks. Often the interview can be brief, because the family has a great sense of relief at being involved as a family; some families, however, may create difficulties for the therapist which need to be resolved before progress can be made.

The opening phase of the interview should be concerned with explaining ward policy and answering the family's questions about exactly what is going to happen while the patient is on the ward. The therapist should state clearly that the ward does not believe that family members are to blame for the patient's difficulties, but that a supportive and consistent family atmosphere can help restore the patient's health. Many families have very firm ideas about the causation of 'mental illness' and will want to share their ideas with the therapist. The therapist should hear them out, but at the same time she should be thinking of ways to build a bridge between her own position and that of the family.

If the family is fairly relaxed as a result of this approach, then the therapist will be able to begin to establish how the patient and the family define the problem that has resulted in hospitalization. Great care needs to be taken at this stage — the family may well wish to deliver a very long pejorative history of the patient. The therapist's skill, on the other hand, hinges around getting a problem-orientated, here-and-now account, which will allow specific treatment goals to be set. This means that she must be able to listen emphatically to each family member's account, but not cut in too early to shift the mood in a positive direction. As Harbin (1982) stresses, allowing the family to ventilate their feelings at length is an essential part of this first interview. They see themselves as being greatly burdened by the often intolerable behaviour of the patient — it is essential therefore that the therapist mobilizes her joining skills so that the family feels that their views have been heard and understood.

In practice such a tactic may well prove difficult for a therapist who may feel more sympathetic towards the patient. It is the task of the live consultant to prevent the therapist from reacting thus. If this phase of the interview is successfully completed then the therapist can begin to shift the focus of the interview away from the problem itself. In practice it is best to take time out in the interview after the 'problem phase' has been completed. This enables the therapist and consultant to confer so that the next phase of the interview can concentrate on (a) reframing the problem; (b) establishing goals for treatment.

Reframing psychiatrically-presented problems is an art in itself. Fortunately the work of Erickson, described in Haley (1973), and, more recently, Bandler and Grinder (1982) provides us with rich examples of how to proceed. Reframing forms an essential phase of the first interview in hospital because it helps to arrest the processes which underpin the move to hospitalize the patient. For example, a patient who has become deeply anxious about the depth of her depression and her inability to 'snap out of it' at the behest of her family can be comforted by the suggestion that her depression may be meaningful and that she should not give it up until she has made the changes in her life which would stop her from becoming depressed.

If the therapist and her supervisor are successful in generating some workable reframes during their time out, then the session continues with these reframes being communicated to the family. If they are accepted by the family, then the interview can move to its final phase — the setting of goals. This part of the interview is primarily concerned with clarifying the underlying issues which need to be worked on. In practice, since long-term admission is rarely advocated as part of this approach, the setting of goals hinges around issues such as the frequency of family sessions, the nature of the topics to be explored in these sessions and the basis upon which discharge of the patient is likely to occur. With more compliant families who are eager to cooperate, such goals can be set easily but it is essential to build the goals to suit the family. For example, a highly anxious family which is also hostile to the ward may only return to a further session on the basis that the therapist is stuck and unable to help the patient unless she gains further information from the family.

It is essential, however, not to move to 'descapegoat' the identified patient at an early stage in the treatment. To do so is to move counter-systemically, and hence to meet the maximum resistance of the family who, at this point, has a large investment in maintaining that it is the patient that is the problem. It is the task of the subsequent interviews to begin to work on this issue.

Consolidation phase

If a successful first interview has been achieved and the family has been successfully joined, then treatment can enter a consolidation (or middle) phase. Goals for discharge are raised and discussed but most of the work is concerned with discussing the patient's brief return visits to home. It may seem paradoxical to some observers that leave of absence from the hospital should be suggested so early, but it is an essential feature of the brief hospitalization approach suggested by Harbin and other workers. The work of Spitzer and his colleagues is particularly significant in this respect, since he has demonstrated the value of very brief hospital stays in enhancing family functioning, helping the earlier resumption of occupational roles and preventing other damaging effects associated with more standard lengths of stay in hospital (Herz et al. 1976; Spitzer et al. 1982). In essence this tactic is designed to prevent the family from engaging in what Scott has described as 'closure', i.e. functioning as though the identified patient was no longer a family member (Scott and Ashworth 1967).

During the leave period the family is invited to undertake homework tasks which are designed to solve the problem which it has reported during prior sessions with the therapist. The advantage of a brief leave of absence is obvious since the family does not feel that it is being forced to make massive changes on a 'go-it-alone' basis. If the experiments prove unsuccessful then the next family session can redesign the tasks, following an appropriate investigation of how they failed. If the tasks succeed, the family's morale will have been strengthened, new therapeutic initiatives can be opened up, and discharge becomes a realistic possibility.

Discharge

Clearly a planned discharge is crucial since there are very real dangers of relapse as the identified patient returns home. A significant remission of the presenting symptom, coupled with concrete evidence that the family has successfully undertaken its homework tasks, form the basis for discharge. However, it is essential that there should be continuity in the treatment, so that the family is not neglected at the point at which the hospital phase of treatment is completed. In practice it may prove very difficult to maintain continuity because of the way mental health services are organized. The hospital may have a very large catchment area so that it would be utopian for the hospital-based therapist to continue therapy with the family on an outpatient basis. If the hospital-based worker cannot offer further sessions to the family, a community-based family therapist needs to be involved. If a transfer is to be successfully achieved, a joint meeting between the two therapists and the family needs to be undertaken. Such 'transfer' meetings can prove very successful if handled correctly, but it is essential that the new therapist and her co-worker are aware of the family's need to disengage from the previous therapists. At the same time she must acknowledge the family's need to engage with her. One of the best ways of achieving the changeover is to invite the family to review the progress of the therapy so far, and in particular to identify which elements of the therapy have proved most successful. By building on these strengths the 'new' therapist can create an alliance with the 'old' and a sense of continuity with previous work.

My outline of the hospital phase of treatment has been very schematic, and I would recommend my readers to consult the more detailed work of Harbin (1982). However, it is essential that I complete this section of the chapter by briefly exploring the role that other forms of treatment may play during the in-patient phase. It should be clear from the emphasis of this chapter that I would expect a family-orientated ward to emphasize the significance of the family therapy session. However, this does not mean that the significance of other forms of treatment is reduced.

Medication clearly plays an important role as far as highly disturbed patients are concerned. Often very acute symptoms can be controlled so that a very disturbed patient is able to keep in touch with his family and others. This is clearly important in preventing mutual rejection — but other positive aspects of medication must also be appreciated by family therapists. If patients find drugs beneficial it is hazardous for any therapist to suggest otherwise; I would generally advocate that family therapists should avoid disputes over medication. As Palazzoli and Prata (1982) have argued, it is best to adopt a respectful attitude to the medication and advise the client to continue taking the drugs. If the client complains about taking the drugs then he should be advised to raise the issue with his doctor who must have felt the drugs were appropriate. By adopting this tactic the family therapist avoids the pitfall of trying to compete with another form of therapy.

A patient's involvement in the social and group life of the ward can also have profound effects (for example, in raising self-esteem), while involvement in occupational therapy may either revitalize old skills or help to create new ones. Concurrent individual psychotherapy can also play its part in boosting self-esteem and enabling the patient to feel legitimate as a person. Truly systemic thinking will encompass all these dimensions of ward life, but the crucial requirement for the systems therapist is that any gains that the hospitalized patient makes should be channelled back into the matrix of the family, so that the gains are not sabotaged by countervailing forces within the family system.

Having completed our review of general tactics for developing family therapy, it is essential that we discuss briefly, the issue of family therapy models.

ADOPTING A FAMILY THERAPY APPROACH
SUITABLE FOR IN-PATIENT UNITS

One of the major problems created by the family therapy movement is the current cornucopia of different theoretical approaches. In choosing which approach to adopt, we may be helped by the observations of Lansky (1981):

> An application of family therapy principles to the predicaments posed by major psychiatric illness must consider the overall goal of coping with the illness and minimizing its effects. It is not sufficient to treat the family in isolation with the sole aim of reducing conflict. A new eclecticism is required based on rational strategies designed to overcome specific psychopathologic obstacles

appearing as specific treatment difficulties. Such obstacles include pathologic features found in schizophrenia, affective disorders, personality disorders and symptomatic manifestations thereof, and organic brain syndromes, as well as the problems of narcissistic vulnerability, medication discontinuance and family psychotherapy in the hospital.

Obviously Lansky's work is not solely concerned with patients who require hospitalization but it is clear that his approach would include hospitalization as part of an overall strategy designed to overcome the specific psychopathological deficits of particular patients. Many family therapists would take exception to Lansky's position because they would insist that it involves abandoning an interactionist perspective, but I would counter this argument by insisting that his approach is potentially compatible with the integrative approaches of therapists such as Feldman (1976; 1979) who have stressed the importance of multi-level models in explaining the behaviour of family systems. Feldman's discussion of depression (1976) is particularly valuable and provides an excellent conceptual framework for integrating individual and marital therapy.

For want of a better term I have chosen to call Lansky's approach the 'specific treatment' approach. Much of the recent work on schizophrenic families can be included in this category. The communication and problem-solving approach developed by Liberman, Aitchison and Falloon (Falloon 1981) is perhaps the most influential, since it is the logical outcome of a long-established research tradition which has focused on the significance of the emotional atmosphere of schizophrenic families and its effects on the rehabilitation of schizophrenic patients (Brown et al. 1972; Hirsch and Leff 1975; Leff 1979). Related work by Anderson and Reiss (1982) is also important, but the pioneering work of Laqueur (1981) with multiple family groups should not be overlooked. Laqueur's programme was specifically designed for the families of hospitalized schizophrenics. This tradition is well established in the United States (Bley 1981), but it is worth remembering that it is less radical than Bowen's approach, which involved the hospitalization of whole families (Bowen 1965).

CONCLUSION

Different types of families require different styles of therapy (see Hudson 1980) so a really well-organized in-patient unit should be able to offer different forms of therapy to suit the needs of its patients and their families. Obviously, there is, at present, a big gap between this ideal and the current situation in British mental hospitals, but like Lieberman and Cooklin (1982), I am optimistic about the future development of family therapy. I believe that, in the long term, the appeal of the approach is irresistible; however, much careful and patient work needs to be undertaken and family therapists must resist forcing the pace. At present family therapists working in mental hospitals need optimism and the survival skills that go with it. Family therapy with adult patients is a very exacting form of therapy, because it goes so much against the grain, but its outcome can be rewarding for both families and therapists alike.

I would like to end this chapter with a word of caution to the enthusiast. Ideally, the would-be family therapist who is intent on working with in-patients and their families should attempt to develop her basic family therapy skills in out-patient settings. Having gained some solid experience in such a setting, it is possible to graduate to working in in-patient settings. Perhaps my position is over-cautious but I certainly believe that all in-patient work is more challenging and more difficult than out-patient work. It would indeed be surprising if family therapy proved an exception.

11

Working Together: Supervision, Consultancy and Co-working

JOHN CARPENTER

In 1962, Haley observed: 'Just as many swimmers who are wary about drowning will associate with a life saver, so do many family therapists prefer company when they dive into a family' (Haley 1962). There is no denying that 'diving into' a family is a difficult task, especially if you work for an agency which is unsupportive or even hostile to your approach — in this case company is especially important. In this chapter I will review the ways in which people can work together, both for mutual support and in order to provide a more effective way of helping families.

Perhaps one of the most striking factors in the use of family therapy has been the extent to which workers have been prepared to practise 'in the open'. I have no doubt that it is this willingness to share their work which enables family therapists to develop their skills and self-confidence. Whether by meeting and discussing in support groups, or by working in pairs or teams, practitioners can create opportunities to help each other in the task of learning to use family therapy. I will begin by reviewing the various forms of co-working and then consider how people can prepare effectively for working together. In the final section I will discuss consultancy and support groups.

CO-WORKING

Family therapists usually distinguish only two methods of co-working: co-therapy and live 'supervision', but the use of the latter term is problematic. As Brown has pointed out, the term 'supervisor' is usually restricted to a person who has formally delegated authority over a supervisee (Brown 1984). The supervision itself has four main functions: managerial, supportive, educational, and consultative. Thus so-called live 'supervision' (which normally involves one worker being in the room with a family while a colleague watches from behind the screen) obviously only meets Brown's criteria if this colleague is functioning as a manager. If the relationship is a peer relationship then 'consultancy' is a far better term, since this implies a voluntary rather than a hierarchical relationship. (It should be noted, however, that the term 'live supervision' should be retained in order to describe training based on live supervised practice. A trainer using live supervised practice carries a responsibility for the families with whom the trainee works and therefore has managerial as well as educational and supportive functions.) Brown classifies the familiar method, in which one worker is behind a one-way screen and the other with the family, as a form of 'participant consultancy'. He defines the consultant's primary task as enabling the worker to help the family more effectively, and notes that she achieves this by giving advice, comments (and sometimes instructions) and by the use of 'time out'. 'Consultancy' is clearly a more accurate term than supervision but it still does not encompass the complexity of the situation in which the consultant is actually present and active.

Thus, although Kingston and Smith (1983) describe their work as 'live consultancy in the room', the 'consultant' does far more than advise the 'therapist'. It is clear from their description, and from my own experience of this method, that the consultant is very much a part of the therapeutic system and is perceived as such by the family. The 'advice' she gives is not for the therapist's ears alone. Similarly, as I will describe later, if the 'consultant' is behind a screen, she can make interventions into the family system in her own right, either by entering the room or by sending 'messages' to the family by telephone or 'bug'. The strategic use of these interventions takes these methods of work beyond 'consultation', and it might be more accurate to refer to them as 'team' methods.

Co-therapy

Different models of family therapy have sired different methods of co-working in accordance with the ways in which change is said to be achieved. Thus, 'psychoanalytic' family therapists make use of co-therapy: two workers, preferably male and female, allow themselves, and their own relationship, to be 'sucked in' to the family system, so 'mirroring' the collusive pathological nature of the marital relationship. The co-therapy couple model a resolution of the collusive relationship for the marital couple by first experiencing and then making explicit the unconscious fears and assumptions of the family. A consultancy group assists the co-therapists in exploring the dynamics of their own relationship and, therefore, frees them to interpret 'the transference' in the next session with the family. Interpretation of the transference is the vehicle of change. (Byng-Hall et al. 1982).

It is probably inevitable that co-therapy enhances transference, encourages identification and provides an influential model relationship for the family. These processes are grist to the analyst's mill and, as I have indicated, are carefully understood and 'worked through'. However, what is essential in this model is either an unnecessary complication or a handicap in another. As we have argued previously, unless the co-therapists intend to process this material, they have no business to enhance its production in the first place (Carpenter et al. 1983). Unfortunately, all too often co-therapy is seized upon either as a convenient solution to the organizational problem of having to provide work for two therapists, or as an inappropriate means of providing mutual support. The relationships so formed are often on an *ad hoc* basis, and with little or no commitment to examining their dynamics and development. It must be remembered that co-therapists take their own relationships, with all their unresolved problems and difficulties, into the formation of the therapeutic system. If the resulting therapy is unsuccessful, it will be quite inappropriate to blame the family.

I do not, therefore, recommend co-therapy as a method for other than psychoanalytically-inspired family therapy. It can be a most unhelpful solution to an organizational problem. If mutual support is what is required, other methods of co-working are more appropriate, as I will describe later.

Live 'consultancy': the structural model

Structural family therapists are concerned to challenge directly the family's patterns of organization. The family's capacity to absorb the therapist is therefore seen as unhelpful, or worse, since she can be 'trapped' into obeying their rules, thus re-inforcing the problematic relationships which brought the family into therapy in the first place. The co-worker, therefore, distances herself from the therapeutic system (family plus therapist) in order to perceive the process of therapy more clearly. Her task is to prevent her colleague being drawn away from her function as change agent, and to help her recover control and direction. Montalvo, in a seminal paper on this subject, stresses the consultant's responsibility not just for the progress of therapy with the family, but also for the working relationship with the 'therapist' (Montalvo 1973).

Montalvo's paper emphasizes the sensitivity required by the consultant. She must not inhibit the therapist's freedom of exploration and operation too much. The suggestions which she makes must be carefully designed to fit the therapist's personal style, so they must be neither too frequent, nor too vague or equivocal. This is a subtle process, for, as he points out, the consultant's input can also be 'strategically correct, well timed and well phrased, yet accompanied by just enough of a discordant mood to disrupt the therapist's performance' (Montalvo 1973, p. 358).

Montalvo's presentation is an important corrective to a prevailing caricature of 'supervision' in structural family therapy. This view sees consultants as intrusive, all-knowing beings who seize upon the therapist's slightest error as an excuse to appear in the therapy room itself and 'take over' the work, thus rendering the therapist incompetent for the remainder of the session. On the contrary, Montalvo asserts that the consultant's job, at its unintrusive best, is to suggest something for the therapist to do which will reveal new aspects of the family's behaviour in such a way that the therapist can react usefully. Almost simultaneously, the family are helped to change and the therapist to regain her effectiveness. Montalvo emphasizes that the model is one of 'mutual consent and collaboration'. His exposition certainly stresses this aspect, and I would agree that it can be a highly effective method of co-working between peers, so long as the emphasis is placed upon collaboration and not competition.

Working as a 'team': a 'strategic' approach

In a number of settings, such as the Day Hospital described by Harry Procter and Trish Stephens (chapter 8), and the Family Institute, Cardiff (Speed et al. 1982), a 'team' approach to therapy has been developed, based on the work of the Milan Group (Palazzoli et al. 1978). The therapeutic method rests on the creation of 'systemic' hypotheses regarding family interaction, the technique of 'circular' questioning, and on 'strategic' interventions, usually delivered at the end of the session in the form of a prescription. In this team approach, it is important to recognise that the 'therapist', the person in the room with the family, only has exclusive responsibility for asking the questions. In fact, because the model does not assume that the 'therapist' will actively try to change the family in the session itself, I prefer to describe her in this method as the 'interviewer', thereby stressing that she is but part of the team. The team, as a whole, has the responsibility for effecting change.

Of course, as Breunlin and Cade (1981) point out, the 'observers' (those members of the team behind the screen) can intervene to unbalance both the family system *and* the therapeutic system. Including the therapist as part of the target system adds a new dimension to the therapy, for as Breunlin and Cade note, the observers can disagree with the therapist, triangulating family, therapist and themselves. This tactic, together with the use of divided opinions and deliberately confusing or mysterious messages, seems to have considerable potential in situations where the therapeutic process has become 'stuck'. (See also Papp 1980.)

Live 'consultancy' in the room

Our colleagues, Donna Smith and Philip Kingston (1980) originally developed this method of co-working, because they did not have the facility of a one-way screen. The co-worker sits in the room a little back from the therapist and family so that she cannot be easily absorbed into the therapeutic system. Like a supervisor behind a screen, she concentrates on the process of the interview and makes interventions through the therapist. Of course, these interventions can be heard by the family; consultancy thus adds a new dimension to the process of therapy. (I shall return to this later.)

Smith and Kingston discovered that this method has clear advantages over co-therapy. There is a clear distinction of roles between the co-workers which reduces competitiveness and enables one of the pair to perceive the process of therapy more clearly. In addition, because the roles can be alternated with different families, both workers can experience the problems and strengths inherent in each role and avoid the difficulty of becoming trapped in fixed complementary roles. Compared with live consultation using a screen, the process and issues in the family appear more immediate and 'alive', and the concentration and commitment of the co-worker can be enhanced. Her interventions can be made much more rapidly, without the delay of a telephone call, and thus the moment to intervene, which is important in some methods of family therapy, will not be lost. On the other hand, this immediacy carries with it a very real danger of the consultant being drawn in as a co-therapist. Because it violates the usual rules of social interaction in that she does not talk directly to the family, the consultant's role requires a lot of practice.

This method, therefore, is far from being a 'second best' for workers in agencies which do not have much in the way of technical resources. The very fact that it does not require video equipment and one-way screens, means that it can be used in a wide variety of situations and settings, from an interview on the ward of a psychiatric hospital to a home visit. I will therefore describe the method in more detail, drawing heavily on the work of Kingston and his colleagues (Smith and Kingston 1980; Ainley and Kingston 1981; Kingston and Smith 1983). In doing so, I will adopt the terms 'therapist' and 'consultant' to describe the two roles in the situation of peers working together.

At the beginning of the first interview, the therapist introduces the consultant to the family: 'My colleague is here to help me to help you. To make sure that I don't miss important points, she will sit a little back from the rest of us and will say something to me if it will help us. Some time during the course of the interview we will take a break in order to put our heads together and share our opinions.' The consultant, for her part, has the somewhat difficult task of joining with the family from a relatively detached position. This process can be helped by the consultant (as well as the therapist) welcoming the family at the beginning of the session, and by her making an intervention to encourage and praise them a short way into the interview. For example, it is often appropriate to say to the therapist: 'It's always difficult for families to talk about their problems in front of people they don't know. I'm most impressed by how frank and open the family are today.'

The range of intervention open to the consultant is similar to that in other methods of co-working (excluding co-therapy). She can help the therapist to structure and focus the interview, point out problems and processes which her colleague has not recognized, and re-frame family members' and the therapist's behaviour and opinions. She can also use her instructions or observations to the therapist as a means of covertly intervening in the family system. The family members are usually most attentive to the consultant's remarks and, because they are not made directly to them, family members do not have a straightforward 'right of reply' to the consultant. Such interventions are, therefore, more difficult to disqualify, so long as the consultant maintains her role.

Therapist and consultant should meet before the interview to share hypotheses and make plans. There should be a pre-arranged meeting, approximately 15 minutes before the end of the session, in order to consider tactics and strategy, and both parties should be prepared to call 'time out' during the session. 'Time out' should always be called if either therapist or consultant is unsure about, or wishes to change, the direction of the therapy. However, Kingston and Smith (1983) suggest that this should not occur more than three times in the interview lest it foster doubts in the family's mind about the competence of their workers!

At the end of the session, the co-workers should meet in order to discuss not only the family and the process of the interview, but also their own relationship. Preparedness to talk about this matter is possibly one of the essential requirements for effective co-working, whatever the method chosen. Since, in my experience, it is such a neglected area, it seems appropriate to round off this discussion of co-working by noting some of the important factors which must be taken into account if two people are to work together successfully.

PREPARING TO WORK TOGETHER

Russell and Russell (1979) stress that a pairing must be a 'workable match'. There is no advantage in two people or a group working together simply because no one else is available — co-working can be used and abused. Kingston and Smith (1983) have listed a number of issues to be resolved *before* agreeing to work together, whatever the method. If these issues cannot be resolved then it is surely better not to begin.

Potential co-workers should first establish:

1   Whether they have (or are prepared to develop) a reasonable
    congruence in the theoretical and practical bases of their
    work, including a belief in the value of co-working. (Since
    labels like 'strategic', 'psychodynamic', or 'systemic' are used
    rather loosely, it is probably a good idea to discuss in detail
    how they might handle a particular case referred to the agency
    and/or to review cases which they have previously dealt with
    separately.) They should also be prepared to rehearse their
    work together, perhaps by role-playing in a support group with
    colleagues, or by attending a training course. They must
    recognize that the development of a good working relationship
    takes time.
2   Whether they respect each other professionally and personally,
    and are prepared to commit themselves to work at difficulties
    as they arise. This includes the open discussion of sex and role
    differences, hierarchical differences, and differences in
    personal beliefs and values. They must recognize that the
    outcome of their work will be a *shared responsibility.*

If a pair, or a team, do agree to work together on this basis, there
are a number of general issues which should be discussed:

1   The fact that all workers have the right 'not to know'. This is
    especially true in live consultation and team work, where the
    consultant or team can become incapacitated by the
    responsibility to provide useful answers. It must be
    acknowledged that there are times when no answers are
    forthcoming — therapy is often a struggle.
2   Arrangements to experience all the different roles used in the
    method.
3   Administrative arrangements, including record-keeping, room
    bookings, correspondence with the family and with other
    agencies, etc.
4   Agreement to work together for a specified length of time or
    with a specified number of families, and to build in occasional
    meetings with a third party to review the co-working
    relationship.

Finally, the co-workers must agree the 'ground-rules' for the
sessions themselves. These will vary somewhat, according to the

method used. (See Walrond-Skinner (1976), chapter 6, on co-therapy; Montalvo (1973) on 'consultation' with a screen; Breunlin and Cade (1981) on team working; and Kingston and Smith (1983) on consultation in the room.) However, some common points can be made:

1 Pre- *and* post-session discussions are essential.
2 Positive and negative comments on each others' performances should be made.

In relation to live consultation and team work, the following should be agreed:

3 How interventions from the consultant or team can be made (e.g. by phone, ear-bug, coming into the room, catching the therapist's eye). Also, the procedure for both parties calling 'time out'.
4 A rule for the status of these interventions, e.g. if 'must' is used, it must be done; if 'may', it is only a suggestion.
5 How to introduce the method to the family (including 'consent' forms, if the interview is to be audio- or video-taped).

In my experience, it is very rare for a family to make objections to co-working. If the workers themselves believe that the method they have chosen is going to be helpful, then their confidence will communicate itself to the family.

ADDITIONAL CONSULTANCY

Any co-working pair or team will need to refer from time to time to somebody outside the co-working system. This situation usually arises because they are 'stuck' with a case and require a consultant's help in identifying and overcoming the problem. The exact source of the impasse can be difficult to establish; it may occur because of difficulties within the supervisory and co-working systems (professional colleagues), as well as in the therapeutic system (therapist plus family). Given this degree of complexity, it is essential that the consultant is familiar not only with the model of therapy being used, but also with the structure of the agency in which it is practised (Carpenter, et al. 1983).

Since Brown (1984) has provided an excellent and detailed

discussion of consultancy, I will confine myself to a discussion of 'support' groups which are probably the most widely used method of consultation in family therapy practice.

Support groups

According to Brown's schema, there are two types of support group. The 'facilitated' support group involves workers meeting together with a designated facilitator or leader who is not their agency supervisor. Peer group consultancy, on the other hand, involves members taking collective responsibility for its functioning. Brown points out that both types of group are, nevertheless, dependent for their success on thorough preparation. They are greatly influenced by the extent to which the members already know one another and whether they come from one or more agencies.

If a support group is to be formed within an agency, it is most important to discuss it with all relevant staff, especially line managers so that the function and membership of the group can be clarified. As Adams (1980) notes, a group cannot function effectively within a team or agency without a mandate. It is essential that the relationship between the consultation group and the supervisors of the consultees is clearly stated: formal authority rests with the agency supervisors — the consultancy provided by the group carries no such authority. To define the relationship otherwise, or to leave it undefined, is to invite suspicion and even hostility. Invoking an old adage, I would observe that the creation of an 'in-group' creates an 'out group'. An in-group which defines itself in terms of special expertise in a new therapeutic approach (which also requires novel methods of 'supervision') defines the out-group of agency supervisors and colleagues most unfavourably. A consultation group which is set up with the agency's blessing is much more likely to be successful than one which threatens to 'subvert' the organization or make line managers 'redundant'.

Adams (1980) reports that a group forming in a social services office found it necessary to 'spell out the reasons why we thought working on family therapy would be helpful in the agency.' This involved them in some lengthy discussion about what they meant by 'family therapy', and was a most appropriate place to start. Having been a member of a number of different support groups of varying duration, I recognize, in retrospect, that the most successful were those which clarified assumptions about knowledge and expectations at an early stage.

In my experience too, support groups often confuse two functions — training and consultation. Thus members will often join a group not so much because they require support and consultation in using family therapy in their work, but rather, because they hope to learn basic skills. (See Mills and Cullum 1982.) If this is indeed the case, then I would recommend either that they attend a training course first, or alternatively, that the group redefines itself as a 'training group'. If one of its members has experience and skills in training, then it is probably best to 'appoint' this member as 'group trainer' and avoid both ambiguity in task and confusion in leadership. If an outside trainer, and funds, are available then this would be the ideal solution but if no one with expertise can be found, then a peer-learning group working to a fixed programme is a possibility.

Some guidelines

I have already noted that peer consultation groups can be facilitated or leaderless. Iveson et al. (1979) describe a facilitated group in a Social Services Department, but most family therapy support groups have no defined leader, and it is to these that I turn my attention. (However, many of the same issues arise in facilitated groups.)

1   Groups can be *closed* or *open*, i.e. with fixed or changing membership. The former usually enable trust and cohesion to develop more quickly. Commitment to attendance is stronger, but long-term closed groups run the danger of becoming inward-looking and stale. Open groups bring in new members with new ideas, but the group has the additional task of coping with changing membership; too frequent changes lead to instability and discontinuity (Brown 1984). There are advantages in a semi-closed group which runs 'closed' for a mutually agreed term, but takes in new members at agreed intervals.

2   The setting up of *multi-agency groups* may require careful negotiation with managers who may be concerned about issues of confidentiality and accountability. (Mills and Cullum 1982).

3   The *task* should be defined as 'consultancy' in relation to the

members' practice of family therapy, covering work with families and other systems, including the members' own agency systems. Attention should be given as to how the group can meet separate interests, needs and aims of the different members.

4 It should be recognized that the group, like all formed groups will go through various *stages of development,* characterized by Tuckman (1965) as 'Forming, Storming, Norming and Performing'. The group will therefore need to pay more or less explicit attention to its own internal processes, but Brown (1984) warns against the 'process trap' in which the group becomes so self-obsessed that it becomes akin to a 'sensitivity' group, and the task of providing a better service to clients recedes into the distance. I might also observe that mere survival is not necessarily proof of usefulness.

5 A consultancy group should agree on the *method* by which it will carry out its task. It should consider how often it needs to meet and how it will allocate the time between its members so that they all have an adequate opportunity to present their own cases and concerns. The *frequency of meetings* will depend on the members' commitment to family therapy, the extent to which they practise, and the size of the group. We recommend that a group meet between one and four times a month, for a period of about an hour and a half. This allows one worker, or pair of workers 45–60 minutes consultancy, with the remainder of the time used to review previous consultations and to deal with business items. I have found that the time can be used much more profitably if *case material* is presented by means of short extracts of video- or audio-tape or by sculpting. Long verbal reports followed by group members' questions rarely generate helpful consultation. A consultancy group is not a discussion group — its task is to provide concrete advice about what to do, and this can only be achieved if the consultees bring specific cases or issues into the group and the other members recommend specific courses of action. It is often helpful to role-play these suggestions and, if possible even to bring a family to the group for a 'live' consultation (Hack and Hindle 1982).

As a further development, Fernandez et al. (1983) have recently described a 'family clinic' set up within a social services area office by members of a support group. They meet for three to four hours each week and work as a team with up to two families each session. There seems much to be said for such a disciplined and thorough approach to mastering new skills, as opposed to isolated and piecemeal attempts by individual practitioners.

Although I have emphasized *practice* rather than *theory,* I do think that it is important to relate the two. Group members, as all therapists, should always keep in mind their own 'theory of change' so that they can estimate what actions on the part of the therapist will promote change. Of course there are many such theories and, unless there is a general agreement amongst the group to restrict their range of suggestions to those which would derive from one, or perhaps two, models of family therapy, the consultee is likely to be frustrated or bemused. There are advantages to a group deciding to work for a specified time using one model only — consultancy is then more straightforward and learning is more usefully promoted.

6 It might seem contradictory to mention *leadership* in a discussion of leaderless groups but, in my experience, it is always an issue. It is frequently a problem for the initiator of a group, who then tends to get left with the organization and administration. These tasks, along with responsibility for the group's process, must be defined rapidly as being shared by all members. Brown (1984) suggests that this usually works best when key functions are identified and allocated to different members, perhaps in rotation. These functions might include: arrangements for rooms and equipment; recording; letter writing; and chairing each meeting. Allocation of these tasks reminds group members that responsibility for consultancy is also shared — members must give as well as take.

7 Finally, we should take note of Adams's observation that, once consultancy groups become cohesive, they will 'disturb their social environments and therefore must negotiate a "foreign policy" ' (Adams 1980). A group can become an alternative power base within an agency and will have to decide the extent to which it can, and wants to, take collective action on identified issues, such as the allocation of the agency's training budget or the job description of a new post.

CONCLUSION

The first step for a worker seeking to use family therapy is to find a friend — someone with whom she can practise and learn. There is as yet no research evidence for the superior effectiveness of co-working compared to 'solo' therapy but, given the complexity of working with families, it is, in my opinion, most advisable to have company when 'taking the plunge'. Similarly, it is very important to establish a consultancy network — either an individual consultant, possibly from another agency, or a support group. Using family therapy presents a challenge not only to the worker's 'technical' skills with families, but also to her creativity in adapting the approach to the requirements of her agency. This is not a task which she should take on in isolation.

Finally, it is important to stress that the process of introducing family therapy to a new setting is more challenging still. In the final chapter of this book we will try to provide some guidelines for the swimmer who sets off alone into uncharted waters.

12

Hindsight

ANDY TREACHER AND JOHN CARPENTER

We hope that the previous chapters in this book have achieved our goal of demonstrating how family therapy can be used in different settings. In this final chapter we will attempt to establish some general conclusions about the process of developing family therapy.

In practice, drawing such conclusions is hazardous because of the genuine disparities between the settings we have compared. Indeed, many readers may feel that it is a mistake to attempt to make broad generalizations from such disparate material. We are sympathetic to such a view but at the same time we are convinced that there are some general principles that can guide anybody who attempts to develop family therapy in a new setting.

SURVIVAL SKILLS

Perhaps the first and most obvious general theme concerns the issue of survival skills. Obviously a well-trained worker who has adequate support from a co-worker, or a family therapy support group, or both, will be able to make progress in work situations that will defeat a less adequately trained worker who lacks support. Our discussion, therefore, presupposes that an innovator will have certain basic skills (through attending some form of training programme), and have established a network of colleagues who will sustain and advise her as the project gets under way. To attempt to develop the project without support would be hazardous. Work that is neither supervised nor reviewed and shared with others is likely to become either stale, or stereotyped, or may involve the therapist in taking risks which place her under great strain.

All therapists need to guard against 'burn out' and it is essential that family therapists should guard against over-extending themselves. At a practical level, the worker who is developing a family therapy approach needs to be careful not to overcommit herself. This may well mean that she chooses to use her newly-developed family therapy framework with only a few of the families on her case-load. Ideally the worker should select relatively simple cases to work on first and this means that she has to learn to say no to requests to undertake work which may be hazardous to her development. This point had already been explored in chapter 11, but we have no hesitation in drawing attention to it yet again — workers need to develop their work at *their own pace* rather than at the pace of others.

ADAPTING THE APPROACH

The second theme concerns the ways in which the theories and techniques of family therapy can most usefully be adapted to particular settings. Thus, whilst all our contributors have found it to be a useful approach, there are clear differences of emphasis in its application.

In some settings the performance of a therapeutic role is relatively straightforward — the issue here is how to establish family therapy as an important and influential part of the therapeutic programme which the agency offers. One way of achieving this is by setting up clinics, as described by Harry Procter (chapter 8) and Brian Dimmock (chapter 7). Alternatively, and perhaps more radically, an attempt can be made to establish a family-orientated service for *all* admissions to a unit (see Hugh Jenkins, chapter 3; Eddy Street, chapter 4; Andy Treacher, chapter 10).

Of course, as we argued in the Introduction, it is essential to extend our analysis, and therefore our range of interventions, beyond the family system, to include schools, neighbours and other members of the helping services (see John Carpenter, chapter 2; Sue Pottle, chapter 9). We suggested that for us family therapy should always be used in the broad sense of a 'systems approach'. As such it has considerable potential for use in the statutory social services and probation — provided that the worker remembers that she is *not* employed as a therapist (see Marjorie Ainley, chapter 6; and David Dungworth and Sigurd Reimers, chapter 7). She may combine a therapeutic role with the other roles required by the agency or, alternatively, use a systems approach to assess 'clients' and, indeed, the network of agencies with which they are involved.

Finally, it should be noted that many of us have found family therapy to be useful in understanding the work systems of which we are a part. For example, Hugh Jenkins discusses an interesting example of the way in which the staff of an adolescent unit replicated the interactional patterns of a family (chapter 3). However, with the benefit of hindsight, it has become clear to us that we have not given sufficient attention to our own agency systems and, in particular, to the crucial issue of how to introduce family therapy.

INTRODUCING FAMILY THERAPY:
TACTICS FOR GETTING STARTED

A third theme that emerges from our authors' contributions concerns tactics for getting started. The importance of starting well with a family in therapy is so obvious and well-recognized a point that it scarcely needs stating. But the same is true of a situation in which an innovator wishes to develop a new way of working within an organization. It is therefore essential to try and establish some guidelines for the initial stages of such a project. Our recommendations are derived partly from our own, and our colleagues', experience, as outlined in this book, and partly from a review of an interesting but rather inaccessible paper by the American therapist Barbara Held (1982).

Held's approach involves developing the analytic tools of family therapy in order to encompass the functioning of professional systems. In particular she focuses her attention on issues which concern the impact that the entry or exit of a member of a system has upon the system as a whole.

> Various proponents of (family) systems theory argue that the anxiety produced by change in a family system . . . can cause its members to develop coping styles or solutions that may create more problems than the anxieties they are attempting to alleviate. More specifically, a system's members' anxieties about being replaced or displaced by a new member, whether a child in a family or a new staff member in an agency, can lead the system into behaviour such as excluding, scapegoating, and forming coalitions against the new member (Held 1982).

Clearly, the extent to which the processes outlined by Held occur will depend on the openness of the system. Some agencies at some points in their development will be especially receptive to new ideas and methods. Others, perhaps because they are going through a phase of consolidation or alternatively because of serious internal conflicts, may be closed, uninterested, or even hostile.

A new member entering a system which is experiencing severe internal conflicts is particularly vulnerable. Established members of the system may have difficulty in including the new member, who appears to represent a threat to the state of equilibrium within the system. She may thus be effectively cast as an outsider whose ideas and expertise can be ignored. Alternatively, she may be coopted by some members of the system in order to form a coalition against others. It is therefore essential that a new member tries to avoid being caught up in these triangular patterns, as her ability to influence the system as a whole will become profoundly impaired.

It is in order to avoid such mistakes that Held formulated a number of axioms which should be observed when entering a new system. We believe that these same principles apply equally well to cases in which a worker returns to her agency following a training course, or has come under the influence of new ideas through attending a family therapy support group. The following four major principles are partly drawn from Held's work and partly from our own experiences.

1 *Proceed slowly*

As Fisch et al. (1982) have observed, therapists should avoid pushing their client to change too much or too rapidly, since this is likely to create resistance or, to use Hoffman's term, 'persistance' (Hoffman 1981). Similarly, the worst temptation when entering a new work situation is the desire to behave like a new broom. This usually takes the form of seeking to advertise and utilize one's skills and competencies without spending time joining the system.

Minuchin's discussion of joining family systems (Minuchin and Fishman 1981, pp. 28–49) can be used on an analogical basis, to guide the new member who joins a professional system. Just as families differ in terms of the 'distance' they take up when a therapist begins her approach to them at the beginning of therapy, so do professional systems differ in terms of the distance they take up in relation to a new member. For example, a highly ebullient therapist who seeks to join a rather 'laid back' staff group would do well to curb her natural enthusiasm and adopt the style of her colleagues.

If successful joining takes place between the worker and her new colleagues she earns her right to contribute to discussions and decision-making. However, it is still essential not to force the pace. The seeding of ideas well ahead of attempts to implement them is a well-respected technique, which was used especially elegantly by Erickson (Haley 1973). It is very valuable in staff groups because it allows the initiator to test out the group's response to new ideas without having to make any commitment to implement them. For this reason it will be especially useful in more closed systems. The technique of 'playing hard to get' is a well-known tactic in courtship, but as Held points out it is not without its hazards when it is utilized (in an analogical way) within professional systems:

> Another way of framing . . . [the] suggestion [to proceed slowly] is for the entering therapist to permit the system to have the chance to request his or her expertise and ideas for change. This obviously requires a delicate balance between making one's competencies apparent while not appearing too presumptious about them. (Playing *too* hard to get can result in not playing at all!) (Held 1982).

However, despite this difficulty, a policy of caution — of refusing to jump to conclusions, and of seeking to gather more information before giving an opinion — can reap its own rewards. A worker who is cautious and thoughtful (and not impetuous) may well become valued precisely for these reasons, particularly if the group has previously suffered from new members who have been too quick off the mark.

We believe that a cautious approach should be based on respect for the existing system. Held has an unfortunate tendency to label systems that need 'slow' joining techniques as 'resistant' and we consider this negative framing can lead to errors. If the system is labelled as resistant then there is a covert implication that it is also bad and dysfunctional. We would prefer to label the system as 'cautious' or 'wanting to look before it leaps', and to assume that there must be good reasons why rapid innovation is not built into the system's ground rules. Ironically, reframing such a system as 'cautious' matches Held's invitation to the new member to proceed with caution; such reframing will enable the innovator to maintain her flexibility. This in turn will enable her to discover the reasons that determine the system's inflexibility. Such knowledge is essential if colleagues are to be approached in the right way and at the right pace.

2 *Be respectful*

This second principle is really an extension of the first. Clients often feel threatened by therapists who peremptorily dismiss their attitudes and ideas. A professional system may feel similarly threatened by a new therapist who arbitrarily dismisses established ways of working. It is therefore best to adopt an 'apprenticeship' approach to staff, inviting them to explain how they think it is best to proceed, rather than jumping in full of bright ideas. In the case of closed systems, Held suggests that the worker takes a strategic 'one-down' position:

> A new member . . . can . . . (a) acknowledge that as a new member there is much to learn about the way the system operates before his or her effective functioning can take place. Seek the help and advice of other staff members. This one-down position should be taken rather quickly since there is usually a 'license' to be uninformed that is granted a new member of a system and which is revoked after the period of . . . acclimation. (b) Acknowledge the . . . expertise of others, particularly in the therapist's own weak areas. Ask (intelligent) questions that permit others to reveal their competencies, thereby validating their sense of worth and so decreasing their fear of displacement by the new member (Held 1982).

Obviously the use of the one-down position cannot be prolonged beyond a certain point because colleagues will rightly become critical of a new member who appears a passenger, reluctant to pull her weight. The new member therefore does need to demonstrate her competence, but in a way that does not alienate other staff. In particular she should not boast about her successful cases in ways which may put other members in a bad light. Treatment failures are also significant since they provide the new member with a chance to gain necessary support and advice. It is therefore essential to avoid the natural tendency to hide one's failures from one's colleagues. Only workers who insist on adopting 'one-up positions' will have difficulty with following this advice. Their internalized injunction,

'I should not fail', will be the stumbling block to gaining help both for themselves and their clients.

3 *Accept and respect criticism*

Held goes as far as suggesting that one way of dealing with persistent criticism is through 'prescribing the symptom'. However, the use of this term when referring to the activities of one's colleagues is an unfortunate example of one-upmanship and could not be better designed to give systems theorists a bad name. We prefer to adopt a position that argues that our colleagues' reluctance to go overboard in favour of our ideas is nothing more than an example of 'do-as-you-would-be-done-by'! We would not expect to abandon our own hard-won ideas easily. Why should we therefore expect others to abandon theirs in favour of ours? To imply that this reluctance is equivalent to symptomatological behaviour is inappropriate and serves to summon up our own (largely instinctive) resistance to the light-minded extention of strategic ideas to inappropriate areas of discourse. Professional systems cannot, and should not, be auto-matically equated with family systems.

At a practical level we would prefer to translate Held's idea of 'prescribing the symptom' into 'inviting positive criticism and exploration'. It is clear that colleagues can be extremely valuable in bringing over-enthusiasm down to earth, but is equally true that their reluctance to accept our ideas can be very beneficial, as Held herself illustrates. She argues that she adopted a tactic of 'prescribing mistrust' when running a new consultation group with colleagues, who differed both in terms of their knowledge of and their expertise in family therapy. Held invited the group to ask her as many questions as they felt necessary to help them decide whether her approach had anything to offer. This tactic worked well because the group was able to build up mutual trust and Held was soon being consulted by group members on an individual basis. However her use of the label 'mistrust' proves our point, because how can 'mistrust' be considered to be a symptom? We would prefer to argue that 'mistrust' or 'resistance' is the appropriate response for a system which finds change threatening. Until the credibility and competence of the new worker has been carefully tested she should not be easily trusted. Just as family therapy can sometimes make families 'worse', so we should assume that it is the *unthinking* adoption of family therapy by some agencies which might make their practice worse.

It is essential, therefore, that the new worker listens hard to the criticisms of her colleagues if she is not to make serious errors. Furthermore, a respectful and flexible approach is more likely to win acceptance. If difficulties remain they are probably concerned with unresolved conflicts within the staff group.

4 *Resist the temptation to be drawn into coalitions*

As we have already noted, an individual entering a new system with unresolved conflicts is extremely vulnerable because she feels isolated and unsupported. She is therefore especially susceptible to falling into the trap of being drawn into coalitions against other staff. The danger of this to a new member is obvious — she can no longer hope to influence the system as a whole because she is drawn inexorably into taking sides over all sorts of issues, including ones which are extraneous to the project of establishing family therapy as a respected and legitimized approach to clients' problems. Held therefore proposes as a basic rule that the innovator should avoid consistently taking one member's side against another.

Avoiding the temptation to become triangulated is especially important in systems with unresolved interprofessional conflicts amongst senior staff. Even if one of these senior members encourages the development of family therapy, it will prove to be a mistake to take her side in the long run. Difficult though it may be at first, it will eventually pay dividends if the worker also seeks the advice of other members of the system, but at the same time keeps the senior staff member informed of any developments.

As Held points out, the formation of alliances is another matter. Alliances (at least in terms of textbook definitions) involve the teaming up of two parties, solely on the basis of shared interests and activities, and with no third party being involved. However, we believe that there is more of a difficulty involved with alliances than Held allows. For example, suppose a new member of a system is successful in gaining active support for her approach and hence forms an alliance with other individuals around the issue of 'interest in family therapy'. Obviously this alliance will inevitably create a third group of staff (those less interested in family therapy) who are potentially isolated from members of the alliance. The latter may well be friendly towards members of the 'less interested' group but because they are, of necessity, less involved with each other, there is a real danger of a split opening up. Obviously such a situation is not irreversible if the two groups make a point of sharing their activities periodically. But if such steps are not taken then a hiving-off process can occur and the alliance effectively becomes a coalition.

Finally we should note that it would be naive to leave this discussion of coalitions and alliances without being prepared to broaden our perspective to include status and organizational issues.

WORKING WITH COLLEAGUES: STATUS AND ORGANIZATIONAL ISSUES

Our review of Held's work has raised many issues concerning the need to be sensitive to colleagues' ideas and feelings. However, the principles outlined in the previous sections of this chapter cannot be applied mechanically and without consideration of the issue of status. If a senior practitioner, who already has a powerful position within an organization, wishes to initiate a new approach the chances of achieving it are much greater than if a more junior practitioner attempts to undertake the same project. For example we suspect that the success of Brian Dimmock in introducing a family counselling service into a general practice had little to do with *Brian's* status but had a lot to do with the fact that his team leader was an enthusiastic member of the group involved. Similarly, senior practitioners such as Marjorie Ainley, Eddy Street and Harry Procter were able to be innovative precisely because they were well established and respected within their settings.

Nevertheless, the ability to innovate is not solely dependent upon status. The more senior grades in professions such as probation, clinical psychology and psychiatry have considerable professional autonomy, especially when compared with their counterparts within social services departments. The degree of autonomy clearly has important implications as far as the role of innovator is concerned. For example, a consultant psychiatrist (who combines high status with high autonomy) can often be genuinely innovative, particularly if she can form a working alliance with the relevant administrative and professional hierarchies with which she works (e.g. nursing and clinical psychology).

These issues centring around status and autonomy in turn form a bridge to wider organizational issues, which have already been discussed in this book. With the benefit of hindsight it is now clear to us that we need to become much more closely acquainted with the body of research on organizational development. A number of family therapists including L'Abate (1974) have explored the effects that work systems can have on family systems, but it is clear that we need to explore organizational structures in much greater detail.

The work of Kahn (1979), is particularly important in this context since it begins to establish a bridge between family systems theorists and the interesting work of theorists such as Argyris (1970), French (1968), Neff (1977) and Perrow (1965). These American researchers have explored many important aspects of organizations including the impact that they have on the mental health of employees (Treacher 1971). Researchers associated with the Tavistock Clinic have pioneered similar work in this country. For example, the classic study of nursing hierarchies by Menzies (1970) was an early contribution to this field. Other work by Emery and Trist (1967) developed the important idea of socio-technical systems which encouraged researchers to investigate the influence that the technical structure of an industry can have on the workers who are employed in it. We have no space to explore this field in any depth, but fortunately there are a number of excellent reviews of the area of organizational research (e.g. Payne 1981). It is obvious to us that family therapists need to be aware of the sophistication of this work if they are to develop an approach that will be able to influence the functioning of complex organizations in more profound ways.

FAMILY THERAPY: WHAT'S IN A NAME?

The primary aim of this book has been to negotiate the first of a long series of hurdles that must be overcome if family therapy is to achieve its true potential. However there is one hurdle which we have still not negotiated ourselves — this concerns the use of the term 'family therapy'.

In the introductory chapter to this book we explored briefly the crucial issue of multiple roles. We argued that since British family therapists are not primarily employed as therapists they need to develop a sophisticated way of distinguishing their therapeutic, change-agent role from the other roles which they need to perform because of the nature of their job descriptions. Many of the chapters in this book have already explored this issue in some detail — for example, in chapter 5, David Dungworth and Sigurd Reimers pay close attention to the multiple roles of the local authority social workers. But this in turn raises the issue of whether we should use the term family therapy to describe our work. We have used it in the title of the book, but it is too narrow a term to suit our purposes. A Bristol colleague of ours, Philip Kingston, has pointed out its inherent difficulties:

> . . . some time ago it became clear to me that the term 'Family Therapy' was, in a number of ways, unhelpful. My concern about the term was related first of all to the word 'therapy'. Therapy implies pathology and the entity which is pathological is now 'the family' instead of 'the individual'. It is interesting to compare someone going into an industrial or commercial organisation for the same purpose. We call the former 'family therapy' but we do not call the latter 'industrial therapy'; we call it 'consultancy'. (Kingston 1982).

So, if we follow Kingston's logic, the term 'family therapy' needs replacing by a term which allows us to overcome our preoccupation both with families, and being therapists. In fact, Kingston is not very helpful in suggesting an alternative — in the end he plumps for the term 'systems change', because 'our work enables people to change and neither we nor they can predict how that will go.'

Whilst being sympathetic to Kingston's aim, we are not sure whether this latter term actually solves the problem. For example, when we have to talk about the professional worker who is involved in 'systems change', we are left with the problem of calling the worker either a 'systems changer' or a 'systems change agent'. Both terms are ugly and have a very technical ring to them, and, if used in professional circles, would have the decided disadvantage of implying that we (the 'systems change agents') are superior beings, very different from our colleagues who are mere social workers, psychologists or doctors.

As a result of puzzling over this apparently thorny issue we have come to the conclusion that the debate is misconceived. In practice we prefer to retain our original professional labels (psychologist and social worker, respectively) rather than adopting new ones. Indeed it might be dangerous or misleading to our clients to make such a change. After all, many of us are not primarily employed as therapists but instead have to perform a number of different roles depending on our profession and the agency for which we work. In some circumstances it may even be unhelpful to describe our activities as 'family therapy' since systems-orientated approaches are, as yet, not widely accepted. Practitioners must therefore avoid the temptation of wishing to force the pace of change. Change will only occur if systems-orientated approaches prove effective in solving the problems of grass-roots workers who carry the brunt of the work within agencies. In order not to distance ourselves from such colleagues we therefore consider it is best to maintain a low profile.

We may well wish to call ourselves family therapists, or problem-solvers, or change agents, in order to preserve our sense of identity and to express our solidarity with like-minded people. However, if we wish to retain our manoeuvrability, and hence our ability to influence uncommitted colleagues, then we would do best to keep such labels strictly to ourselves. Of course, at a practical level we need to describe what we do, and we may well retain the term 'family therapy' because it is recognized. Nevertheless, we need to understand that it means what we want it to mean — such a term is, as far as we are concerned, only shorthand for a much wider (and we hope far-seeing) approach, whose usefulness will ultimately become self-evident.

Bibliography

Ackerman, N. (1966) *Treating the Troubled Family*. New York. Basic Books.

ACPP (1978) *Directory of School Psychological and Child Guidance Services*. Association for Child Psychology and Psychiatry. London.

Adams, R. (1980) Naming of parts: support groups for family therapy practice. *Social Work Service*, 22: 24—28.

Adams, R. and Hill, G. (1983) The labours of Hercules: some good reasons why social workers should not try to be different and practice family therapy. *Journal of Family Therapy*, 5: 71—80.

Ainley, M. (1979) An exploration of the place of post-qualifying training opportunities within the Avon Probation Service and an evaluation of the impact of courses upon officers' subsequent work. Personal Social Services Fellowship Report (unpublished). Bristol University.

Ainley, M. and Kingston, P. (1981) Live supervision in a probation setting. *Social Work Education*, 1: 3—7.

Anderson, C. M. and Reiss, D. J. (1982) Family treatment with chronic schizophrenia: the inpatient phase. In: H. T. Harbin (ed.) *The Psychiatric Hospital and the Family*. New York. Spectrum Publications. Medical and Scientific Books.

Aponte, H. (1976) The family-school interview: an ecostructural approach. *Family Process*, 15: 303—311.

Argyris, C. (1970) *Intervention Theory and Method*. Reading. Mass. Addison-Wesley.

Arie, T. and Isaacs, A. D. (1978) The development of psychiatric services for the elderly in Britain. In: A. Isaacs and F. Post (eds) *Studies in Geriatric Psychiatry*. Chichester. Wiley.

Asen, K. et al. (1982) A day unit for families. *Journal of Family Therapy*, 4: 345—358.

Ashley, J. J. A. (1971) The challenge of another million by 1991. *Modern Geriatrics*, 2: 320—329.

Balint, M. (1957) *The Doctor, his patient and the illness*. London. Pitman.

Balint, M. et al. (1970) *Treatment or Diagnosis: a Study of Repeat Prescriptions in General Practice*. London. Tavistock.

Bandler, R. and Grinder, J. (1982) *Reframing.* Moab, Utah. Real People Press.

Barclay, P. M. (1982) *Social Workers, Their Roles and Tasks.* London. Bedford Square Press.

Bennet, D. et al. (1976) Towards a family approach in a psychiatric day hospital. *British Journal of Psychiatry,* 129: 73—81.

Bentovim, A. (1979) Theories of family interaction and techniques of intervention. *Journal of Family Therapy,* 1: 321—345.

Black, D. (1979) Family therapy as a setting for other treatment modalities. *Journal of Family Therapy,* 1: 183—192.

Black, D. (1982) Child guidance clinics. In: A. Bentovim, G. Gorell Barnes and A. Cooklin (eds), *Family Therapy. Complementary Frameworks of Theory and Practice.* London. Academic Press.

Blau, P. and Scott, W. (1963) *Formal Organizations — a Comparative Approach.* London. Routledge & Kegan Paul.

Bley, C. R. (1981) Multiple family therapy with schizophrenics. In: M. R. Lansky, *Family Therapy and Major Psychopathology.* New York. Grune and Stratton.

Borowitz, G. H. (1970) The therapeutic utilization of emotion and attitudes evoked in the caretakers of disturbed children. *British Journal of Medical Psychology,* 43: 129—139.

Bott, E. (1976) Hospital and Society. *British Journal of Medical Psychology,* 49: 97—140.

Bowen, M. (1965) Family psychotherapy with schizophrenia in the hospital and private practice. In: I. Boszormenyi-Nagy and J. L. Framo (eds), *Intensive Family Therapy.* Hagerstown, Maryland. Harper and Row.

Bowlby, J. (1949) The study and reduction of group tensions in the family. *Human Relations,* 2: 123—128.

Boyd, J. H. (1981) Family therapy in short-term inpatient hospitals. In: A. S. Gurman (ed.), *Questions and answers in the practice of family therapy.* New York. Brunner/Mazel.

Breunlin, D. and Cade, B. (1981) Intervening in family systems with observer messages. *Journal Marital and Family Therapy.* 5: 453—460.

British Association of Social Workers (BASW). Child Guidance Special Interest Group (1975) *The Child Guidance Service.* Report of the 1969 Survey, Birmingham. BASW.

British Psychological Society (1980) *Psychological Services for Children in England and Wales.* Occasional Papers 4, nos 1 and 2.

Broder, E. A. and Sloman, L. (1982) Comparison of three training programmes. In: R. Whiffen and J. Byng-Hall (eds), *Family Therapy Supervision: recent developments in practice.* London. Academic Press.

Broderick, C. B. and Schrader, S. S. (1981) The history of professional marriage and family therapy. In: A. S. Gurman and D. P. Kniskern (eds), *Handbook of Family Therapy.* New York. Brunner/Mazel.

Brodey, W. (1959) Some family operations and schizophrenia. *Archives of General Psychiatry,* 1: 371—402.

Brown, A. (1984) *Consultation for Social Workers,* London. Heinemann Educational.

Brown, G. W. et al. (1972) Influence of family life on the courses of schizophrenic disorders: a replication. *British Journal of Psychiatry.* 121: 241—258.

Brown, L. and Levitt, J. (1979) A methodology for problem-system identification. *Social Casework,* 60: 408—415.

Bruce, T. (1982) Family Work in a Secure Unit. In: A. Bentovim et al. (eds), *Family Therapy: Complementary Frameworks.* Vol. 2, 497—513. London. Academic Press.

Bruggen, P. and O'Brian, C. (1982) An Adolescent Unit's Focus on Family Decisions. In: H. T. Harbin (ed.) *The Psychiatric Hospital and the Family.* Lancaster. MTP Press.

Bruggen, P., Byng-Hall and Pitt Aitkens (1973) The Reason for Admission as a focus of Work for an Adolescent Unit. *British Journal of Psychiatry,* 122: 319—329.

Burck, C. (1978) A study of families' expectations and experience of a child guidance clinic. *British Journal of Social Work,* 8: 145—158.

Burden, R. (1978) Schools' system analysis: a project-centred approach. In: B. Gillham (ed.), *Reconstructing Educational Psychology.* London. Croom Helm.

Butler, J. et al. (1982) Task-centred casework with marital problems. In: A. Clare and R. Corney (eds), *Social Work and Primary Health Care.* London. Academic Press.

Byng-Hall, J. (1973) Family myths used as defence in conjoint family therapy. *British Journal of Medical Psychology,* 46: 239—250.

Byng-Hall, J. and Bruggen, P. (1974) Family admission decisions as a therapeutic tool. *Family Process,* 13: 443—459.

Byng-Hall, J. et al. (1982) Evolution of supervision: an overview. In: R. Whiffen and J. Byng-Hall (eds), *Family Therapy Supervision.* London. Academic Press.

Cade, B. (1978) Family violence: an interactional view. *Social Work Today,* 9: 26.

Campbell, D. (1975) Adolescents in Care: A model for work with the family. *Social Work Today,* 6: 265—269.

Carpenter, J. and Treacher, A. (1982) Structural family therapy in context-working with child-focussed problems. *Journal of Family Therapy,* 4: 15—34.

Carpenter, J. and Treacher, A. (1983) On the neglected arts of convening and engaging families and their wider systems. *Journal of Family Therapy.* (in press).

Carpenter, J. et al. (1983) 'Oh no! Not the Smiths again!' An exploration of how to identify and overcome 'stuckness' in family therapy. Part II: Stuckness in the therapeutic and supervisory systems. *Journal of Family Therapy,* 5: 81—96.

Carter, R. E. (1981) Using family therapy to plan the discharge of a hospitalised family member. In: A. S. Gurman (ed.), *Questions and answers in the practice of family therapy.* New York. Brunner/Mazel.

Cartwright, A. and Anderson, R. (1981) *General Practice Revisited.* London. Tavistock Publications.

Chase, A. M. et al. (1979) Treating the throwaway child: a model for an adolescent service. *Journal of Contemporary Social Work,* 20: 538—546.

Cheek, F. (1966) Family socialisation techniques and deviant behaviour. *Family Process,* 5: 199—217.

Child Guidance Trust (1982). Interdisciplinary Standing Committee. *Interdisciplinary Work in Child Guidance.* London. Child Guidance Trust.

Children and Young Persons Act (1969). London. HMSO.

Children's Act (1980). London. HMSO.

Churven, P. (1978) Families: parental attitudes to family assessment in a child psychiatry setting. *Journal of Child Psychology and Psychiatry,* 19: 33—41.

Clare, A. (1980) *Psychiatry in Dissent,* 2nd edn. London. Tavistock.

Clare, A. and Corney, R. H. (eds), (1982) *Social Work and Primary Health Care.* London. Academic Press.

Clough, R. (1982) *Residential Work.* London. Macmillan.

Combrinck-Graham, L. (1980) The role of family therapy in child psychiatry training: Why and how. In: K. Flomenhaft and A. Christ (eds), *The Challenge of Family Therapy.* New York. Plenum Press.

Cook, D. and Skeldon, I. (1980) The use of a hospital admission procedure in an acute psychiatric admission ward. *British Journal of Psychiatry,* 136: 463—468.

Cooklin, A. (1974) Exploration of the staff-patient 'contract' in an acute female admission ward. *British Journal of Medical Psychology,* 47: 321—335.

Corney, R. H. (1980) Factors affecting the operation and success of social work attachment schemes to General Practice. *Journal of the Royal College of General Practitioners,* 30: 149—158.

Corney, R. H. and Bowen, B. A. (1982) Referrals to social workers: a comparative study of a local authority intake team with a general practice attachment scheme. In: A. Clare and R. H. Corney (eds), *Social Work and Primary Care*. London. Academic Press.

Criminal Justice Act (1948). London. HMSO.

Daines, R. et al. (1982) *Child Guidance and Schools — a Study of a Consultative Service.* DHSS Research Report (unpublished).

Dare, C. (1981) Psychoanalysis and family therapy. In: S. Walrond-Skinner (ed.), *Developments in Family Therapy.* London. Routledge & Kegan Paul.

Dare, C. and Lindsey, C. (1979) Children in family therapy. *Journal of Family Therapy,* 1: 253—269.

Davies, M. (1981) *The Essential Social Worker.* London. Heinemann.

Davis, G. (1982) Conciliation: a dilemma for the Divorce Court Welfare Service. *Probation Journal,* 4: 123—128.

Department of Health and Social Security (1968). *Report of the Committee on Local Authority and Allied Personal Social Services.* (Seebohm report) London. HMSO.

Department of Health and Social Security (1974). *Social Work support for the Health Service.* London. HMSO.

Dessent, T. (1978) The historical development of school psychological services. In: B. Gillham (ed.), *Reconstructing Educational Psychology.* London. Croom Helm.

Dimmock, B. and Dungworth, D. (1983) Creating manoeuvrability for family/systems therapists in social services departments. *Journal of Family Therapy,* 5: 53—69.

Dingwall, R. (1979) Problems of Teamwork in Primary Care. In: T. Briggs et al. (eds), *Teamwork in The Health and Social Services.* London. Croom Helm.

Emery, F. E. and Trist, E. L. (1965). The causal texture of organisational environments. *Human Relation,* 18: 21—32.

Esterson, A. et al. (1965) Results of family-orientated therapy with hospitalised schizophrenics. *British Medical Journal,* 2: 1462—1465.

Falloon, I. R. H. (1981) Communication and problem solving skills training of acute schizophrenia. In: M. Lasky (ed.), *Family therapy and Major Psychopathology.* New York. Grune and Stratton.

Feinstein, S. C. et al. (eds) (1980) *Adolescent Psychiatry. Developmental and Clinical Studies.* Chicago. University of Chicago Press.

Feldman, L. B. (1976) Depression and marital interaction. *Family Process,* 15: 389—395.

Feldman, L. B. (1979) Marital conflict and marital intimacy: an investigative psychodynamic-behavioural-system model. *Family Process,* 18: 69—78.

Fernandez, C. et al. (1983) True/False. Practising family therapy in a local authority setting. *Community Care,* 456: 24—25.

Ferreira, A. J. (1960) The 'double bind' and delinquent behaviour, *Archives of General Psychiatry*, 3: 359—367.

Fisch, R. et al. (1982) *The Tactics of Change, Doing Therapy Briefly.* San Francisco. Jossey Bass.

French, J. R. P. (1968) The conceptualisation and measurement of mental health in terms of self-identity theory. In: S. B. Sells (ed.), *The Definition and Measurement of Mental Health.* Washington. National Centre for Health Statistics.

Friedman, A. S. (1969) Delinquency and the family system. In: O. Pollark and A. S. Friedman (eds), *Family Dynamics and Female Sexual Delinquency.* Palo Alto. Science and Behaviour Books.

Fromm-Reichman, F. (1948) Notes on the development of treatment of schizophrenia by psychoanalytic psychotherapy. *Psychiatry*, 11: 267—277.

Gath, D. (1968) Child Guidance and the General Practitioner. *Journal of Child Psychology and Psychiatry*, 9: 213—227.

Gath, D. et al. (1977) *Child Guidance and Delinquency in a London Borough.* Oxford. Oxford University Press.

Glick, I. P. and Kessler, D. R. (1981) *Marital and Family Therapy*, 2nd edn. New York. Grune and Stratton.

Goffman, E. (1968) *Asylums.* Harmondsworth. Penguin.

Goldberg, D. and Huxley, P. (1980) *Mental Illness in the Community — the Pathway to Psychiatric Care.* London. Tavistock.

Goldberg, M. et al. (1977) Towards accountability in social work. *British Journal of Social Work*, 7: 257—287.

Gordon, S. B. and Davidson, N. (1981) Behavioural parent training. In: A. S. Gurman and D. P. Kniskern (eds), *Handbook of Family Therapy.* New York. Brunner/Mazel.

Hack, E. and Hindle, D. (1982) Nottingham live supervision workshops. *Association for Family Therapy Newsletter* (Aug.) 6—11.

Haley, J. (1962) Whither family therapy? *Family Process*, 1: 69—100.

Haley, J. (1973) *Uncommon therapy — the Psychiatric Techniques of Milton H. Erickson, MD.* New York. Norton.

Haley, J. (1975) Why a mental health clinic should avoid family therapy. *Journal of Marriage and Family Counselling.* 1: 3—13.

Haley, J. (1976) *Problem Solving Therapy.* San Francisco. Jossey Bass.

Haley, J. (1980) *Leaving Home: The Therapy of Disturbed Young People.* New York. McGraw Hill.

Hallet, C. and Stevenson, O. (1980) *Child Abuse: Aspect of Interprofessional Co-operation.* London. Allen & Unwin.

Harbin, H. T. (1979) A family-oriented psychiatric in-patient unit. *Family Process*, 18: 281—291.

Harbin, H. T. (1982) *The Psychiatric Hospital and the Family.* New York. S. P. Medical and Scientific Books.

Harms, E. (1962) Defective parents, delinquent children. *Corrective Psychiatry,* 8: 34—42.

Harwin, B. G. et al. (1970) Prospects for Social Work in General Practice. *Lancet,* 2: 559—561.

Held, B. (1982) Entering a mental health system: A strategic—systemic approach. *Journal of Strategies and Systemic Therapies,* 1: 40—50.

Herbert, M. (1982) *Behavioural Treatment of Problem Children — a practical manual.* London. Academic Press.

Herr, J. J. and Weakland, J. H. (1979) *Counselling Elders and Their Families.* New York. Springer.

Hersov, L. and Bentovim, A. (1976) In-patient units and day hospitals. In: M. L Rutter and L. Hersov (eds), *Child Psychiatry: Modern Approaches.* Oxford. Blackwell Scientific Publications.

Herz, M. I. et al. (1976) Brief versus standard hospitalisation: the families. *American Journal of Psychiatry,* 133: 795—801.

Hirsch, S. R. and Leff, J. P. (1975) *Abnormalities in Parents of Schizophrenics.* London. Oxford University Press.

Hoffman, L. (1981) *Foundations of Family Therapy.* New York. Basic Books.

Holman, R. (1975) The place of fostering in social work. *British Journal of Social Work,* 5: 3—30.

Home Office Criminal Statistics (1980). London. HMSO.

Howard, J. and Shepherd, G. (1982) Conciliation — new beginnings? *Probation Journal,* 29: 87—92.

Hudson, P. (1980) Different strokes for different folks: a comparative examination of behavioural, structural and paradoxical methods in family therapy. *Journal of Family Therapy,* 2: 181—198.

Hunt, H. J. (1972) The Renaissance of general practice. (The Lloyd Roberts Lecture 1957). *Journal of the Royal College of General Practitioners.* 22, Supplement 4.

Huntington, J. (1981) *Social Work and General Medical Practice — Collaboration or Conflict.* London. George Allen & Unwin.

Hurley, P. (1982) The therapeutic advantage to the family therapist of intervening in the family—clinician system. *Family Process,* 21: 435—441.

Iveson, C. et al. (1979) A family therapy work-shop: a review of a two-year experiment in a Social Services Department. *Journal of Family Therapy,* 1: 397—408.

Jack, B. (1983) Out from the geriatric ghetto. *Social Work Today,* 14, No. 20: 7—10.

Jacobs, J. (1982) *In the Best Interest of the Child. An Evaluation of a Child Assessment Centre.* Oxford. Pergamon Press.

Janzen, C. and Harris, O. (1980) *Family Treatment in Social Work Practice.* Illinois. Peacock.

Jarvis, F. V. (1980) *Probation Officer's Manual.* London. Butterworth.

Jenkins, H. (1981) 'Can I (let you let me) leave?' Therapy with the adolescent and his family. *Journal of Family Therapy,* 3: 113—138.

Johnson, F. (1974) Hooking the involuntary family into treatment: family therapy in a juvenile court setting. *Family Therapy,* 1: 79—82.

Jones, H. V. R. (1980) Methods of treatment in a psychiatric unit for adolescents. In: R. Walton and D. Elliott (eds), *Residential Care.* Oxford. Pergamon Press.

Jordan, W. (1981) Family Therapy — an Outsider's View. *Journal of Family Therapy.* 3: 269—280.

Kahn, M. (1979) Organisational consultation and the teaching of family therapy: contrasting case histories. *Journal of Marital and Family Therapy,* 1: 69—80.

Kingston, P. (1979) The social context of family therapy. In: S. Walrond-Skinner (ed.), *Family and Marital Psychotherapy.* London. Routledge & Kegan Paul.

Kingston, P. (1982) Power and influence in the environment of family therapy. *Journal of Family Therapy,* 4: 211—228.

Kingston, P. and Smith, D. (1983) Preparation for live consultation and live supervision. *Journal of Family Therapy,* 5: 219—233.

Kirschner, C. (1979) The ageing family in crisis. *Social Casework,* 60: 209—216.

L'Abate, L. (1975) Pathogenic role rigidity in fathers: some observations. *Journal of Marriage and Family Counselling,* 24: 69—79.

Laing, R. P. and Esterson, A. (1964) *Sanity, Madness and the Family.* Harmondsworth. Penguin.

Langsley, D. G. and Kaplan, D. M. (1968) *The Treatment of Families in Crisis.* New York. Grune and Stratton.

Lansky, M. R. (1981) *Family Therapy and Major Psychopathology.* New York. Grune and Stratton.

Laqueur, H. P. (1981) Multiple family therapy. In: M. Lansky (ed.), *Family Therapy and Major Psychopathology.* New York. Grune and Stratton.

Leeunhorst Conference Working Party (1972). *The Future General Practitioner: Learning and Teaching.* London. Royal College of General Practitioners.

Leff, J. (1979) Developments in family therapy of schizophrenia. *Psychiatric Quarterly,* 51: 216—232.

Lerner, B. (1972) *Therapy in the Ghetto.* Baltimore. John Hopkins University Press.

Levin, J. and Levin, W. C. (1980) *Ageism: Prejudice and Discrimination against the Elderly.* Belmont. Wadsworth.

Lieberman, S. and Cooklin, A. (1982) Family therapy and general psychiatry. In: A. Bentovim et al. (eds), *Family therapy: Complementary Frameworks of Theory and Practice.* London. Academic Press.

Looney, J. G. et al. (1980) A family-systems model for in-patient treatment of adolescents. In: S. C. Feinstein et al. (eds), *Adolescent Psychiatry: Developmental and Clinical Studies. Vol. VIII.* Chicago. University of Chicago.

Lorion, R. P. (1978) Research on Psychotherapy and Behaviour Change with the Disadvantaged. In: S. L. Garfield and A. E. Bergin, (eds) *Handbook of Psychotherapy and Behaviour Change.* New York. Wiley.

Madanes, C. (1980) The prevention of rehospitalisation of adolescents and young adults. *Family Process.* 19: 179—191.

Madanes, C. (1981) *Strategic Family Therapy.* San Francisco. Jossey Bass.

Martin, F. and Knight, J. (1962) Joint interviews as part of intake procedure in a child psychiatric clinic. *Journal of Child Psychology and Psychiatry,* 3: 17—26.

Mattinson, J. and Sinclair, I. (1979) *Mate and Stalemate.* Oxford. Blackwell.

Mayer, J. and Timms, N. (1970) *The Client Speaks: Working Class Impressions of Casework.* London. Routledge & Kegan Paul.

McDermott, J. and Char, W. (1974) The undeclared war between child and family therapy. *Journal of the American Academy of Child Psychiatry,* 13: 422—436.

Mechanic, D. (1969) *Mental Health and Social Policy.* Englewood Cliffs. Prentice-Hall.

Menzies, I. (1970) The functioning of social systems as a defence against anxiety. *Tavistock Pamphlet,* No. 3. London. Tavistock.

Merrington, D. and Corden, J. (1981) Families' impressions of family therapy. *Journal of Family Therapy,* 3: 243—261.

Mills, G. and Cullum, E. (1982) First year of a family therapy group. *Association for Family Therapy Newsletter.* Spring. 1—4.

Minuchin, S. (1974) *Families and Family Therapy.* Cambridge, Mass. Harvard University Press.

Minuchin, S. and Fishman, C. (1981) *Family Therapy Techniques.* Cambridge, Mass. Harvard University Press.

Minuchin, S. et al. (1967) *Families of the Slums: An Exploration of their Structure and Treatment.* New York. Basic Books.

Minuchin, S. et al. (1978) *Psychosomatic Families, Anorexia Nervosa in Context.* Cambridge, Mass. Harvard University Press.

Montalvo, B. (1973) Aspects of live supervision. *Family Process,* 12: 343—359.

Montalvo, B. and Haley, J. (1973) In defence of child therapy. *Family Process,* 12: 227—244.

Mortimer, J. A. and Schuman, L. M. (1981) *The Epidemiology of Dementia.* Oxford. Oxford University Press.

Neff, W. S. (1977) *Work and human behaviour,* 2nd edn. New York. Atherton Press.

Olie, D. A. (1982) The integration of family therapy in a psychiatric day hospital. *Journal of Family Therapy,* 4: 329—344.

Orvin, G. H. (1974) Intensive treatment of the adolescent and his family. *Archives of General Psychiatry,* 31: 801—806.

Palazzoli, M. S. (1982) *Behind the Scenes of the Organisation.* Unpublished presentation in Cardiff, 28 Oct. (Available on audiocassette from The Family Institute, Cardiff.)

Palazzoli, M. S. and Prata, G. (1982) Snares in family therapy. *Journal of Marital and Family Therapy.* 8: 443—450.

Palazzoli, M. S. et al. (1978) *Paradox and Counterparadox.* New York. Jason Aronson.

Palazzoli, M. S. et al. (1980) Hypothesizing, circularity and neutrality — guidelines for the conductor of the session. *Family Process,* 19: 3—12.

Papp, P. (1980) The Greek chorus and other techniques of paradoxical therapy. *Family Process,* 19: 45—57.

Parsloe, P. (1967) Families who do not come to clinics. In: *Child Guidance from Within: Reactions to New Pressures.* London. NAMH.

Patterson, G. (1971) *Families: Applications of Social Learning to Family Life.* Champaign, Illinois. Research Press.

Payne, R. (1981) Organisational Behaviour. In: M. Herbert (ed.), *Psychology for Social Workers.* London. Macmillan.

Perrow, W. (1965) Hospitals, technology, structure, and goals. In: J. G. March (ed.), *Handbook of Organisations.* Chicago. Rand McNally.

Pincus, A. and Minahan, A. (1973) *Social Work Practice: Model and Method.* Itasca, Illinois. Peacock.

Power, M. et al. (1967) Delinquent schools? *New Society.* 19 Oct., 542.

Power, M. et al. (1974) Delinquency and the family. *British Journal of Social Work,* 4: 13—35.

Procter, H. G. and Pottle, S. (1980) Experiences and guidelines in running an open couples psychotherapy group. *Journal of Family Therapy,* 2: 233—242.

Reder, P. (1983) Disorganized families and the helping professions: 'who's in charge of what?' *Journal of Family Therapy,* 5: 23—36.

Reder, P. and Kramer, S. (1980) Dynamic aspects of professional collaboration in child guidance referral. *Journal of Adolescence.* 8: 165—173.

Rees, S. (1979) *Social Work Face to Face.* New York. Columbia University Press.

Rehin, G. (1972) Child guidance at the crossroads. *Social Work Today,* 2: 21—24.

Reifler, B. V. and Eisdorfer, C. (1980) A clinic for the impaired elderly and their families. *American Journal of Psychiatry,* 137: 1399—1403.

Roberts, W. (1968) Working with the family group in a child guidance clinic. *British Journal of Psychiatric Social Work,* 9: 175—179.

Roberts, W. (1979) Family or agency network — where to intervene. *Journal of Family Therapy,* 1: 203—210.

Robinson, M. (1968) Family based therapy. Some thoughts on the family approach. *British Journal of Psychiatric Social Work,* 9: 188—192.

Rosenberg, J. (1978) Two is better than one: use of behavioural techniques within a structural family therapy model. *Journal of Marriage and Family Counselling,* 4: 31—39.

Rowlings, C. (1981) *Social Work with Elderly People.* London. Allen & Unwin.

Russell, A. and Russell, L. (1979) The uses and abuses of co-therapy. *Journal of Marital and Family Therapy,* 3: 39—46.

Rutter, M. (1975) *Helping Troubled Children.* Harmondsworth. Penguin.

Rutter, M. (1982) Psychological therapies in child psychiatry: issues and prospects. *Psychological Medicine,* 12: 723—740.

Rutter, M. et al. (1970) *Education, Health and Behaviour.* London. Longman.

Rutter, M. et al. (1979) *15,000 Hours.* London. Open Books.

Sainsbury, E. (1980) *Client Need, Social Work Method and Agency Function in a Research Perspective.* London. DHSS.

Sampson, O. (1980) *Child Guidance: its History, Provenance and Future.* London. British Psychological Society.

Satir, V. (1964) *Conjoint Family Therapy.* Palo Alto. Science and Behaviour Books.

Satir, V. (1972) *Peoplemaking.* Palo Alto. Science and Behaviour Books.

Scheff, T. (1966) *Being Mentally Ill: a Sociological Theory.* Aldine, Chicago.

Scott, R. D. (1973) The treatment barrier. *British Journal of Medical Psychology,* 46: 45—55.

Scott, R. D. and Ashworth, P. L. (1967) 'Closure' at the first schizophrenic breakdown: a family study. *British Journal of Medical Psychology,* 40: 109—145.

Scott, R. D. and Starr, I (1981) A 24-hour family orientated psychiatric and crisis service. *Journal of Family Therapy,* 3: 177—186.

Sedgwick, P. (1982) *Psychopolitics.* London. Pluto Press.

Segal, L. (1981) In: The focus and activity of family therapists, R. Meltzer (ed.), In: E. R. Tolson and W. Reid (eds), *Models of Family Treatment.* New York. Columbia University Press.

Serrano, A. C. et al. (1962) Adolescent maladjustment and family dynamics. *American Journal of Psychiatry,* 118: 897—901.

Shapiro, R. L. (1967) The origins of adolescent disturbance in the family — some considerations in theory and implications for therapy. G. H. Zuk and I. Boszormenyi-Nagy (eds), *Family Therapy and Disturbed Families.* Palo Alto. Science and Behaviour Books.

Shepherd, M. et al. (1971) *Childhood Behaviour and Mental Health.* London. University of London Press.

Short, R. and Gray, G. (1982) Foster families must be trained. *Community Care,* 416: 14—16.

Singh, N. (1982) Notes and observations on the practice of multiple family therapy in an adolescent unit. *Journal of Adolescence,* 5: 319—332.

Skynner, A. C. R. (1969) A group-analytic approach to conjoint family therapy. *Journal of Child Psychology and Psychiatry,* 10: 81—106.

Skynner, A. C. R. (1976) *One Flesh: Separate Persons.* London. Constable.

Smith, D. and Kingston, P. (1980) Live supervision without a one-way screen. *Journal of Family Therapy,* 2: 379—387.

Spark, G. M. and Brody, E. M. (1970) The aged are family members. *Family Process,* 9: 195—210.

Speck, R. V. and Attneave, C. L. (1973) *Family Networks.* New York. Pantheon.

Speed, B. et al. (1982) A team approach to therapy. *Journal of Family Therapy,* 4: 271—284.

Spitzer, S. P. and Denzin, N. K. (1968) *The Mental Patient: Studies in the Sociology of Deviance.* New York. McGraw-Hill.

Spitzer, S. P. et al. (1982) Family reactions and the career of the psychiatric patient: a long-term follow-up study. In: H. T. Harbin (ed.), *The Psychiatric Hospital and the family.* New York. Spectrum Publications. Medical and Scientific Books.

Stanton, A. and Schwartz, M. (1954) *The Mental Hospital.* New York. Basic Books.

Street, E. (1981) The family therapist and staff group consultancy. *Journal of Family Therapy,* 3: 187—199.

Thomas, H. A. (1982) The road to custody is paved with good intentions. *Probation Journal,* 29: 93—97.

Timms, N. (1968) Child guidance service: a pilot study. In: G.

McLachlan (ed.). *Problems and Progress in Medical Care* (3rd series). London. Oxford University Press.

Treacher, A. (1971) *Mental Health in Industry. A Report to the Committee on Safety and Health at Work.* Robens Committee. (Unpublished).

Treacher, A. and Carpenter, J. (1982) 'Oh no! Not the Smiths again!' An exploration of how to identify and overcome 'stuckness' in family therapy. Part I: Stuckness involving contextual and technical aspects of therapy. *Journal of Family Therapy,* 4: 285—305.

Tucker, B. Z. and Dyson, E. (1976) The family and the school — utilizing human resources to promote learning. *Family Process,* 15: 125—141.

Tuckman, B. (1965) Developmental sequences in small groups. *Psychological Bulletin,* 63: 384—399.

Umbarger, C. (1972) The paraprofessional and family therapy, *Family Process,* 11: 147—161.

Underwood Report, (1955) *Report of the Committee on Maladjusted Children.* London. HMSO.

Van de Lande, J. (1979) Multiple family therapy in a residential setting for adolescents. *Journal of Family Therapy,* 1: 241—252.

Walker, G. and Procter, H. G. (1981) Brief therapeutic approaches: their value in contemporary day care. In: *New Directions for Psychiatric Day Services.* London. NAMH.

Walrond-Skinner, S. (1976) *Family Therapy. The Treatment of Natural Systems.* London. Routledge & Kegan Paul.

Walrond-Skinner, S. (1981) *Developments in Family Therapy.* London. Routledge & Kegan Paul.

Watzlawick, P., Weakland, P. and Fisch, R. (1974) *Change: Principles of Problem Formation and Problem Resolution.* New York. Norton.

Wendorf, D. J. (1978) Family therapy: an innovative approach to the rehabilitation of adult probationers. *Federal Probation,* 42: 40—44.

Whitehead, J. M. (1974) *Psychiatric Disorders in Old Age: a Handbook for the Clinical Team.* London. Harvey Miller and Medcalf. Oxford University Press.

Williams, P. and Clare, A. (1982) Social workers in primary health care: the General Practitioner's viewpoint. In: A. Clare and R. Corney *Social Work and Primary Health Care.* London. Academic Press.

Wilson, H. (1980) Parents can cut the crime rate. *New Society,* 54: 456—458.

Index of Subjects

)

Index of Authors